WEAPONS OF THE TRENCH WAR 1914–1918

WEAPONS OF THE TRENCH WAR 1914–1918

ANTHONY SAUNDERS

SUTTON PUBLISHING

First published in the United Kingdom in 1999 by
Sutton Publishing Limited
Phoenix Mill · Thrupp · Stroud · Gloucestershire GL5 2BU

Reprinted 1999

British Library Cataloguing in Publication Data
A catalogue record for this book is available from the British Library.

ISBN 0 7509 1818 7

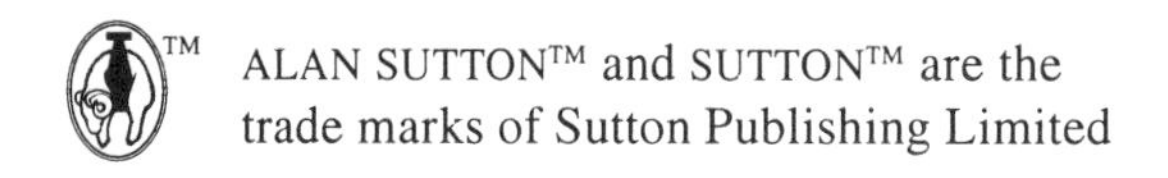

Typeset in 10/12pt Times.
Typesetting and origination by
Sutton Publishing Limited.
Printed in Great Britain by
MPG, Bodmin, Cornwall.

Contents

Acknowledgements

I could not have written this book without the help of a number of people who kindly gave up their time to assist me. My friend Derek Rackett generously found the time to read some of the First World War memoirs and mark the sections that might be of interest to me. Without the kindness of Mrs Joan Harper, who allowed me to stay in her home and looked after me while I was in London, I would have been unable to do any of the research at the Public Record Office, the Science Library or the Imperial War Museum. The staff at the Public Record Office were always very obliging and often went out of their way to help me no matter how near it was to closing time. I am particularly grateful to the staff of the Reprographic Department who supplied me with a missing page at the eleventh hour. I am also grateful to the staff at the Science Library and at Exeter Reference Library for their assistance. I would like to thank David Penn, Keeper of the Department of Exhibits and Firearms, Imperial War Museum, and his colleague Mike Hibberd for their assistance. The UK patent drawings are reproduced by permission of the Stationery Office and courtesy of Alan Grant of the Ideas House, Taunton, who kindly allowed me to use one of their scanners. I have cleaned up the drawings by removing the labelling which, without the full specification to refer to, serves no useful purpose here.

Introduction

Much has been written about the First World War. As far as I am aware, this is the first book devoted solely to the weapons designed specifically for use in the trenches. Such weapons played an important part in the trench war from late 1914 onwards. Without them, the outcome of the First World War might have been very different. Some, like the Mills hand grenade and the Stokes mortar, made major contributions to Britain's victory in 1918 as they significantly increased the offensive capabilities of the British Army. However, when the British Expeditionary Force (BEF) went to France in August 1914, it possessed no rifle grenades, no trench mortars, indeed no equipment of any kind designed for trench warfare. All it had was a meagre supply of unsuitable hand grenades.

This was not due to incompetence. Rather, it was because the likelihood of such equipment ever being needed had seemed extremely remote since a prolonged period of entrenchment was not predicted. Although trenches had been a feature of warfare for a very long time, trench warfare was virtually unheard of before October 1914. Digging in by soldiers to protect themselves from small arms fire had been common practice for about forty years but fighting that could be described as trench warfare had never followed. However, ten years before the outbreak of the First World War, embryonic trench warfare had occurred during the Russo-Japanese War in Manchuria but it was of short duration and had arisen under siege conditions. Neither side had weapons suitable for this kind of warfare so they had to be improvised; the grenade and the trench mortar emerged as potent killers. The British Army did not foresee itself getting involved in sieges in any future European war.

The European powers had all sent observers to Manchuria. Although there were lessons to be learned from the Russo-Japanese War, no one saw it as a warning of what might happen in a future European war. What was not fully appreciated at the time was why trench warfare had arisen in the first place. There had been a revolution in small arms and artillery in the last decades of the nineteenth century during which firepower and accuracy had increased enormously. Tactical developments, on the other hand, had not kept pace with this revolution. The result was the slaughter of exposed infantry. When the BEF went to France in August 1914, it expected the fighting to follow the principles set out in its training manuals, which described tactics that were better suited to the middle of the nineteenth century than to the second decade of the twentieth. Infantry would engage each other at 1,200–1,500 yd, closing to 800–1,000 yd for the main battle. It was anticipated that the decisive range would be 400–500 yd, the battle going to whichever side could 'develop the most accurate and rapid rifle fire'. Concentrated small arms fire was seen to be the most important factor in deciding the outcome of a battle, while artillery was viewed as an ancillary instrument to aid this process.

What this failed to take into account was the intensity of the small arms fire that could be brought to bear with modern, magazine-fed, high-velocity rifles which made an exchange of fire at 400–500 yd deadly to both sides. Neither did it consider the devastating effect of modern, quick-firing artillery shooting high-explosive shells against unprotected infantry in the open. Although the fighting of the first few months of the war more or less followed the expected pattern, these two factors, combined with essentially outmoded infantry (and artillery) tactics, made it impossible for either side to bring about a decisive battle that would defeat the enemy. (One of the most remarkable achievements of the war was the revolution in tactics that allowed an Allied victory in 1918.) The British, French, Belgian and German Armies suffered appalling casualties and became exhausted by seemingly endless fighting, marching, fighting and countermarching in a vain effort to outmanoeuvre the enemy. During October they came to a standstill. Where they stopped, they dug in.

By late 1914 a line of trenches curved across France from the Swiss frontier and into Belgium, terminating on the North Sea coast. The result was stalemate and mutual siege, a situation that remained largely unchanged for about three and a half years despite battles of ever-increasing intensity being fought to try to break the deadlock. With the entrenchment of the armies, the nature of warfare changed almost overnight. Suddenly, not only had the tactics set out in the training manuals become redundant but it became apparent to private soldier and general alike that different types of weapons and equipment were needed. What had happened in Manchuria ten years earlier was now happening in France and Belgium on a massive scale.

The First World War was the first war – indeed the only one – in which massive opposing armies were entrenched opposite each other, separated by a strip of No Man's Land, for an extended period. It caused a radical change in the way the war was fought. During that time, the weapons of siege warfare assumed an importance not seen since the days of Marlborough when sieges were more common than battles. It was no accident that some of the weapons that emerged during late 1914 and throughout much of 1915 were ancient siege weapons such as catapults. Hand grenades, which had last seen widespread use in the eighteenth century, suddenly became essential; by the end of the war, the hand and rifle grenade had practically supplanted musketry as the principal means by which the infantry attacked the enemy. Captain Dunn, the medical officer of the 2nd Battalion, Royal Welch Fusiliers, referred to the 'cult of the bomb' in 1916 and Frank Richards wrote of 1917 that 'The young soldiers that were now arriving had been taught more about the bomb than about the rifle, which some of them hardly knew the way to load'. And the trench mortar became not only indispensable but decisive.

Weapons suitable for trench warfare had to be designed, tested, developed, trialled at the front, modified, sometimes redesigned, and retested and retrialled before finally being manufactured and supplied in large quantities to the front-line troops. For the British, this was neither a smooth nor easy process for much of 1915 and 1916 because of their lack of experience with such weapons and because of conflicting opinions at the Front about what form they should take. Trial and error was sometimes a painful process and for much of 1915 improvisation was the rule rather than the exception. Moreover, there was always a problem finding engineering companies that could take on the manufacture of things such as hand grenades, detonators and mortar ammunition at short notice and make them to the correct specifications. To a large extent, matters were eased by the Second Army Workshop set up by Captain Newton in 1915; many of the grenades and mortars supplied to the Front during 1915 came from this source.

During the course of the war, a profusion of departments came into being to examine the ideas and inventions submitted by members of the public and soldiers serving at the Front. Their brief also included designing new weapons. These departments included the Trench Warfare Department, the Trench Warfare Supply Department, the Design Department and the Munitions Inventions Department (MID), as well as various committees like the Trench Warfare Committee and the committees of the Munitions Inventions Panel, not to mention the Royal Arsenal at Woolwich and the Ordnance Board. The responsibilities of these departments and committees changed at various times as new departments were created, sometimes by division and amalgamation of existing departments and committees. Duplication of effort was rather more common than it might have been had there been better coordination between them. As late as May 1917 this duplication led General Headquarters (GHQ) France to issue 'Notes on Inventions and New Stores' that described equipment currently under test by GHQ to help prevent such duplication. On the inside front cover it stated:

> It has been found that much waste of time and labour results through experimental work being carried out on patterns of stores which have already been approved for manufacture. In order to obviate this the following notes on some of the more important inventions and new patterns dealt with at General Headquarters . . . are issued for information.

This book is about the weapons that became indispensable to trench warfare – grenades, trench mortars and bomb-throwers. More effort was put into developing these than any other trench warfare store. It focuses on British weapons and equipment simply because lack of space prevents more than a cursory glance at similar equipment adopted by the French and German Armies; this is a vast subject that has been largely unexplored by previous writers about the First World War. Not everything described in what follows was necessarily adopted by the British Army. Much of the effort that went into devising and evaluating new equipment eventually came to nothing, sometimes because the ideas were unsound and sometimes because good ideas could not be made to work effectively and safely; this was uncharted territory and inevitably mistakes were made. It was a constant process of learning and improvement. Sometimes promising weapons were ultimately rejected because they were too difficult to manufacture in quantity despite having undergone successful trials at the Front. Anything that required precision engineering and very tight tolerances was liable to be rejected. And there were a lot of hare-brained ideas that ranged from the Heath Robinson to the outright bizarre.

A huge number of ideas and suggestions came before the trench warfare departments. The MID is a case in point. During February 1918, 982 inventions were submitted to it, of which 880 were considered or sent to a more appropriate department if the submission did not come within its scope (including things related to naval and aerial warfare). In addition, 1,059 inventions were evaluated by the various committees of the Munitions Inventions Panel, 124 of which were considered to be worth further investigation. The MID's monthly report for May 1918 stated that since August 1915, 43,987 inventions and ideas had been submitted to it. Of these, 42,811 were considered by the department or sent to other departments; the panel committees evaluated 39,717 of them and produced reports on 3,549 that appeared to justify further development. By the end of the war, a total of 47,949 submissions had been made to the MID. Not all of these inventions and ideas were related to trench warfare, of course, but the figures give an idea of the enormity of the task of separating the wheat from the chaff. In the end, only 226 proved to be of any use. On the whole, the MID seems to have done a good job although rejection was not always accepted gracefully as all inventors tended to believe that their own project had war-winning potential.

In preparing this book, I have used two principal sources of information: War Office, Ministry of Munitions and Treasury files held at the Public Record Office at Kew, and UK patents that were applied for between August 1914 and November 1918 and subsequently granted, which are kept at the Science Library at Chancery Lane. The UK patents fall into the following classes: 9 (i) ammunition; 92 (i) ordnance and machine-gun carriages and mountings; 92 (ii) ordnance and machine-guns; and 119 small arms.

There are several hundred relevant patents dating from this period although relatively few of them formed the basis of a weapon that was even trialled at the front let alone officially adopted by the Army. Yet, it is highly probable that most of them were submitted to the MID or some other department for consideration at some stage – otherwise there would have been little point in the invention or in applying for the patent, although some of them related to improvements to existing weapons. However, few submitted inventions were identified as being the subject of patents. Some patents relate to important inventions such as the Mills hand grenade and the Stokes mortar.

Because of the large number of patents, it was not possible to look at all the complete specifications so the patent abridgements had to suffice in many cases and even then it was not possible to examine them all. Unlike the patents, which are arranged numerically irrespective of subject, the abridgements are volumes of extremely shortened versions of the specifications, being grouped numerically by class. They are intended as search tools and provide just enough information to show the nature of an invention to 'a person skilled in the art', i.e. someone who was familiar with the state of the art in a particular field at that time. Until 1916, patents were numbered from 1 at the beginning of each year. To correctly identify these, the year must be added to the number, e.g. 1,234/15. From 1916 the numbers became continuous.

The First World War was a time of great innovation. A tremendous amount of time and effort went into the search for new weapons for the trench war. This book is about the fruits of those labours.

CHAPTER 1

Jam-Tins, Pitchers and Balls – Hand Grenades 1914–15

The Russo-Japanese War made a much greater impression on the German observers than it did on those of Britain or France. This was not because the Germans were more receptive to new ideas than the British or the French but because the German Army had a somewhat different perspective. For one thing, it saw a future war as one of conquest, in which it might go east into Russia or west into France (in fact, it did both). Irrespective of which way it chose to go, a series of border forts would have to be destroyed if an invasion was to succeed. The siege of Port Arthur, which brought grenades and trench mortars to the fore, suggested to the Germans that similar situations its army might face when it invaded its neighbours could be resolved effectively with similar weapons. Consequently, the German

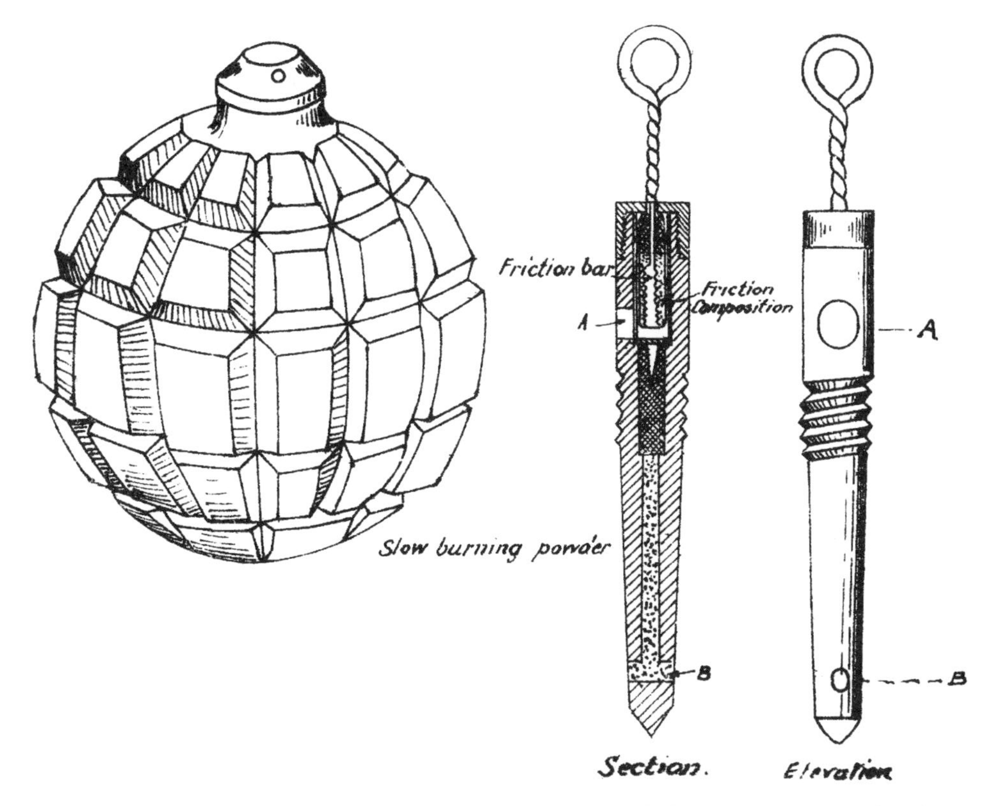

The German ball grenade was about 3 inches in diameter and varnished. The cast iron was about ⅓ inch thick. Explosive was black powder. The friction igniter of this example was fired by pulling the wire using a wrist strap with a swivel hook. (The Training and Employment of Grenadiers)

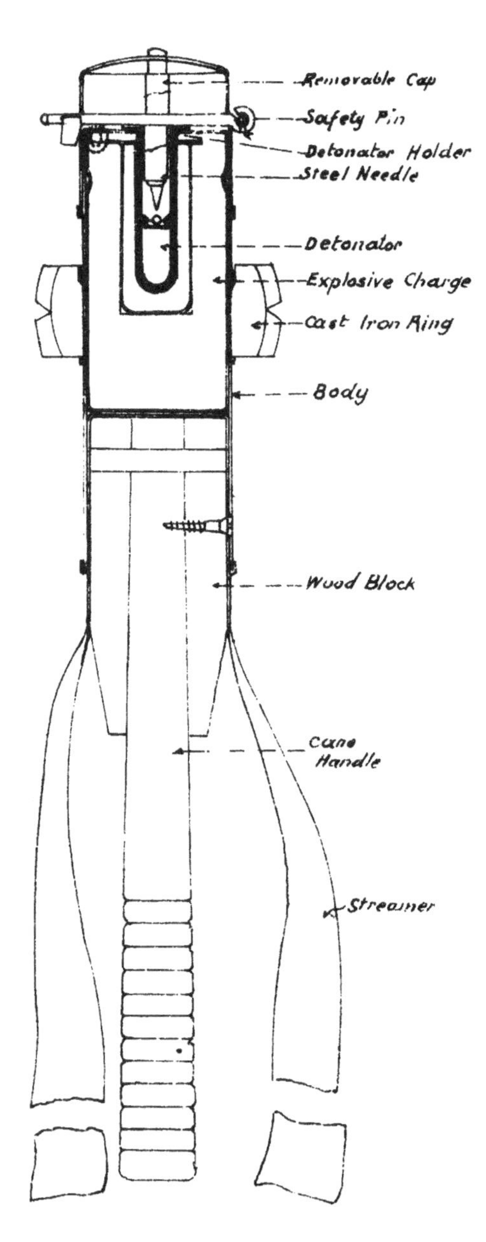

No. 1 Mk III percussion hand grenade. The handle of the No. 1 Mk I was much longer than this. (The Training and Employment of Grenadiers)

Army adopted heavy siege mortars and these later proved their effectiveness as they were responsible for the destruction of the Belgian forts at Namur and Liège in 1914. The German Army also saw the potential of hand and rifle grenades as well as lighter trench mortars, and decided to equip its army with them. It entered the First World War well supplied with grenades and, although the number of trench mortars available at the start of the war subsequently proved inadequate, they were nevertheless much better equipped than either the British or French Armies.

The start of trench warfare in late September to early October 1914 presented the British Army with a series of problems that could not be resolved quickly. In fact, it took until about the spring of 1916 to get on top of them. At the heart of these problems was the sudden and desperate need for trench mortars and hand and rifle grenades, a need that grew more pressing with each passing week. Although the British Army had adopted a percussion hand grenade in July 1908, the supply of them was quite inadequate to meet the demands received by the War Office from the increasingly desperate BEF. Moreover, the No. 1 percussion grenade had not been designed with trench warfare in mind and it was causing problems in the field.

Devised by the Royal Laboratory, the No. 1 stemmed from the report on the Japanese hand grenade by Lieutenant-General Sir J.L. Haldane, Britain's representative at the Japanese headquarters in Manchuria, and examples that he brought back to Britain on his return. In appearance, the No. 1 resembled a medieval mace with its 16 in wooden handle topped by a brass cylinder, around which was a segmented double ring of cast iron. Its overall length was just short of 22 in and it weighed nearly 1.75 lb. The cylinder contained the explosive. It had a removable cap to which a firing pin was fixed and held in a safe position by a removable safety pin. Until the grenade was required for use, the detonator was kept separate from the grenade. To arm it, the cap was removed, the detonator inserted and the cap replaced. All that was then required was removal of the safety pin and it was ready. A yard of webbing was wound around and attached to the lower part of the handle. Its purpose was to stabilize the grenade in flight by streaming out behind it as a tail, ensuring that the grenade landed on its head. It needed to do this to activate the impact fuse. The grenade needed to be handled with extreme care once it was armed.

Herein lay its most serious drawback: the percussion fuse was inherently dangerous. The No. 1 was prone to accidents once it had been armed. An impact with any surface would cause it to explode, as was witnessed by Robert Graves in early 1916 when he was an instructor at the base camp at Harfleur. While waiting for the bombing instructor to arrive, a group of soldiers about to be given a grenade demonstration watched as one of their number, a sergeant in the Royal Irish Rifles, picked up a No. 1 from the selection laid out on a table and proceeded to give an impromptu lesson. 'Now, lads, you've got to be careful here! Remember that if you touch anything while you're swinging this chap, it'll go off.' He then hit the edge of the table with it to emphasize the point. The result of this foolish act of bravado was predictable. The grenade exploded, killing the sergeant and a man standing beside him, and severely wounding twelve others.

But surfaces likely to detonate the grenade also included less avoidable things than the edges of tables. During late 1914 and well into 1915 there were numerous accidents caused by the thrower hitting the wall of a trench with the armed grenade while in the act of throwing. Unfortunately, this was all too easy to do because of its length, no matter how careful its users were, especially in the heat of the moment. One solution was to shorten the handle to half its original length but although this reduced the number of accidents it did not eliminate them, because it did not address the fundamental problem – the hazardous nature of the percussion fuse.

Part of the problem was lack of care by inadequately trained personnel. It had been assumed in 1908 that grenades would be used by trained specialists, Royal Engineers, familiar with handling explosives. In the reality of the trenches, however, they were handled by a far wider range of soldiery who tended to be much less aware of the potential hazards and have much less respect for them until taught otherwise by unfortunate example, as demonstrated by the Royal Irish sergeant at Harfleur. Systematic training did not really get under way until the middle of 1915. Before then, selected officers were given a brief period of instruction on a bombing course and were then expected to pass on their knowledge to others in the battalion. The Second Battalion of the Royal Welch Fusiliers received a demonstration from Second Lieutenant Murphy in January 1915 just after he attended such a course:

> the bomb was a Hale's long-handled stick-grenade [No. 2 hand grenade]. Murphy explained it with characteristic gravity and precision to a somewhat impatient, if not frivolous, audience. He showed us the use of the tail of tape to make it fall on its detonator, withdrew the safety-pin with due solemnity, and then, informing us that the proper action of throwing was that of bowling a cricket-ball, with a good round-arm action he bowled it across into the plough on the other side of the road. The explosion was not very startling, nor the displacement of soil considerable. We trooped across to look at its effect. Someone did say that it might be useful in trench-to-trench fighting.

Clearly, the audience was not impressed. When it came to using one in earnest, the erstwhile bomber might never have thrown one before, in which case he had to rely on remembering what he had seen someone else demonstrate behind the lines. Captain Attwater, another Royal Welch officer, recalled Murphy's demonstration when he found himself in a situation in which he had to throw a bomb on the spur of the moment, never having thrown one before. Fortunately, he was not in a trench and he got it right.

Left: *Throwing percussion grenades at a Bombing School,* c. *1915. You can just make out the streamers. Note the bowling action of the man on the left.* (ILN)

Below: *Although this photograph from* The Training and Employment of Grenadiers, *issued by GHQ in October 1915, is not very clear, it demonstrates how the percussion stick grenade should be thrown from a trench to avoid hitting the trench wall. The head of the grenade is held rather than the stick part and it is thrown like a dart. This was not the most efficient way of delivering a grenade but at least it was safe.*

A grenade-throwing contest. In view of the screen and unconcerned officer on the right, they are probably practice grenades without explosive. (ILN)

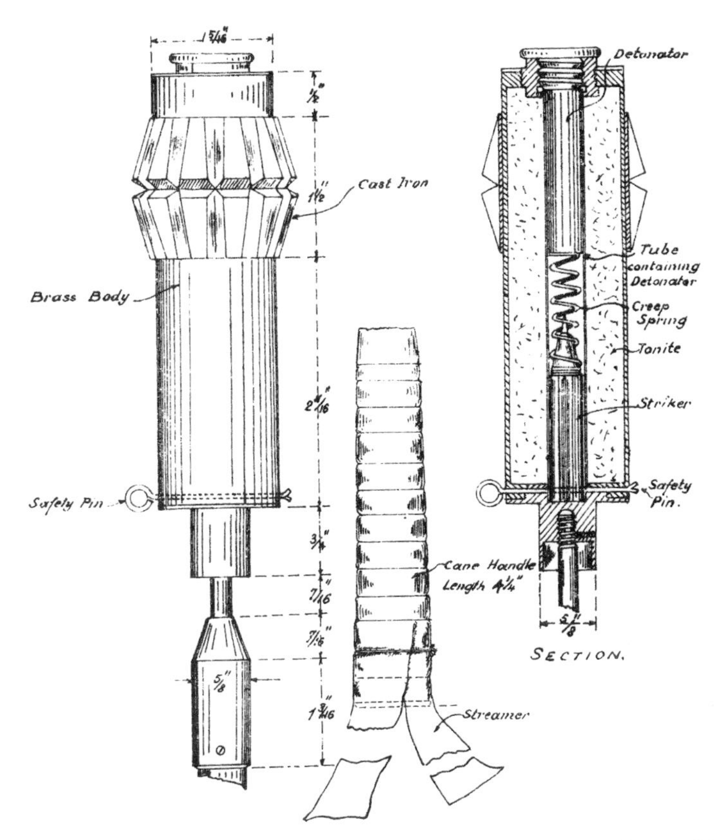

No. 2 percussion grenade. The detonator for this grenade was very similar to that used in the No. 3 rifle grenade, which sometimes caused confusion. It was an extremely sensitive grenade and not popular. (The Training and Employment of Grenadiers)

The bowling action was the standard way to toss all forms of hand grenade throughout the war. In time, bombers were taught how to do this from kneeling and prone positions as well as standing up. The grenade went further when bowled than when thrown. Moreover because bowling imparted a high-angle trajectory to the bomb, it helped to ensure that the bomb dropped onto the target trench rather than hitting the parapet. Bowling also had the added advantage of getting the bomb clear of the grenadier's own trench; throwing imparted a low-angle trajectory, which tended to result in disaster because the bomb often hit the side before it cleared the trench. Such an incident occurred during the Battle of Arras in 1917 when the Royal Welch Fusiliers were holding a captured German trench. During an exchange of grenades, a Royal Welch grenade failed to clear the trench, hit the top, dropped back into it and 'blew into fragments the feet of a young private'.

There were other problems with the grenade, or more specifically with supplies of the detonator – a problem that persisted throughout 1915 and which was the main cause of delays in production and ultimately of supply to the BEF. By October 1915 the grenade was being produced by the Ordnance Factories at the rate of 8,000 a week but this was far short of the 63,000 a week demanded by Field Marshal French in August. The limiting factor was the rate at which detonators could be made. Orders for 570,000 grenades were placed with various firms, 'the trade', most of which were unaccustomed to making armaments. In any case, they would be supplied without detonators. Since only the Ordnance Factories had facilities to make the detonators, the trade orders could not significantly improve the supply problem.

If the rate of production of detonators could be increased, the rate of production of completed grenades could be increased. Before the war, there were no more than eight or nine sources of detonators and half of them were German companies without production facilities in Britain. It was also discovered that if commercial companies undertook the manufacture of grenade detonators, this would compete with production of detonators for coal and gold mining, both important to the war effort. Of the commercial companies capable of making the detonators, only Nobel had the capacity to produce large numbers, but it too had problems. It could only make the required number if it stopped making commercial detonators; and the grenade detonators could only be made at one-tenth the rate of commercial detonator production. The situation was further complicated by the fact that the demand for hand grenade detonators competed with the demand for detonators for rifle grenades, which were also percussion-fused.

In September 1915 Nobel's weekly production of detonators for percussion grenades was only 5,000. By October Nobel had been prevailed upon to sacrifice the production of commercial detonators so that it could produce 20,000 grenade detonators a week but most of these were intended for rifle grenades, the need for which had become more pressing than for percussion hand grenades by the middle of 1915 – the demand for hand grenades had been satisfied by other means. In the meantime, Kynoch, the ammunition manufacturer, began the installation of plant to make 40,000 detonators a week but it was not expected to start production before January 1916. Again, most of these were destined for rifle grenades.

The Trench Warfare Department began experimenting with commercial detonators to find an alternative to the 'special' one needed for the percussion grenades as soon as the department was set up in June 1915. The problem was to find a detonator that would ignite the explosive in the grenade which was not the same as the commercial explosives used in mining; it was the explosive that determined the composition of the detonator charge. The trade argued that its commercial detonators would be unsuitable for grenades but it was not as familiar with military explosives as it was with commercial explosives and Trench Warfare Department experiments showed that some commercial detonators would do the job. While these experiments were under way, the department also looked into the possibilities of getting detonators from America but nothing seems to have come of it.

The Trench Warfare Department eventually designed an alternative percussion grenade, the No. 19, with a different detonator but this was not officially adopted until June 1917, although it had seen trials at the front some time before this. Although still a stick grenade, it was quite different from the No. 1. It had a segmented cast-iron pear-shaped body with a stubby extension on the top containing the striker which was topped by a disc, like a very large drawing pin. The Trench Warfare Department was confident that once this grenade went into production, 50,000 a week could be made. Meanwhile, the Royal Laboratory modified the No. 1 Mk III, which had a short handle, to take a different detonator and this was introduced as the No. 18 at the same time as the No. 19.

The British percussion grenades were, it seems, ineffectual. According to reports from German prisoners, captured by the French at Ypres during 1–15 January 1916, the British percussion grenades were deflected by the Germans with the distinctly unsophisticated means of wooden boards set up specifically for the purpose. They even caught some of them in flight and threw them back. The German grenades, on the other hand, were provided with touch cords and were consequently more effective.

The intense demand for hand grenades led to various short-term solutions, some of which introduced new problems or worsened existing ones. The initial response to the demand was to look for an existing supply of grenades that could be made immediately available to the Army. Such a supply was found. In August 1914 the Cotton Powder Company had been making grenades with percussion fuses under a contract for the Mexican government (Mexico had been going through a period of violent revolution since 1911). The company was making both hand and rifle versions of a grenade that was based on a design by Frederick Marten Hale, an engineer and General Manager of Explosive Trades Ltd (later taken over by Nobel), who patented his grenade in 1911 (UK patent 4,925/11 referred to rifle grenades but the mechanism was just as applicable to hand grenades). On 16 February 1915 this officially became the No. 2 hand grenade but it was also known as the Mexican pattern and the Hale's.

It was very similar to the No. 1. Both had long wooden handles with streamers to ensure that they landed head first. Both had cylindrical brass bodies. Both had segmented rings of cast iron for fragmentation (in the case of the No. 2 it was barrel-shaped as opposed to the thick disc on the No. 1). And both were percussion grenades. Unfortunately, the No. 2 also suffered from the same drawback as the No. 1 in that it required a special detonator that was slow to make. As with the No. 1, there were accidents because of the length of the handle so a shorter-handled version had to be produced.

In October 1915 the Cotton Powder Company was producing the No. 2 at the rate of 5,000 a week but this was about to be increased to 20,000 a week. To further increase output of the No. 2, Roburite & Ammonal began production in 1915 but whereas the Cotton Powder Company made its own detonators, Roburite & Ammonal had to get them from Nobel, which caused delays because Nobel was reluctant to supply them. Although on the face of it, the production of the No. 2 should have increased the supply of grenades to the BEF; in reality it did little to help the situation because of the difficult detonator. Indeed, this may have made the supply problem worse because of the increased competition for the 'special' detonators.

An alternative way of increasing the rate of production of the No. 2 was to change the explosive it contained so that a simpler detonator that was quicker to make could be employed; this appears to have been done. The Trench Warfare Department suggested that the explosive Tonite could be used and the Cotton Powder Company agreed that this would make a simpler detonator a feasible proposition. Meanwhile, the department put pressure on the company to modify its factory to increase its output of detonators and continued to exert pressure on it to ensure that the company fulfilled its promises.

Although there was a huge demand for grenades, paradoxically their real value was not appreciated before the middle of 1915. This was partly because the shortage of grenades at battalion level meant that few men had much experience of them. Even after nearly twelve months of trench warfare some officers remained sceptical of their value but again this stemmed from inexperience rather than outright prejudice. The situation was not improved when unfamiliar grenades were supplied to a battalion whose bombers were trained in the use of some other type. By the time of the Battle of Loos in September 1915 there were twelve different patterns of hand grenade. According to James Jack of the Cameronians, writing in October 1915 (when he was a captain), 'few had mastered completely the mechanism of all of them'. Come to that, few had even seen all of them. Lieutenant-Colonel O.F. Brothers, the Acting Controller of the Trench Warfare Department in August 1919, writing of the hand grenade in a report entitled 'Development of Weapons used in Trench Warfare', noted that 'the development of a war store is never likely to be rapid, unless its value is recognised and practical experience in its use is available'. Before the Battle of Loos 'the Grenade was

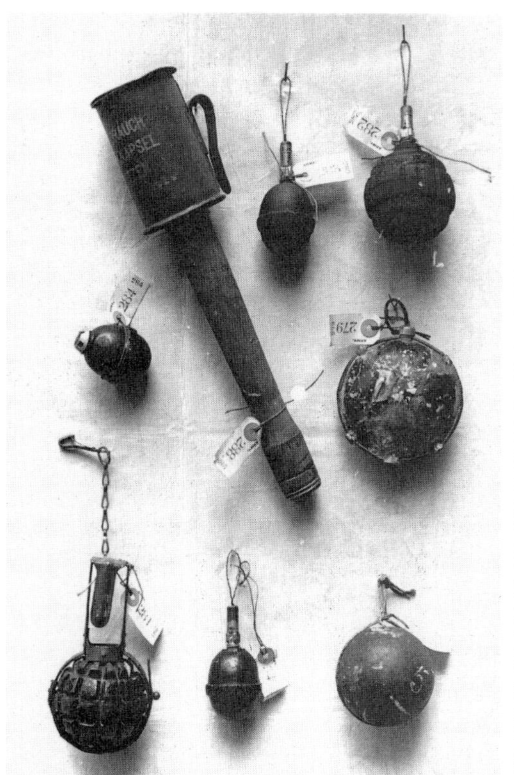

German grenades. Note the belt hook on the stick grenade. The smallest are egg grenades. A Diskusgranate *is in the middle on the right and a* Kugelgranate *(ball grenade) is at the lower left-hand side. It has a throwing handle which pulled the friction igniter as it was thrown.* (IWM)

A German grenadier late in the war. Note the 'special' at his feet, which has the cylinders of six stick grenades attached to the cylinder of a seventh complete with handle. This was probably intended for dealing with strong points or dugouts. Note also the instructions on the cylinders and the fuse type printed on the handles of those hooked on his belt. (The Times History of the War)

considered a "side-show"' and very little research was carried out. The main expenditure of energy was on providing expedient solutions to immediate problems and this was the main reason why there were so many different patterns of hand grenade. By the spring of 1916 most of the twelve had been withdrawn from service because they suffered from serious deficiencies. As Brothers ruefully pointed out in 1919 'The development of Grenades during this war has been on somewhat different lines to the normal lines of development of war stores'.

As soon as the German dominance in grenades and trench mortars became apparent in late 1914, Sir John French requested that someone be put in charge of developing equivalent British weapons as a countermeasure. The man chosen was Colonel Louis Jackson, the Assistant Director of Fortifications and Works (because trench warfare was a form of siege, it came under the remit of Fortifications), and it became his job to come up with equipment suitable for trench warfare. He was a good choice. Jackson could spot a good idea with potential. He was resourceful and inventive while at the same time a capable organizer. Under his direction, the search for new weapons quickly began to bear fruit.

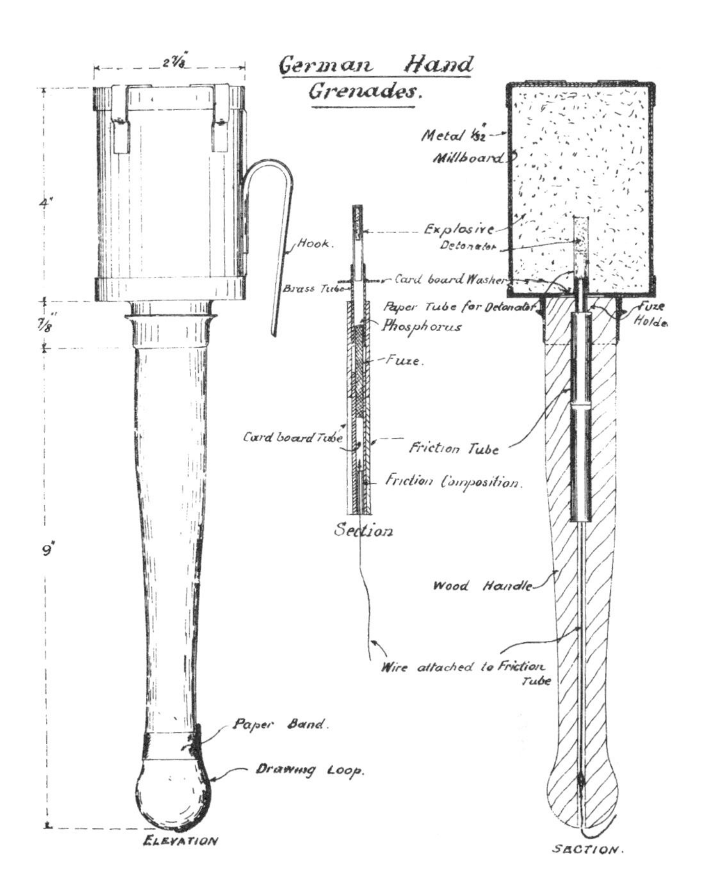

The 1915 German stick grenade, also known as the cylindrical grenade. The lid of the tin cylinder was held in place by four clips. Vor Gebrauch Sprengkapsel Einsetzen *was printed on the outside of the cylinder instructing the user to insert the detonator before use. The paper band at the base of the handle held the pull wire by which the friction igniter was fired. The fuse burning time of 5½ or 7 seconds was marked on the handle.* (The Training and Employment of Grenadiers)

Jackson had been trained at the Royal Military Academy, Woolwich, and had served overseas for much of his career, starting in Afghanistan in 1879. From 1895 to 1902 he was an instructor in fortifications and military engineering at the School of Military Engineering, Chatham, and from 1907 to 1910 he was the Assistant Director of Fortifications and Works before becoming the Chief Engineer of the London District in 1910. He retired from the Army in 1913. On the outbreak of war in August 1914 he was reappointed as an assistant director at the War Office. In 1915 he became a director-general in the Ministry of Munitions and between 1916 and 1917 he was Controller of Trench Warfare Research. He was to play an important role in the development of new weapons for trench warfare.

Jackson was responsible for the introduction of several of the hand grenades in service in 1915, as well as for helping to improve on others of the twelve. Each of them was a stopgap measure designed to provide a quick and ready supply of grenades that were easy to make in large numbers. They all dispensed with the percussion fuse, partly because of its inherent dangers and partly because of the problems that already existed in supplying suitable detonators. The time fuse that these reintroduced (all grenades prior to the twentieth century had used time fuses) remained the standard type used in hand grenades throughout the war, although the nature and operation of the fuse became more sophisticated. Later in the war attempts were made to reintroduce percussion-fused hand grenades but by then the time fuse was master.

Two of the grenades that owed their existence to Jackson have become synonymous with the spirit of improvisation at the front – the Jam-Tin and the Hairbrush grenades. It is clear from Jackson's account about early research that the Jam-Tin, or jam-pot, and the Hairbrush were his inventions, rather than unofficial improvisations created in France that were subsequently adopted on an official basis and manufactured under contract in Britain. The genesis of both had been a discussion with Lieutenant-General Sir Stanley von Donop, the Master-General of Ordnance, about the problem of supplying enough grenades. Jackson volunteered that he could 'make some' and was promptly given the opportunity to prove it.

Jackson obtained information from France about the quantity and type of explosive that would be likely to give the best results and set about designing hand grenades. In the end, his two designs contained ammonal. The idea for the Jam-Tin came from his knowledge of the 'quick manufacture of tin' through his earlier dealings with the Ammonal Company, which subsequently became the main contractor for both the Jam-Tin and the Hairbrush grenades. The Jam-Tin was officially known as the Double Cylinder grenade and it came in two versions. For some reason, rather than giving them Mk I and Mk II designations they were assigned different series numbers, so were born the No. 8 and No. 9 patterns. The difference between them was slight and amounted to little more than the No. 9 being heavier than the No. 8 by about 7 oz. Not surprisingly perhaps, the No. 8 was known as the Light Pattern and the No. 9 as the Heavy Pattern.

A group from the 2nd Battalion, Argyll and Sutherland Highlanders, spring 1915. Several grenades are on show including examples of the No. 2 and the Jam-Tin. (IWM)

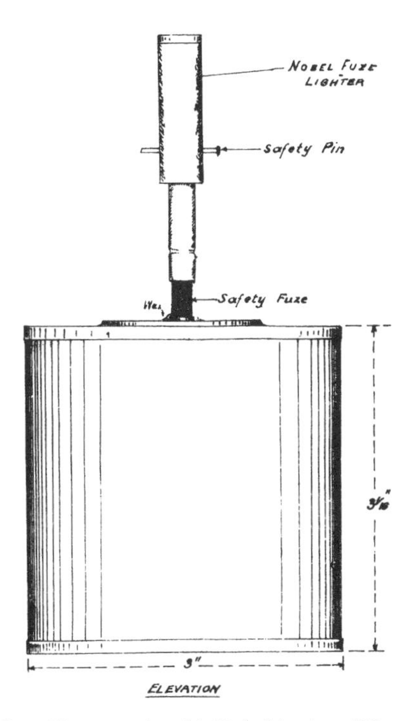

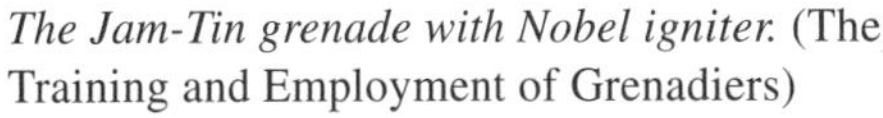
The Jam-Tin grenade with Nobel igniter. (The Training and Employment of Grenadiers)

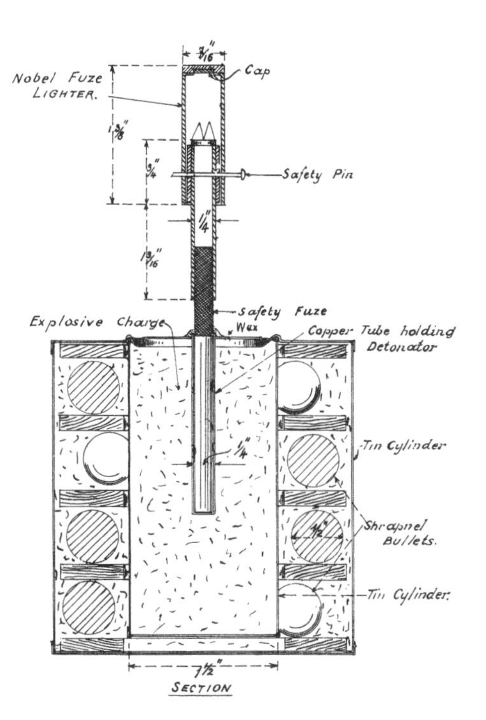

The Jam-Tin (No. 8) in section showing the shrapnel bullets and cast iron rings. The explosive was ammonal. (The Training and Employment of Grenadiers)

The Jam-Tin grenade was basically two cylinders or tubs of soldered tin, one inside the other, with 0.5 in steel shrapnel balls set in resin between them, the smaller, inner tub being filled with explosive, with a copper detonator holder in the centre of it to take a No. 8 Mk VII detonator (a development of commercial detonators). When the detonator was inserted immediately prior to use of the grenade, two lengths of copper wire, attached to the grenade's upper lid of tin, were used to secure it in place. The shrapnel filling was similar to that used in artillery shells. The No. 8 contained circular spacers of wood about 0.5 in thick, one at the top (the tops of the two tubs were both soldered to the upper lid) and one at the bottom of the outer casing, whereas the No. 9 dispensed with them and incorporated more shrapnel balls instead. It was these extra balls that made the grenade heavier (it weighed 2 lb as opposed to 1.5 lb). The heavier No. 9 was intended to be thrown by catapults and bomb-throwers as well as by hand, the extra weight allowing it to travel further than the lighter version.

Fusing for both grenades was extremely rudimentary but functional. Initially, Jackson tried Bickford fuse but trials showed it to be unsuited to the trench conditions; if it got damp it would not light. Bryant & May, Brock and others designed various fuses for the grenades to get round this problem. Brock produced a matchhead that was rubbed on an arm brassard to ignite it. When Bickford fuse was used, a portfire was intended as the means of ignition but in practice burning cigarettes were more often used, as recounted by Captain Hitchcock of the 2nd Battalion, Leinster Regiment. During an incident at Hooge in 1915 'Algeo [another officer] and his half-dozen bombers did wonders. With cigarettes in their mouths for lighting the fuses of their jam-tin bombs, they drove back over thirty Huns armed with Krupp's latest pattern bomb.'

Throwing a grenade from the kneeling position, demonstrating the bowling action. It is not easy to see which grenade the soldier is holding but it appears to be a No. 6, No. 7 or Jam-Tin. The range was expected to be a minimum of 20 yd from this position when in the open. In 1915, it was suggested that those men who enjoyed outdoor games would make the best bombers, especially if they were tall – the taller the man, the longer his reach and the further he could toss the grenade. (The Training and Employment of Grenadiers)

The Jam-Tin bomb was simple to extemporize by Royal Engineers who were encouraged to improvise from late 1914 onwards and throughout 1915. It is not clear whether the bomb acquired its name because it resembled a jam tin or because empty jam tins were used to make the grenade at the Front. There is no doubt that it was improvised from empty jam tins in France as well as in the Dardanelles, where grenades of any kind were in very short supply. Under such circumstances, the tins were filled with scrap metal of all kinds including cut lengths of barbed wire. The explosive filling was usually gun cotton and the fusing was usually Bickford safety fuse. The book *The War the Infantry Knew* suggests that improvised Jam-Tin bombs appeared in December 1914 but a 'demonstration with a new kind of bomb, a tin canister said to contain an almost unbelievable number of shrapnel bullets' carried out by Second Lieutenant Murphy in March 1915 seems more chronologically accurate and clearly refers to the No. 8 or No. 9 grenades rather than improvised Jam-Tins which, if Jackson's account is correct, must have come later.

The Hairbrush grenade was an oddity. Not only did it look even less like a bomb than the Jam-Tin but it was extremely heavy, weighing in at around 3 lb. Its crude appearance was no reflection on its effectiveness, however, although its weight meant that it could not be thrown as far as the lighter grenades. Also known as the Box Pattern, it was introduced as the No. 12 hand grenade at the same time as the Jam-Tin bombs in the spring of 1915. It resembled a woman's hairbrush because of its bat-shaped wooden paddle. A rectangular tin box was attached to the broad portion of the paddle by two heavy-gauge wire clamps that passed through it to be

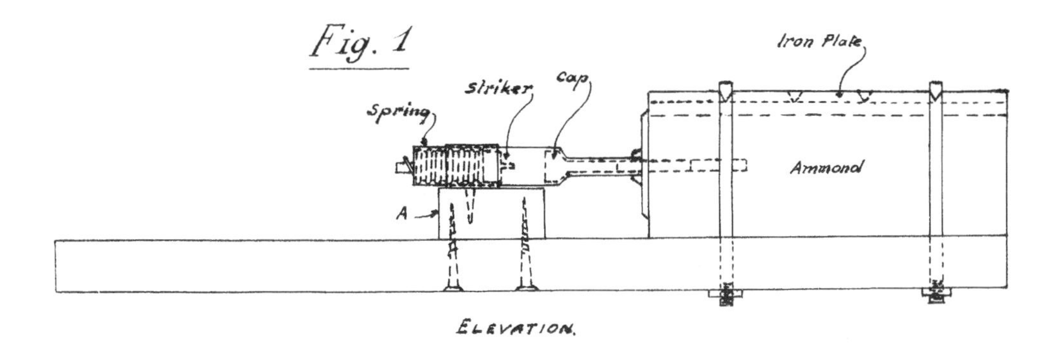

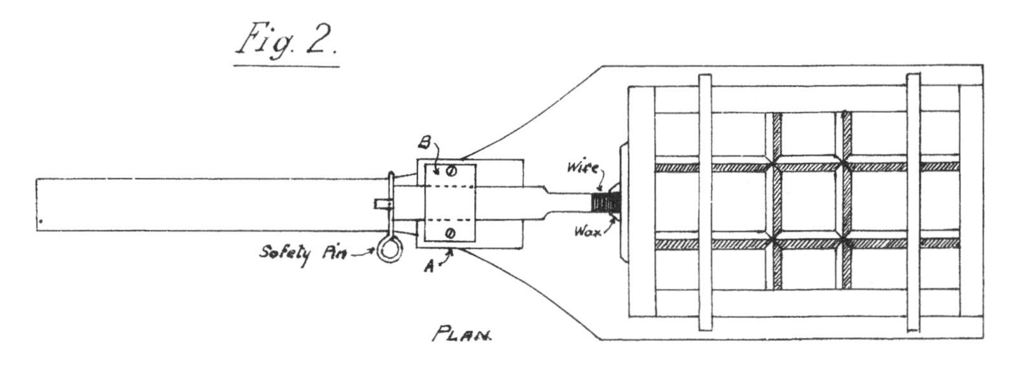

The Hairbrush grenade, one of Colonel Louis Jackson's designs, illustrated in The Training and Employment Grenadiers.

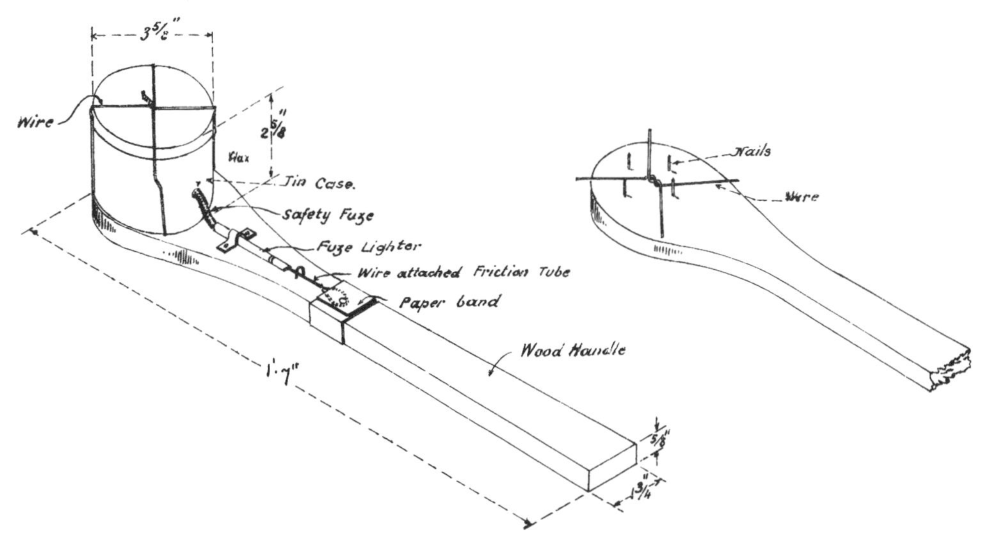

A French variation on the Hairbrush, an officially sanctioned improvisation made locally, known as a 'petard'. This one had a jam-tin body that was fixed to the wooden bat with nails and wire. Another variation had a rectangular tin box instead of the jam tin. In both cases, the container was not attached to the handle until the grenade was required for use. They needed to be handled with care. (The Training and Employment of Grenadiers)

A posed demonstration of how to throw the French version of the Hairbrush – and not very far by the look of it. Note how the grenades are held on a string over his shoulder. (ILN)

secured on the reverse by nuts. The top and bottom of the box were made of steel plates into which vertical and horizontal grooves had been cut to weaken them so they would fragment into evenly sized pieces on detonation (research since the Second World War has shown that putting such grooves into the body of a grenade has little effect on the size, shape or number of the fragments). Inside this box was another smaller one for the explosive. That the box within a box of the Hairbrush was similar to the double cylinder principal of the Jam-Tin is not surprising considering that they were designed by the same man at the same time and for the same reason, namely expediency.

This grenade also took the No. 8 Mk VII detonator, which (as with the Jam-Tin) was secured in place by copper wires. However, unlike the Jam-Tin, the safety fuse was ignited by the 'igniter, safety fuze, percussion' that consisted of a brass tube, containing a striker inside a compressed spring which was held above a percussion cap by a removable pin, and a shorter, narrower brass tube into which the safety fuse was fitted so that when the cap was struck it would ignite the fuse. This form of igniter was a copy of the sort used by the Germans on their grenades. It was more reliable than match-headed fuses or lighted cigarettes because it was less susceptible to deterioration by moisture. The igniter was secured to the handle of the paddle by a metal bracket.

Like the Jam-Tin, the Hairbrush was improvised at the front, using slabs of gun cotton as explosive and it seems that the extemporized Hairbrush was not confined to the British. The German version of the Hairbrush was probably what Edmund Blunden meant when he referred to '"windy bombs" with their bat-handles'. *The Times History of the War* (hereafter referred to as *The Times History*) recorded that 'The British, French, and Germans used the "fives-bat" form . . . which consists of a cake of explosive, to which is attached a fuse ignited just before it is thrown'. Grenades were used in such large numbers by both sides that approved supplies dried up at times leaving improvisation the only recourse to remedy the situation. Such grenades might be made from virtually anything that came to hand. There were reports of bottles being filled with explosive, stoppered with a rubber plug through which a length of safety fuse was inserted. According to *The Times History* 'All sorts of contrivances were at first used to form improvised grenades. . . . Meat tins, mess-tins, and, in fact, anything that would hold a charge'.

Generally, these improvisations were made by Royal Engineers but because they were not made under the same strict manufacturing conditions as were imposed on the contractors in

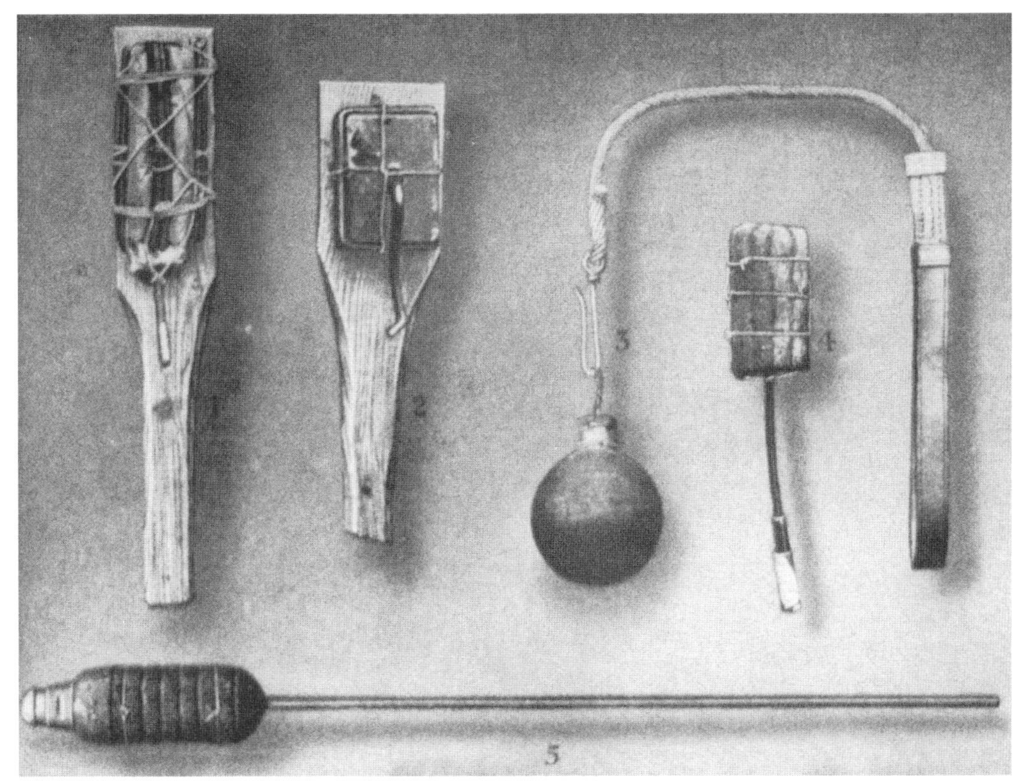

A selection of grenades, 1915. The two on the left are improvised copies of the Hairbrush; the larger one is French, the smaller one is German. The ball is a French bracelet grenade. The right-hand grenade is an improvised British device with a twist friction igniter. The rifle grenade at the bottom is German. (The Times History of the War)

Britain, there was plenty of scope for error. Many of the improvisations were more lethal to their users than the enemy as they had an alarming tendency to explode prematurely or for the resulting explosion to be excessively large. Some simply did not detonate, while on others the fuse went out before they were thrown. If a partly burned fuse was relit, there was a very strong likelihood that the grenade would explode too close to the thrower. *The Times History* recounted such an incident at the Dardanelles in which the thrower relit a Jam-Tin grenade that quickly exploded and severely injured him.

Another improvisation was the Battye bomb, made in Béthune. It is not clear whether this was made by Royal Engineers or a French firm but the evidence suggests the latter. Judging from its name, the inventor was someone called Battye. It must have been made in reasonably large numbers as the Trench Warfare Department was asked to look into the possibility of supplying different igniters for the Bickford safety fuse. The suggestion appears to have been initially turned down as impractical but Nobel igniters were subsequently fitted.

In December 1915 the use of any improvised or unapproved grenade was forbidden because of the high number of accidents. No doubt this was greeted with some relief by all concerned. Fortunately, by then the supply of grenades of an approved pattern had greatly improved. The pattern in question was the No. 5, the first version of the Mills bomb.

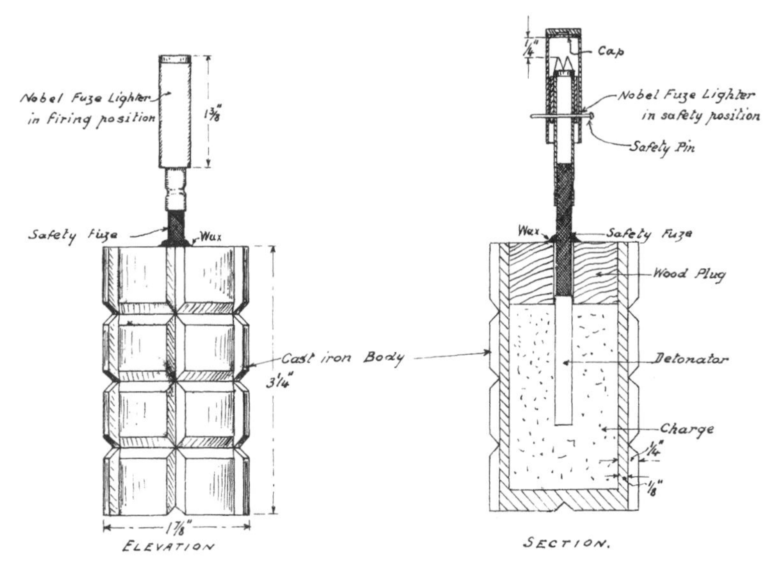

The Battye bomb, an interim measure of 1915, consisted of a grooved, cast iron cylinder, containing 1.5 oz of explosive and weighed 1 lb 2 oz. The detonator was only inserted immediately prior to use. The wax was to keep out moisture. (From The Training and Employment of Grenadiers, issued in October 1915)

Another posed demonstration, this time of throwing the bracelet grenade. His grenades are in the satchel. Inset left is a disassembled German rifle grenade. (ILN)

Although this was introduced in about May 1915, it did not entirely replace the other patterns until about December or even the spring of 1916. The Mills was, of course, one of the twelve to which James Jack had referred, another two of which were the No. 1 and No. 2 percussion grenades; the Jam-Tins and Hairbrush were three more. Although none of these was intended to remain in service for long – they were only stopgap measures until research came up with the elusive perfect grenade – the other six were quite different from these and included the Lemon grenades, the Pitcher grenades and the Ball and Oval patterns. They were all introduced in the first half of 1915. The Pitchers gained a reputation for lethal unsafeness, earning the bombers who used them the unenviable nickname of the Suicide Club, and the Ball and Oval patterns were so unreliable that they nearly caused disaster at Loos and were no sooner issued than they were withdrawn.

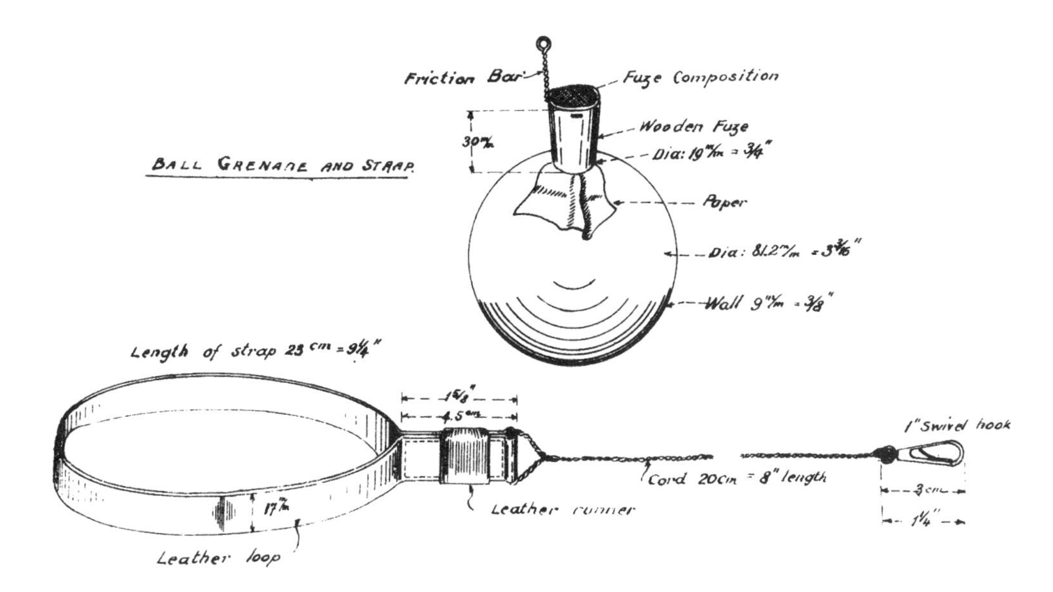

The French bracelet or ball grenade, also known as the Fortress Artillery Grenade. It was filled with black powder and ignited by friction. The strap was worn on the right wrist and paper covering the wooden plug or fuse was torn back to the body of the grenade. The wire was bent upwards and the swivel hook of the strap was clipped to the ring in the wire. The grenade was held with the fuse to the rear and thrown with the arm fully straightened until the friction bar or wire had been pulled. Extreme caution had to be exercised when straightening the wire to avoid premature ignition. (The Training and Employment of Grenadiers)

Of these, excepting the Mills, the No. 6 and No. 7 Lemon friction patterns were perhaps some of the more reliable grenades but were not without their problems. Made at Woolwich, they had been designed by the Royal Laboratory as temporary expedients like the Jam-Tin and the Hairbrush. Unlike the other grenades, they had a friction igniter that had been specially designed by the Royal Laboratory. The name 'lemon' was derived from their shape, although they did not look at all like lemons. Approximately 4 inches tall and 2.3 inches in diameter, both the No. 6 and the No. 7 had outer cylindrical casings of soldered tin, the top and bottom caps of which were shallow flattened domes so that the grenades looked rather more like modern soft drink cans than lemons. The Light Pattern, the No. 6, contained only explosive whereas the Heavy Pattern, the No. 7, had an inner casing for the explosive and the space between the inner and outer casings was filled with steel scrap as rudimentary but functional shrapnel. However, the Light Pattern was preferred over the Heavy Pattern because it could be thrown further and a bomber could carry more of them.

This reasoning was always used whenever there was a choice between light and heavy versions of grenades. However, there was a little more to it than that. Grenades that contained no added shrapnel were not only lighter but safer to the thrower and his companions, especially if the casing was soldered tin, since the grenade's effect was achieved almost exclusively by blast. Consequently, there was little risk of getting hit by shrapnel from a friendly bomb. On the other hand, a shrapnel grenade tended to hurl large pieces of metal over a greater distance than it could be thrown. If it was used in the open, the thrower and his companions were forced to take cover to avoid injury.

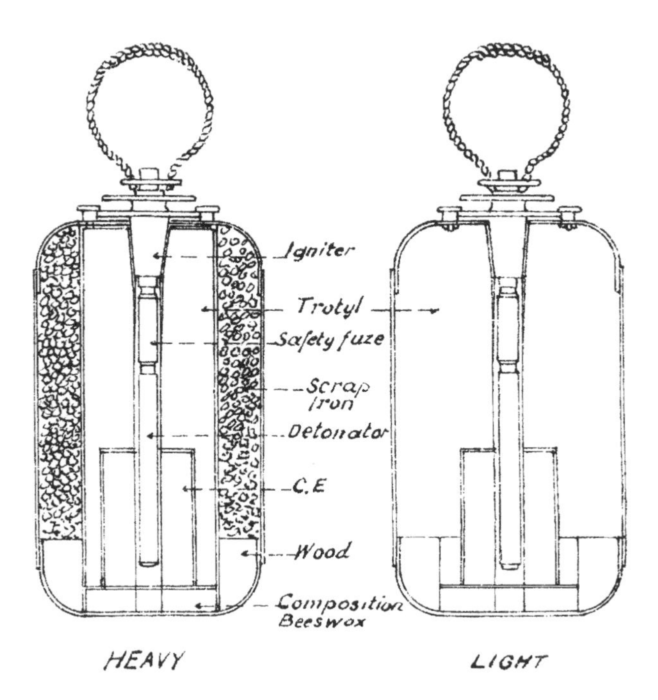

Nos 6 and 7 Lemon grenades. Immediately prior to use, the igniter was inserted and the flange clipped under the studs. The papier maché transit cap was then replaced until the grenadier was ready to ignite the grenade. To throw it, the grenade was held with the loop towards the wrist, the cap was removed and the loop was pulled out sharply according to The Training and Employment of Grenadiers *issued in October 1915. However, in practice this did not always work.*

Two studs on the upper cap of the casing of the Lemon engaged a notched flange with springs on the friction igniter to hold the latter in place, rather than the cruder copper wires used on the Jam-Tin for the similar purpose of securing the detonator (a method that was almost guaranteed to result in a high proportion of failures due to the wires being inadequately tied so that the detonator fell out). This same igniter had been proposed as a modification to the Battye bomb but because a flange with studs capable of withstanding a 30 lb pull needed to be fitted to the Battye in order to accommodate the igniter, the proposal was dropped. The igniter consisted of a metal holder with a friction bar and an ignition composition inside attached to a No. 8 Mk VII detonator via a short length of safety fuse. The composition was secret and this caused some difficulties when the Ordnance Factories tried to get the grenades made by the trade because they were not at liberty to divulge its make-up, although Jarman & Co and Ewart & Son did make some of the outer casings under contract. Moreover, the friction igniters were rather too sensitive for rough treatment in the field. When fitted in the grenades, the igniters made them almost as dangerous to handle as the percussion patterns. A sharp blow to an armed grenade could fire the igniter and there was only a 5-second delay before it exploded.

In theory, the igniter was fired by a sharp pull on a loop of tarred whipcord attached to a knob fitted to the end of the friction bar. However, a letter dated 20 May 1915 from Lieutenant-General R.C. Maxwell, writing to the War Office on behalf of Sir John French, pointed out that the pull on the loop was often too much for one man and sometimes needed

Bombing practice at a Bombing School, c. *1915.* (ILN)

the strength of two to make it work, hardly a recommendation for the grenade. The most effective method of firing it was to hold the grenade between the knees to pull the cord as though drawing a cork from a bottle but this often resulted in cut fingers. The problem was not encountered with all Lemon grenades, which served only to make it all the more frustrating because it only became apparent when a bomber came to use one. This was a far from satisfactory state of affairs and it needed to be put right, but it never was. The Lemon grenades were declared obsolescent at the end of December 1915.

Problems with friction igniters were by no means confined to the Lemon grenades. Far more serious difficulties were found with the so-called Pitcher grenades, difficulties that resulted in a lot of accidents, which were often fatal. The Pitcher was a commercially designed grenade and although it is not clear how it came to be adopted by the Army, it is likely that it was one of the inventions put before one of the committees or departments set up to examine ideas from the public. It has been suggested that the name 'pitcher' was derived from its

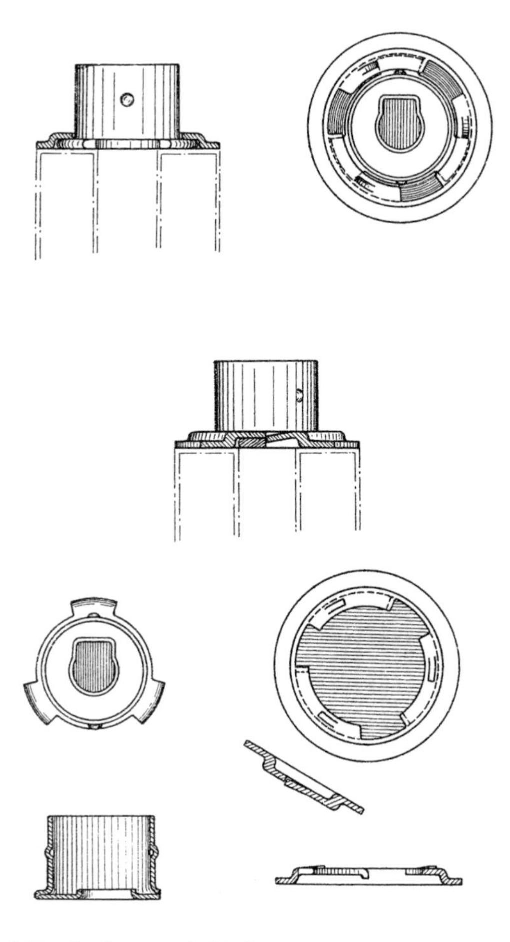

The drawings from one of Charles Sangster's Pitcher patents (5,901/15). These show 'means for connecting and locking the fuse-cap . . . to the charge-container'.

appearance. However, it seems more likely that the name was picked up from the wording in the two UK patents, 5900/15 and 5901/15, the statements of invention of which start 'This invention has reference to military hand or pitcher grenades'. 'Pitcher' clearly refers to the method of throwing grenades rather than the appearance of these particular patterns.

The Pitcher was the invention of Charles Thomas Brock Sangster, a Birmingham engineer. He applied for his two patents on 20 April 1915, predating their official introduction by only a matter of weeks. This raises the question of whether the grenade was entirely his idea or the result of collaboration with someone else. The method of making the outer casing and the shape of its segments (the subject of 5900/15) and the method of attaching the friction igniter to the casing (the subject of 5901/15) may have been refinements of something that was already under development. Unfortunately, the patents give no clue since arguments for either position can be made from the information they contain. There is a slight twist to this. Colonel Jackson claims that he designed the friction pull pattern of fuse on the Pitcher grenade, a claim that predates its introduction (in other words, it was not a modification at a later stage). It would appear that the Pitcher was a collaborative effort between Jackson and Sangster.

The two versions of the Pitcher were about the same size and weight as the Lemons, the No. 14 Pitcher being slightly heavier than the No. 13. The reason for the difference in weight was that the outer casing of the No. 13 was made of steel while that of its sister was made from cast iron. The significance of using steel for one and cast iron for the other was not made clear. Each had an internal tin cylinder filled with explosive, the space between the inner and outer casings being filled with lead wool in the case of the No. 13 and pitch in the case of the No. 14. Again it is not clear why one used lead wool and the other used pitch. Certainly, neither would have added to the fragmentation effect.

Even fragmentation of the outer casing was at the heart of Sangster's first patent. It was also his intention to 'provide an improved grenade-shell which can be more cheaply manufactured and assembled with the charge container without involving any machining operations'. The casing was cast with one enclosed end, the 'thinning grooves along and around the exterior . . . being produced or formed in the walls in or by the casting process so that all machining operations are obviated'. An essential feature of the casing was the shape of the segments. These were pyramidal with a thickened middle section, the idea being that these would cause more serious injuries by virtue of being heavier than similarly sized fragments that were of uniform thickness. Moreover, by dividing the casing into pyramidal

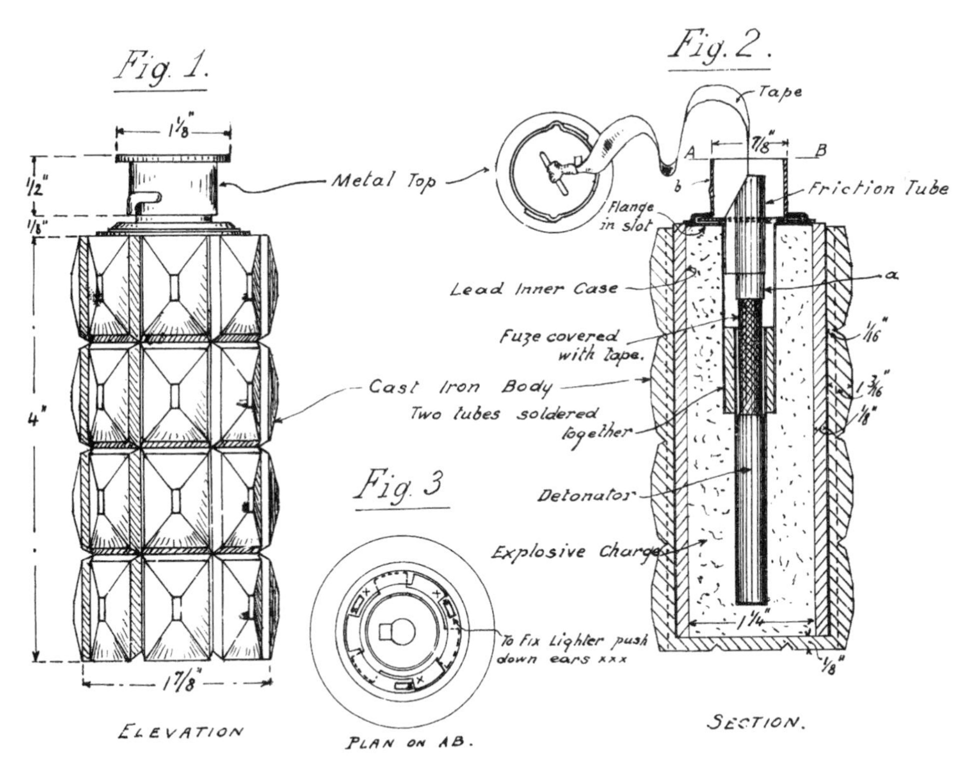

The infamous Pitcher invented by Charles Sangster. According to The Training and Employment of Grenadiers, *it was quite a rigmarole to assemble and arm it. The instructions and precautions described in the manual were intended to avoid more of the fatal accidents that had already occurred with the grenade. However, it had built-in dangers, including the cap – the parts marked with Xs (Fig. 3) needed to be firmly pushed down to avoid pulling out the lighter.*

segments, the theory was that fewer small and relatively harmless fragments would be produced on detonation. The War Office fondly believed that thirty-five fragments would be the result but as mentioned above, segmenting grenade casings in this way had no effect on the number or size of the fragments that were produced on detonation.

On the face of it, the Pitchers looked to be serviceable grenades that would perform under most trench conditions. But the friction fuse was frighteningly dangerous. In fairness to Colonel Jackson, this does not appear to be a design fault but rather a manufacturing one, caused to a large extent by poorly controlled production methods. The main contractors, Roburite & Ammonal, which made the No. 13, and Decimals Ltd, which made the No. 14, may not have had pressure put on them to conform to the strict manufacturing codes because of the increasingly difficult job of policing commercial businesses involved in war work. Altogether only about 10,000 No. 13s and 20,000 No. 14s were produced.

The friction igniter was basically a tube with a piece of safety fuse and a bead of a matchhead composition at the top. A piece of silk tape covered with the abrasive composition used on the outside of matchboxes was located in a groove that ran up the side of the tube, past the matchhead composition, and was tied to the igniter's removable cap. The igniter was supposed to work by pulling off the cap with a slight turn and a sharp jerk, thereby causing the tape to rub against the matchhead composition to produce a flame and light the fuse, much like striking a match on a matchbox. It sounded good.

By September 1915 Field Marshal French was demanding that the supply of Pitchers be stopped immediately because of the number of accidents with them. On 8 September 1915 Lieutenant-General Maxwell wrote to the War Office on French's instructions to describe the defects of the Pitcher grenades, most of which related to the friction igniter. He cited, as an example, an accident in August when a grenade had exploded as soon as the tape was pulled – there should have been a 5-second delay – killing the unfortunate bomber. Maxwell pointed out that the officers on the spot had determined that the accident was not because of a faulty grenade, although quite how this could have been determined after the grenade had exploded is hard to imagine. It was probably caused by a spark bypassing the safety fuse and jumping directly onto the detonator although a tape binding was already supplied to prevent this very thing happening. It was suggested that the tape may have worked loose. This was not an isolated incident; there had been many similar accidents. A court of inquiry held on 4 July into a death caused by an accident with a Pitcher made it plain that these grenades were too dangerous and that they should be withdrawn from service.

Another serious defect was the amount of pull on the tape that was necessary to make the igniter work. The tape sometimes broke without igniting the detonator because of the excessively strong pull that was needed. The tin cylinder containing the explosive, inside which was the detonator to which the igniter was attached, was sometimes so insecurely fixed to the outer casing that it was tugged out when the tape was pulled, a rather alarming, not to say dangerous, occurrence. Worse still, the flame from the igniter was found to vary from 2 to as much as 6 inches in length; 6 inches was far too powerful and tended to burn the bomber's fingers and made the grenades quite unsuitable for night work. Maxwell made it clear that because of these defects the troops in 1st Division had been instructed by their commander to light the fuse with a fusee instead.

And if all that was not bad enough, Maxwell informed the War Office that Pitchers produced large fragments that flew back into friendly troops; there was a danger zone of about 200 yd and they were therefore unsuitable for throwing in the open. The brigades were told not to use the grenades any more. By the middle of September the issue of Pitchers from Britain had been stopped.

French grenadiers, c. *July 1915. Yet another posed picture. Note that these French stick grenades are suspended from the belt by hooks.* (ILN)

These French soldiers (from summer 1915) carry two sorts of grenade: stick grenades with lever/striker mechanisms, suspended from their belts; and the man on the right is holding a ball grenade in each hand. All three wear steel caps that go under the kepi; two wear Daigre body shields. The man on the right also carries what appears to be a short sword with a single-edged blade. The man on the left is wearing a simple gas mask. (ILN)

Writing to the War Office in June 1915, Sir John French went to some pains to reiterate his request for greater numbers of hand grenades to be supplied to the BEF. Trench fighting had created a greater demand than supplies could satisfy because men were relying more and more on the grenade. They found that the rifle and bayonet were not easy to use effectively in the confined spaces of the trenches and the only alternative was the hand grenade. Moreover, attack and counter-attack by parties of bombers meant that grenades were consumed in enormous quantities. French cited as an example a French Army corps that had got through 30,000 grenades in 24 hours at Arras. That he did not cite an example from his own army suggests that he did not know the figures, a rather curious state of affairs. He also wanted all infantrymen to be trained as bombers. Many who were untrained in the specialization of bombing were resorting to the bomb. He asked for the standardization of grenades because men were being trained in one type, only to be supplied with another.

It was a forlorn request. In June 1915 there were simply no facilities to produce one type of grenade in sufficiently large numbers to satisfy the demand. Moreover, this was still a period of 'suck it and see'; no one was certain which grenade would ultimately become the standard pattern – if, indeed, any of those currently in production and being supplied to the BEF was suitable. All of them had drawbacks.

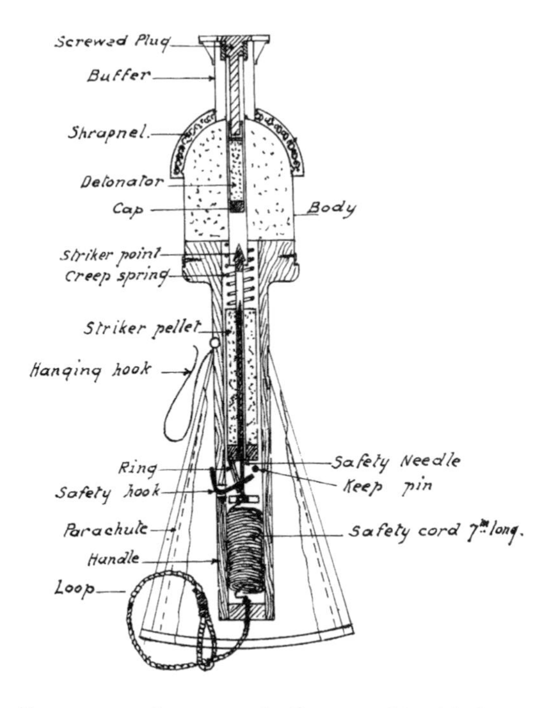

German parachute grenade. Compare this with the grenades carried by the French soldier in the photograph on the previous page. In The Training and Employment of Grenadiers *it is described as German but the photograph clearly shows French poilus. However, captured equipment was utilized by both sides. The black-painted, tin body had a cone of shrapnel. The buffer ensured that the grenade exploded above ground and the parachute made sure that it landed head first – it was a percussion grenade. The 12–13 ft safety cord inside the handle was attached to a safety needle and the loop was held in the hand when the grenade was thrown upwards. When it reached a height of about 12–13 ft, the needle was jerked out freeing the safety hook, which fell away and released the ring that was attached to the striker pellet thus arming the grenade.*

In August Maxwell wrote to the War Office with the estimated daily expenditure of grenades. According to him it was 220 rifle grenades, 120 percussion grenades and 240 time-fused grenades for each division. As there were forty-eight fighting divisions in the BEF at this time, this came to a daily expenditure of 17,280 grenades of all types and 10,560 rifle grenades. In addition, he wanted reserves per division of 4,500 rifle grenades, 7,000 percussion grenades and 7,000 time-fused grenades. These figures did not take into account the daily requirement of twenty grenades per bomb-thrower and catapult, which for each division evidently amounted to 160 grenades for the West Spring Gun and 160 for the Leach catapult. According to Maxwell, this came to 7,500 of each per day but this would only supply forty-seven divisions not forty-eight. Interestingly, these figures indicate that there were on average eight West Spring Guns and eight Leach catapults in each division.

In September 1915 French launched the BEF into the Loos offensive. The No. 15 Ball Pattern or Cricket Ball grenade was intended to play an important role in this attempt to breach the German defences and break through to open country beyond. In the event, not only was the offensive unsuccessful but the failure of the grenade nearly led to disaster. 'A number of regiments were supplied with the "Cricket Ball" Grenade. . . . Owing to the rain, in about 18 out of every 20, the igniter failed to light' was how the débâcle was described in 1919. The Ball grenade had originally been designed to meet an urgent request for bombs in the Dardanelles, where there was a severe grenade shortage. Its design was influenced by the need for fast production and it fulfilled its purpose admirably. In early September the rate of production was more than 200,000 a week.

The No. 15 was a 3 in diameter sphere of cast iron, segmented internally for fragmentation. It had either a 5-second or a 9-second fuse, the latter being intended for use with catapults and bomb-throwers with which it was considered to be very useful. Both used a Brock matchhead igniter that was struck against an arm brassard to light it and both had a lead pull-off cap to protect the fuse prior to use. In the Dardanelles, where the weather was hot and dry, the grenade fulfilled its expectations, which no doubt led the Home Authorities

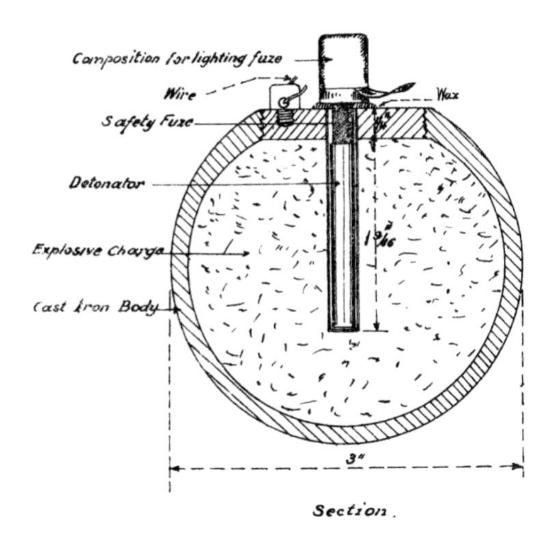

The infamous No. 15 Ball grenade that failed so abysmally at Loos in September 1915. (The Training and Employment of Grenadiers)

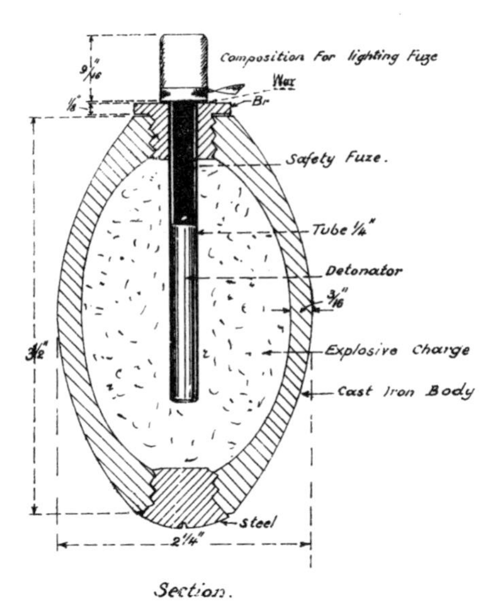

The No. 16 Oval grenade fitted with a Brock lighter. 'The lighter consists of a small cardboard cup filled with friction composition, covered with waterproof paper.' The small tag on the right is used to pull off the cover. An armlet was used to light the fuse. (The Training and Employment of Grenadiers)

to believe that it would perform equally well in France. Its only drawbacks were the size of the explosive charge and its 3 in diameter, both of which were considered to be too big. The solution to the size problem was the No. 16 Oval Pattern, which was essentially the same as the Ball differing only in shape, although the Oval Pattern had a brass plug in the base to close the charge-filling hole. The Oval was supposed to replace the Ball around September but because the ignition system was same for both grenades, the Oval suffered from the same problems as its sister in wet weather.

A memo from Louis Jackson in mid-September 1915 explained that the problem of the excess charge had been addressed by replacing some of the explosive with sand. This modification had evidently been undertaken before September because Lieutenant-General Maxwell noted the increased lethality of the Ball grenade if only half the ammonal charge was used (about 2.5–3 oz) in a letter to the War Office at the beginning of the month. The effect of this was to increase the size of the fragments.

Significantly, in view of what was about to happen at Loos, Maxwell also noted the inferiority of the Ball (along with the Lemon patterns) compared to the Mills and expressed the hope that the supply would soon discontinue. The Mills, however, although being produced at the rate of 33,000 a week, was not being delivered effectively. Only 10 per cent of the Mills that should have been delivered by the beginning of September had arrived. So Maxwell and French were stuck with the Ball pattern, like it or not.

The 2nd Battalion, Royal Welch Fusiliers was one of the regiments supplied with the Ball grenade at Loos. Captain Dunn recorded that they were equipped with 'several new and unwieldy bombs known as "cricket balls". The match-striker on which the bomb fuse had to be lighted had become so wet as to be useless.' Robert Graves recalled that survivors of the two leading

Stick grenade carrier, October 1915, as illustrated in CDS 74 The Training and Employment of Grenadiers. *It consisted of a belt 3 ft long and 3 in wide tied at the back with tapes, with supporting straps over the shoulders. There were eight loops for grenades.*

The waistcoat designed for the Nos 6 and 7 grenades was intended to hold ten bombs. The waistcoats were packed in the grenade boxes used to transport the grenades to the Front. (The Training and Employment of Grenadiers)

Two slightly different patterns of waistcoat worn in summer 1915 for carrying grenades. The men appear to holding Ball grenades. (The Times History of the War)

companies of the neighbouring Middlesex Regiment sheltering in shell holes near the German wire 'had bombs to throw, but these were nearly all of a new type issued for the battle. The fuses were lighted on the match-box principle, and the rain had made them useless.' Jack recorded, of a diversionary attack at the same time, that 'the fuses of the bombs became damp from rain and would not light'.

On 20 November 1915 the Army Council made it clear that the only time-fused type of grenade it wanted was the Mills No. 5 and that the Ball Pattern should be discarded forthwith because it had shown itself to be quite useless. Not surprisingly, the men had lost confidence in it, although it is doubtful that there was ever any confidence to lose. The Army Council proposed that the entire stock should be returned to Britain unless a damp-proof ignition system could be supplied very quickly. Such a system was not a feasible option and on 25 November all outstanding contracts for the No. 6, Ball and Pitcher grenades were cancelled. The year 1915 had not been a good one.

Nearly twelve months later, by which time Loos had been over-shadowed by the Somme, Edmund Blunden came upon a mildewed old store of Cricket Balls and Hairbrushes that had lain untouched and long forgotten. Wisely, he decided to leave them alone.

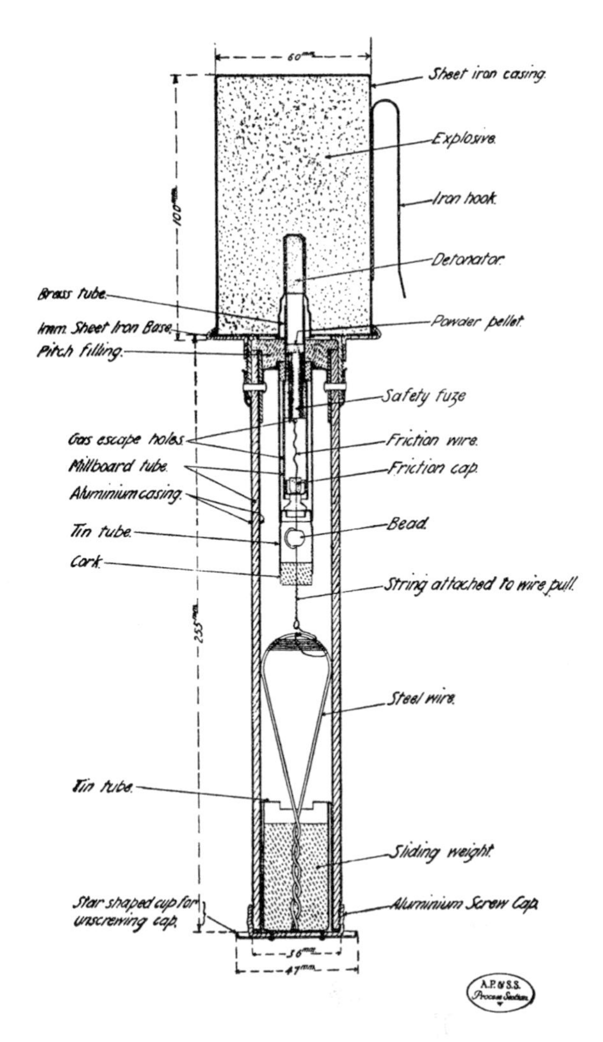

Drawing of a 1917 German stick grenade from SS 566 showing its mechanism. The screw cap at the base of the handle is removed and the weight falls, pulling the wire and operating the friction igniter. Armed by the act of throwing. (MUN 4/3589)

CHAPTER 2

Drainpipes, Toffee-apples and Flying Pigs – Trench Mortars 1914–15

The German trench mortar was loathed right from the start. It was unlike any other weapon. Its bomb was big and brutal and it seemed to those on the receiving end to move through the air with a perceptible and unnerving malevolence. In late 1914 it came as something of a shock to the soldiers of the BEF to find themselves bombarded in their trenches with bombs that dropped right on top of them with little warning. Not only had they never encountered such a weapon before but at first they had no means of countering it. In 1914 the Germans had over a hundred trench mortars while the British had not a single one.

A medium German trench mortar and one of its shells captured by the British near Nieuport in 1915. The cylinders above and below the barrel are part of the recoil system. It had a rifled barrel. (ILN)

The loathing for German trench mortars and their bombs led to them acquiring a variety of nicknames, all designed to lessen the fear they induced and make them appear less sinister. As the German term was *minenwerfer*, which translated as mine-thrower, they were often referred to as 'minnies'. Siegfried Sassoon called them canisters, while Graves dubbed them sausages. Because of their size, they were sometimes ironically called flying pigs, a term that was later applied to the bombs used by the 9.45 in trench mortar in British service from about 1916. They were sometimes reduced to a cipher, Toc Emma, using the phonetic alphabet of the time. Edmund Blunden described them as rum jars. An Irishman in the Leinsters imaginatively referred to them as 'the lads with the rubber heels'. When asked to explain what he meant he answered, 'Sure, them trench mortars do steal across so soft-like, sorr, they do be on top of us before we know where we are' according to Hitchcock's rendition of the man's Irish brogue. On the other hand, Stephen Graham reported one of

German trench mortars ready for transport, captured on the Somme, July 1916. Left: *75 mm light mortar with a rifled barrel.* Right: *medium mortar.* (ILN)

his fellow guardsmen as saying that the bomb sounded 'like a row of houses rushing through the air' but this impression was probably based on the noise the bomb made as it descended.

Guy Chapman described the noise of their descent as a hum. Hearing it, he looked up and 'saw a monstrous minenwerfer shell tumbling out of the air'. Captain James Jack called the big German mortars 'oilcans'. They made a huge explosion when they went off. On one of his daily rounds, Jack 'came on four of our men killed in a bay of the support trench by one "can"'. Because of their size they could be spotted fairly easily. According to Jack, it was possible to see them high up and therefore dodge them 'by a display of agility if there is time to run round a traverse'. This kind of thing was very trying on the mind, however.

The trench mortar as something of which an author was on the receiving end is rarely mentioned in war memoirs without a sense of how frightening it could be. The trench mortar made an impact on the imagination. Captain Dunn remarked that the 'bombs lurching through the air are peculiarly demoralizing' and referred to the 'wobbling flight of this demoralizing charge of high explosive'. James Jack expressed what many felt when he stated that 'These heavy trench mortar shells, with their terrific explosions, are intensely disagreeable'. The bigger bombs arced almost inaudibly across the sky, looking for all the world like black dustbins until they landed with devastating explosions. Guy Chapman was caught in the blast of a mortar bomb in which 'a furious hot whirlwind . . . seized me and flung me violently back against the earth'. Showered with dirt and the remains of others less fortunate than himself, he was just missed by 'something which whizzed viciously and stuck quivering in the trench wall', an 18 in splinter of steel. He was 'scared out of my ten wits'. Captain Hitchcock of the Leinsters described how 'One trench mortar got a direct hit into one of [the] fire bays, knocking out all the occupants and completely obliterating the trench. One of the unfortunate men got a terrible wound in the leg; in fact, it was almost severed but for a piece of skin.'

What helped to make the German trench mortar so unpleasant was the size of some of the bombs. A relatively simple piece of ordnance could toss a heavyweight bomb a fair distance, in the case of the later German mortars, more than 1,000 yd depending on the calibre. Because of the relatively low pressures generated in the barrel of a mortar, the casing of the bomb could be thinner than that necessary for artillery shells which had to withstand much higher pressures. Therefore, the bomb could hold a lot more explosive than

The smooth-bored 9.45 in Flügelminenwerfer *in its pit 6.5 ft long by 5 ft wide and 18 in deep. A layer of sand or gravel was used where the foundation was poor. Note firing lanyard. Drawing from SS 634, a translation of a captured German manual dated July 1917.* (MUN 4/3590)

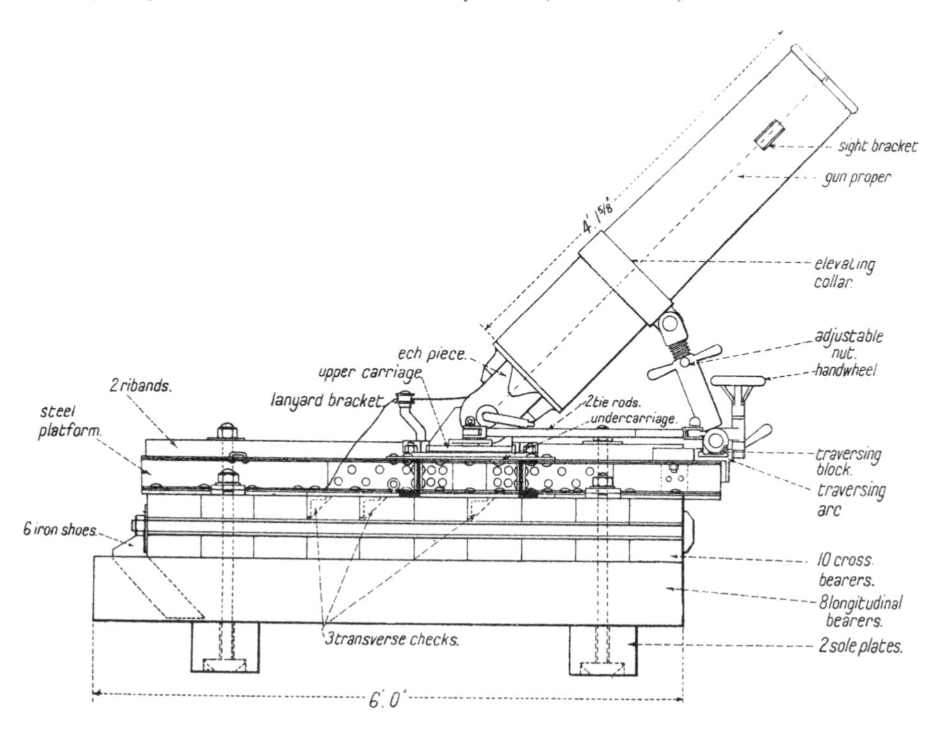

Side view of the Flügelminenwerfer *from SS 634. Its rate of fire was twenty rounds per hour and it weighed 25 cwt.* (MUN 4/3590)

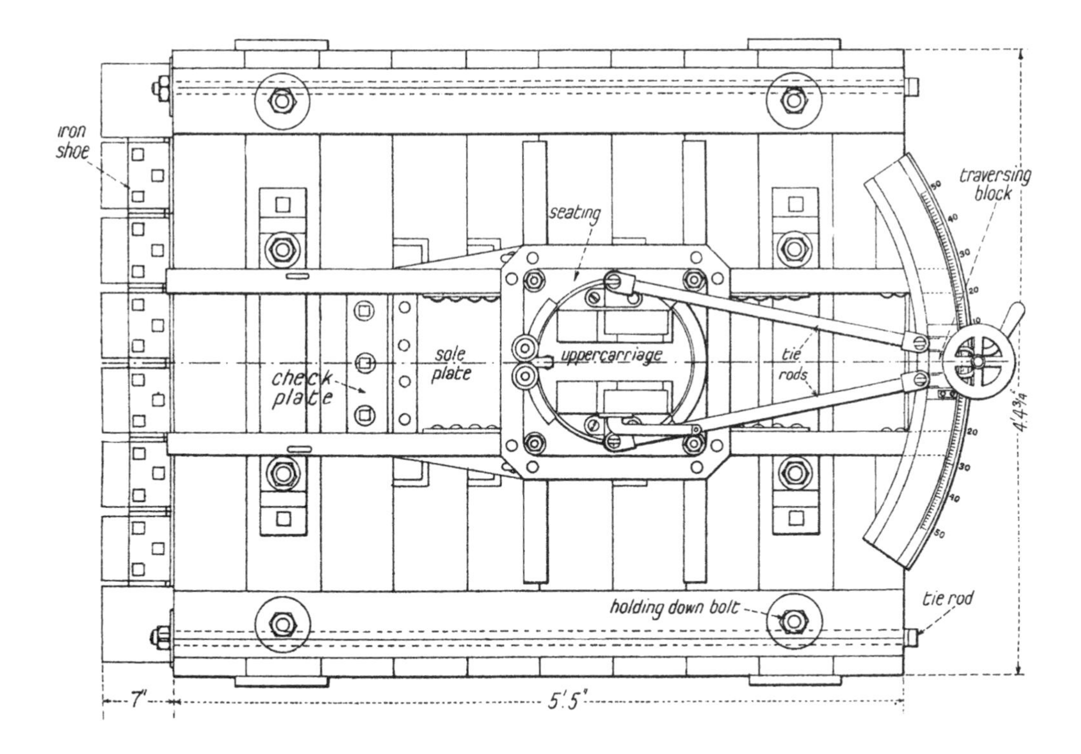

Top view of the Flügelminenwerfer*'s platform. Its traverse was ±28°.* (MUN 4/3590)

an artillery shell of a similar calibre. While in the trenches in May 1915 Hitchcock 'could see the trench mortars coming through the air. They weighed about 60 lb and made a colossal explosion on striking the ground. The craters they formed were about the same size as a 5.9.' Writing of 1916, he remarked that they were 'Colossal great bombs waddling across through the air, with their long timber tails waving – to explode with a deafening roar, which re-echoed through the valley'. Sometimes they contained more than explosive as the Leinsters discovered when a dud landed in a trench; it was found to be 'full of broken razor blades and nails'. That the bomb could be seen as it travelled was due to its relatively low velocity. They could even be seen at night because of the trail of red sparks they left behind them.

Edmund Blunden was in no doubt as to the effectiveness of the German *minenwerfer* when he wrote, 'I have heard it ruled that the minenwerfer was unimportant, and its effect was principally . . . moral. But in stationary war it seemed to me to make large holes not only in the nervous but also in the trench system.' His first sight of a German mortar bomb was of 'a small black cask wabbling over and over in the air at a great height above us' which he mistakenly thought to be a large rifle grenade. Robert Graves remarked that '"Sausages" are easy to see and dodge, but they make a terrible noise when they drop'. The noise of the explosion contrasted with the almost inaudible sound of a trench mortar firing which Graves likened to a 'faint plop'.

MINENWERFER AND THEIR AMMUNITION
(from GHQ-translated German document, 1917)

Table 1. Old Pattern Minenwerfer

Minenwerfer Designation	Shell Designation	Shell Weight (lb)	Charge Weight (lb)	Most Favourable Range (yd)
Heavy Minenwerfer Calibre: 26 cm (9.84 in) Weight in action: 11.25 cwt Personnel required to move it: 21 men Rate of fire: 20 rounds per hour	Full-sized heavy HE shell	207.2	103.6	219–601
	Half-sized heavy HE shell	134.4	44	492–897
Medium Minenwerfer Calibre: 17 cm (6.69 in) Weight in action: 9.5 cwt Personnel required to move it: 17 men Rate of fire: 30–35 rounds per hour (HE shell); 40–45 rounds per hour (gas shell)	Medium HE shell	109.1	26.4	164–984
	Medium gas shell	92.6	22–24.2 (liquid)	328–1,094
Old pattern light Minenwerfer Calibre: 7.6 cm (2.99 in) Weight in action: 2 cwt Personnel required to move it: 6 men Rate of fire: up to 20 rounds a minute for short periods	Light HE shell	9.9	1.23	328–1,094
	Light gas shell	9.9	about 1.76 (liquid)	328–1,094

Table 2. New Pattern Minenwerfer

Minenwerfer Designation	Shell Designation	Shell Weight (lb)	Charge Weight (lb)	Most Favourable Range (yd)
1916 pattern heavy Minenwerfer Calibre: 25 cm (9.84 in) Weight in action: 15 cwt Personnel required to move it: 28 men Rate of fire: 20 rounds per hour	1916 pattern full-sized heavy HE shell (with or without delay action)	207.2	103.6	547–1,094
Heavy Minenwerfer (Flügelminwerfer) Calibre: 24 cm (9.45 in) Weight in action: 25 cwt Personnel required to move it: 42 men Rate of fire: 20 rounds per hour	Heavy HE shells fitted with vanes (with or without delay action)	220.5	92.6	492–1,312
1916 pattern medium Minenwerfer Calibre: 17 cm (6.69 in) Weight in action: 11 cwt Personnel required to move it: 21 men Rate of fire: 30–35 rounds per hour (HE shell); 40–45 rounds per hour (gas shell)	1916 pattern, medium HE shell (with or without delay action)	109.1	26.4	328–1,258
	Medium gas shell	92.6	22–24.2 (liquid)	437–1,750
New pattern light Minenwerfer Calibre: 7.6 cm (2.99 in) Weight in action: nearly 3 cwt Rate of fire: up to 20 rounds a minute for short periods	Light HE shell	9.9	1.23	328–1,094
	1916 pattern light HE shell	9.9	1.23	328–1,422
	Light gas shell	9.9	about 1.76 (liquid)	328–1,422

An artist's impression of a German heavy mortar dating from early 1915. Although the mounting is more or less accurate the barrel is pure fantasy and German mortars never fired toffee-apples. (ILN)

An unusual German 10 cm mortar made from wood wound with wire. Although this was captured on the Somme in July 1916, there is an uncanny resemblance to some forms of the Livens Projector which did not appear until some time later (see *Chapter 9).* (ILN)

Tables 1 and 2 (*see* opposite) 'Minenwerfer and their Ammunition' are taken from a translated German document of 1917. They give details of mortars then in German service. They periodically recorded the effects of their mortars and circulated the information, although it was expressly forbidden to take such documents into the front line (presumably in case the British got hold of them and realized the full extent of the damage that was being done to them). Not surprisingly, the heavy mortars were the most destructive. The full-sized heavy high-explosive shell, the 1916 pattern full-sized heavy high-explosive shell and the heavy *Flügelminenwerfer* high-explosive shell, all fitted with non-delay fuses, had a 'great moral and destructive effect due to the force of the bursting charge; annihilating effect due to concussion, even against troops in dug-outs, as long as these are not too deep'. Deep dugouts were relatively safe but the British were not so well off for such dugouts as the Germans who, even before they withdrew to the Hindenburg Line in 1917, constructed some virtually indestructible shelters. Single fragments from these large projectiles could travel up to 440 yd and a direct hit could clear an area 33 ft in diameter in a barbed wire entanglement. What this did not record, however, was that craters would be inevitable when clearing wire. The delayed-action versions of these projectiles could penetrate 23–30 ft of earth cover of a dugout to destroy it and form craters 16–20 ft deep and 26–33 ft in diameter.

The small-sized heavy high-explosive shell with a non-delay fuse had a 'good burying effect' but was not very effective if penetration was called for. However, its concussion was formidable. Against barbed wire entanglements, it was as destructive as the full-sized heavy high-explosive shell. Medium high-explosive shells were effective against exposed troops in open trenches because of concussion and their fragmentation. It is not surprising that they had a considerable psychological effect. Their effectiveness against wire entanglements was described as reasonable if the heavy mortars were not available, but at a heavy price of increased ammunition consumption – more than double the number of rounds were required to inflict the same level of damage as the heavies. When fitted with delayed-action fuses, the mediums could penetrate to 10–13 ft.

The light mortar shells, when fired at close range and high angles of elevation, were very effective against troops. The new model light mortar, introduced by the Germans in 1916, had a base plate which allowed a 360° traverse, a feature that was never adopted by the British. Each shell took between 14 and 20 seconds to reach its target giving ample opportunity for them to be spotted, but because it had a rate of fire of twenty rounds a minute, as many as six shells could be in the air at once.

The fact that the bombs could be spotted in the air made the job of avoiding them a macabre game of tag. Various strategies were devised to avoid mortar bombs. Later in the war, in sectors where trench mortar activity was hot, platoon lookouts might be posted to spot mortar bombs and blow a whistle to warn the rest of the platoon, a strategy adopted by the Royal Welch Fusiliers. When a warning was given, men 'barged to the right or left accordingly, sometimes in dire peril, sometimes with linked arms in the mood of a jovial Bank Holiday party' according to Dunn. But despite Graves's assertion that the bombs were easy to dodge, an opinion shared by Hitchcock, it was not always so if there were several in the air at the same time because it was much more difficult to predict where the safest place might be. Frank Richards described how they had 'necks like giraffes' from watching for mortar bombs after they had been in the hot sector of the Cuinchy brickstacks in 1915 for a short time. A company sergeant major took to shooting at the bombs with a rifle but he failed to make one explode in flight.

The German dominance with trench mortars was not easy to counter and the first crude devices used by the British in late 1914 and early 1915 were almost as frightening to the British troops as the *minenwerfers*. Graves described the British trench mortars of 1915 as 'dangerous and ineffective'. Although there was always a tendency to underestimate the effect of British mortar fire on the Germans, the mortars were certainly prone to bursting and other accidents. Frank Richards described them as clumsy, complaining that they had only a short range, 'the shell often bursting in the gun'. At the beginning of January 1915, the Royal Welch Fusiliers attended a trench mortar demonstration along with the rest of the division but they were far from impressed with the mortar. Captain Dunn dismissed it with the comment, 'A rotten show, very inaccurate'. Another reason for their unpopularity was that a latrine looked just like a mortar position from the air and German reconnaissance flights invariably misidentified them as mortars with the result that some unfortunate answering the call of nature could find himself on the receiving end of an artillery barrage.

Dunn remarked that in the early days, 'Our Army probably lost more men from accidents with its drainpipes than from the enemy's mortars'. He was still of the same opinion in September 1915. The disparaging terms 'drain pipe' and 'gas pipe' were coined by the infantry because as far as they could see that was exactly what they were. The names never lost their currency and the later and much more effective Stokes was not immune from the same insults. The infantry never quite managed to overcome its prejudice of mortars and tended to distrust all of them irrespective of whether they were British or German. To begin with, before the use of trench mortars became more systemized, the troops sent to man the mortar teams were often the rejects not wanted in the platoons manning the fire-steps.

As soon as the War Office became aware of the BEF's desperate need for trench mortars, it approached Vickers and asked the company to design a 'trench howitzer' as quickly as possible. At the same time, the War Office instructed the Woolwich Arsenal to do likewise. In the meantime, the problem of supplying 'trench guns' had to be resolved some other way. During 1915 and much of 1916 the mortars were confusingly called trench howitzers, trench guns and bomb-throwers (and later to add to the confusion the Stokes was referred to as both a mortar and a gun). It was not until 1917 that the trench mortar became the officially accepted term. Later still, the word trench was dropped and they became just mortars.

Although bombs could be made on the same lines as impact-fused grenades, the improvisation of a mortar to fire them was much less easy from a technical standpoint. Nevertheless, from about October 1914 onwards, the first trench mortars were under development at the front using, in Louis Jackson's words, 'tin cylinders' to fire improvised bombs. The propelling charge was black powder – gunpowder – or cordite, although the latter often caused problems. According to Dunn, the first British trench mortars were indeed made out of pipes originally intended to carry water 'closed at one end by a fused-on breech'. The barrel was supported by a couple of legs attached to it via a ring that encircled the barrel below the muzzle. 'Only the most adventurous cared to handle these contraptions. After loading with great care, the team took cover behind a traverse and used a long lanyard to fire.' The 15th Field Company, Royal Engineers are reported as making such a mortar from a length of drainpipe, one end of which was welded over. A crude touch hole was drilled at a suitable point and black powder was used as a propellant, ignited by a match via the touch hole. It allegedly fired Jam-Tin bombs a reasonable distance, but inaccurately. Not surprisingly, it was prone to accidents and was somewhat unreliable. The British were not the only ones to improvise. The Germans did so too, relying on a similar source of piping as the British – gaspipe.

One solution to the lack of mortars was to press into service ancient nineteenth-century mortars, stubby little bomb-throwers that looked more like desktop models than serious weapons for trench warfare. The French certainly did this and so did the British to a limited extent although theirs were mostly French in origin. In August 1915 the Leinsters captured a German mortar at Hooge which they were expected to turn over to the corps staff for inspection. However, they had no intention of handing it over – they wanted to use it themselves to give the Germans a taste of their own medicine – substituting one 'with "Paris 1888" stamped on the muzzle'. The fact is, this 'German mortar' had been used in the trenches to shoot at the Germans. However, it is unlikely that such anachronistic museum pieces found widespread use.

A more realistic but equally imaginative solution to the mortar shortage was to bore out 6 in naval shells to a 4 in calibre, an operation that was carried out in Britain. These muzzle-loaded devices had rifled barrels, the only British mortars of the war to be rifled. All the others were smooth-bore. The 4 in, rifled, muzzle-loaded light trench mortar was not outstandingly accurate but had a range of about 900 yd. Only 168 of these found their way into action before they were withdrawn in the spring of 1916, replaced by the superior Stokes. The propelling charge was loaded first, followed by the bomb. The firing mechanism was similar to that used on artillery pieces, a friction-operated T-tube inserted in a vent in the breech. The crosspiece of the T contained the friction igniter which had an eye on the end of it to take a lanyard. Once fired, the tube was removed and a new one fitted for the next round. The tube had to seal the vent on detonation of the charge which it did on the same principle of obturation as the small arms cartridge case, rapid expansion, otherwise gas would escape through the vent and erode it, eventually causing problems that might result in a burst barrel.

Left: *a French 1840s Louis-Phillipe 150 mm mortar with 'horns' on the muzzle.* Right: *French ingenuity, September 1915: German shell cases made into mortars. The mountings are fashioned from timber. The mortar was known as the Taupia.* (ILN)

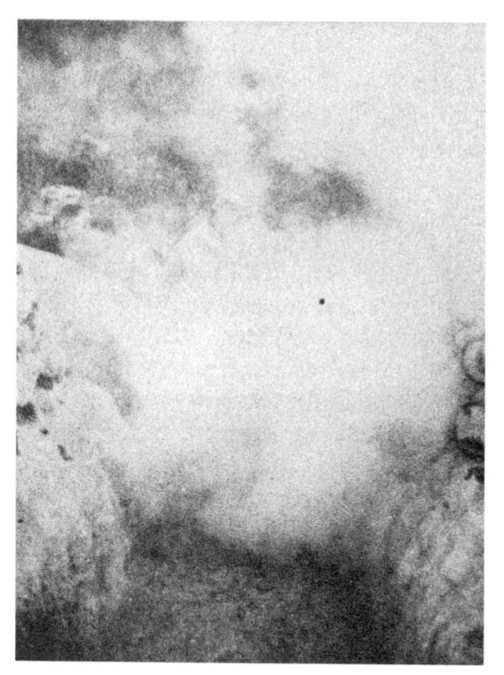

Two shots showing the Taupia mortar in action, taken in the Argonne in the summer of 1915. Left: *a French soldier lights the fuse with the end of a burning cigarette.* Right: *smoke produced on discharge. Presumably, the soldier beat a retreat before the propellant ignited.* (ILN)

Whereas artillery breeches were precision-made by highly skilled workers, the same could not be said of mortars at this time and the precision of the barrel vent was often not all it should have been.

However, the problem was not one of carelessness or slipshod workmanship. Rather, it was, as Lieutenant-Colonel Brothers explained after the war, a fundamental difficulty of having to work with 'comparatively inferior metals and the employment of unskilled labour' that plagued the production of mortars throughout the war. High-grade metals were needed for other essential war products and the firms that were contracted to make mortars did not usually employ the skilled labour force of a Vickers or an Armstrong Whitworth. Moreover, some of the skilled labour had left munitions work to serve in France following Kitchener's call for volunteers, so that there was a shortage of skilled labour, although this was later stopped. This handicap influenced the design of both the mortars and their ammunition. A complex design that amounted to precision engineering was simply out of the question. The materials to make it were not likely to be available and the skilled labour certainly was not. In 1917 two excellent designs, one by Vickers and one by Armstrong Whitworth, were both rejected simply because they were 'very finely made pieces of ordnance' and could not be manufactured in quantity with the available resources.

Time was also a factor, not only in terms of how long it might take to make a weapon but also in terms of how long it would take to train personnel in its use. Therefore, complex weapons were unrealistic. Speed was of the essence; the time available for training was limited. Then the question of repairs in the field had to be considered. The repair workshops were already heavily loaded with work repairing 'perhaps more important weapons' and they could not be expected to shoulder the extra burden of repairing another and complex weapon which, in addition, would inevitably slow down everything. The design and manufacture of mortars and mortar bombs was a matter of making the best with what was available. Nevertheless, some ingenious solutions to the problem were cooked up, the one devised by Captain Newton being especially inspired when faced with making trench mortars at the Second Army Workshop.

Early in 1915 Captain Newton was a 35-year-old company commander in the 5th Sherwood Foresters and occupied himself out of the line by designing and making various trench warfare devices, such as rifle batteries (several rifles fixed in a holder to fire in one direction, either independently or simultaneously), in a local blacksmith's shop. Division was made aware of what he was up to and Major-General Furse, who at that time was in command of 2nd Corps, was particularly taken with his work. Furse instructed him to set up a workshop at Armentières to increase the scale of production so that the benefits could be spread among the whole of 2nd Corps and eventually the Second Army. This was the Second Army Workshop and it came to play a crucial role in trench warfare, as did Newton himself who was an inventive and imaginative engineer with a keen mind for problem solving. He served as commanding officer of the workshop from 1915 to 1917 when he became a member of the newly created Trench Warfare Committee. He also became a deputy controller of the Trench Warfare Department and from 1917 he was Chief of Design in the Mechanical Traction Department.

These Royal Engineer workshops were set up in a technical school, chosen because of the machinery and plant it possessed. Although termed a workshop it was, in fact, more of a factory and although it conducted experimental work, this was undertaken with a view to designing an effective device that could be put into production at the factory. It was manned by officers and men drawn from various units but the majority of the workers were Frenchmen who by about July 1915 numbered perhaps 200. The only drawback to the location of the workshop was its proximity to the front – it was within range of German artillery.

In late June Major Todhunter, the Experimental Officer at the School of Musketry in Hythe, visited the workshop to see what sort of things were being made there; his job at Hythe brought him into contact with similar devices. He reported, rather obliquely, that

> the reason that these shops were established on this scale was that it was found that the Ordnance did not supply either manufactured articles or material and in consequence of this failure it was found necessary to undertake local manufacture and no further attempt was made to secure war material through the usual channels of supply.

In other words, the workshop became self-sufficient. It also implies that the quantity of 'manufactured articles' produced by the workshop was enough to satisfy the demands of the Second Army. He reported that the workshop appeared 'to be performing excellent service'. As noted by Lieutenant-Colonel Brothers in 1919, both grenades and mortars were largely made behind the lines in France from 1914 to 1915. The majority were undoubtedly made at the Second Army Workshop at Armentières.

At the time he established the workshop, Newton was well aware of the shortage of mortars and he set about improving on the design of the 3.7 in currently in service which had a tendency to misfire, causing casualties (Todhunter saw the workshop's experimental design which was undergoing trials when he visited). But there was a problem: where to get the metal to make mortars? Newton later wrote 'It is a matter of interest to recollect that the only suitable metal which could, under the circumstances be worked, was brass'. A ready source of brass was empty small arms ammunition cartridge cases, of which there was an abundance. He came up with a remarkably astute answer to the problem of supplying mortars to the Front and of how to get the empty cases to make them – barter. In exchange for the cartridge cases he offered to supply mortars made from them. Four furnaces were built, each with a 200 lb capacity crucible, to melt and cast the brass. The casting was then machined.

The 3.7 in muzzle-loaded mortar, which Newton proposed to improve, had not been in service in France for long. It was one of three mortars that were now being supplied to the BEF in response to its urgent requests. The others were the 4 in rifled mortar and its smooth-bored sister, although this was not made from old naval shells. The 3.7 in and the smooth-bored 4 in were both fired by the same method as that used on the rifled 4 in. However, because of problems with this method, a new way of firing them was developed using the mechanisms of Lee Enfield rifles to fire a specially designed blank cartridge to ignite the propelling charge. It is not clear where the idea originated but it is possible that this was another of Newton's inventions, in which case the development of the special cartridge came later, but the idea may have been developed by the Woolwich Arsenal. Certainly photographs of Newton's improved 3.7 in, taken at the Second Army Workshop, show this mechanism which was supposed to have been introduced in late 1915.

Newton's improvements consisted of providing the 3.7 in with a means for a wider traverse which was extremely limited on the original 3.7 in, as well as a means to make registration more accurate. He did this by adding a rudimentary ball-and-socket joint to the base of the mortar barrel which was given index marks so that inclinations of the mortar could be precisely noted for registering targets. It worked very effectively. However, there were limitations inherent in all smooth-bored mortars which were not immediately apparent when the mortars were first introduced, the most significant of which were concerned with range and accuracy. Range was determined by the pressure in the barrel generated by the black powder or cordite propellants and there was a limit to the quantity of explosive that could be used to propel the bomb out of the barrel. Too much and the barrel would burst, with dire consequences for anyone in the vicinity. Although the propellant was provided in bagged charges like those used with artillery, there was a tendency to attempt to increase the range of the mortar by loading more propellant than recommended. Such hazards helped to give trench mortars and their operators a bad name.

There was little that could be done to increase range but Newton felt that he might be able to do something to improve the accuracy. This was not only related to how well the mortar was laid and registered but also to how well the bagged charges were prepared which, in turn, determined how often the pressure in the barrel was what it was supposed to be. It became clear that the pressure was not consistent for a given charge. Newton tried various expedients with the 3.7 in to improve this, including the use of shear pins of metal or wood inserted through the barrel wall. The idea was that the pins would 'retard progress of the projectile until ignition and combustion of the propellant charge were deemed to be satisfactorily advanced'. In this way, a consistent pressure could be built up in the barrel each time. However, before this bore fruit, the 3.7 in mortar was withdrawn from service.

Meanwhile, in March 1915, a couple of examples of an experimental 2 in mortar designed by the Woolwich Arsenal were sent out to France for trials and within a matter of weeks it had been approved. Its origins were evidently German and was based on a Krupp mortar that had been described in a technical article published four years before the outbreak of war. Whereas the bombs of the 3.7 in and 4 in mortars fitted inside the barrels, that of the 2 in was fitted with a 2 ft long solid drawn steel tail that went inside the barrel with the sphere containing the business end protruding from the muzzle like a metal balloon. This was the toffee-apple or plum pudding mortar, the bombs sometimes also being called footballs. It did

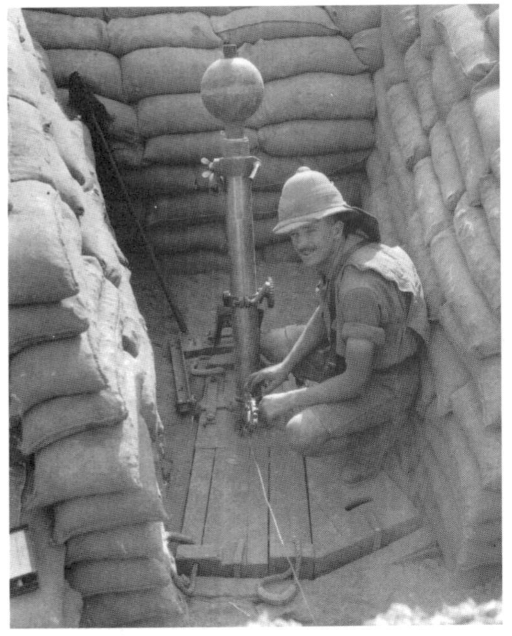

The 2 in toffee-apple mortar was the standard British medium 1915–16. The Lee Enfield firing mechanism is clearly visible with a lanyard running down the centre of the picture. The empty periscope holder is on the left-hand side of the muzzle, just below the wing nut. This pristine mortar position is in Mesopotamia, 1917. Similar mortar pits existed in France. The operator is wearing a quilted spine pad to protect himself from fragments. (IWM)

British troops training Russians how to operate the 2 in trench mortar in 1916. (The Times History of the War)

not start to make an impact on trench warfare until about the end of 1915 and by the time of the Somme offensive in the summer of 1916 about 800 had been made, but not all of these would have found their way to France as other theatres of war also made demands on them. In the autumn of that year the 2 in toffee-apple was phased out and replaced by the Stokes.

The Woolwich mortar had a maximum range of only 500–600 yd. Shorter ranges could be accommodated by altering the elevation of the barrel and by using different amounts of propellant. Like the other mortars in British service, it used a modified Lee Enfield rifle mechanism to fire it and had the added refinement of a periscope so that targets could be located and the fall of shot observed without the mortarman having to expose his head above the parapet. However, just how useful this was is open to question since in the opinion of Newton 'the oscillations . . . during adjustment between rounds must have frequently afforded gleeful satisfaction to those of the enemy who watched'. The periscope also had the disadvantage of pinpointing the position of the mortar to a sharp-eyed German observer who was no doubt using a periscope of his own, although the application of camouflage such as hessian from sandbags may have reduced its silhouette to some extent.

With a rate of fire of between two and three rounds a minute, a battery of 2 in mortars firing bombs containing about 12 lb of explosive could put down an effective barrage which Newton described as 'a most powerful influence where it might be felt'. This rate of fire was not impressive, however, especially when compared with the Stokes that could fire twenty or thirty rounds in the same time. The reason for its slow rate of fire was the number of operations in loading and firing the mortar. Firstly, the charge was inserted, then driven home with a ramrod in the manner of a Napoleonic canon. The bomb was then inserted. There next followed the laborious process of laying or training the mortar with the aid of the periscope before firing the round.

Captain Newton considered the 2 in mortar to be 'an excellent weapon in its time but its limitations were pronounced'. Apart from only being capable of hitting targets that were comparatively close – and 500 yd in trench warfare was indeed close – it was a heavy piece of equipment and thus not easily moved. Worse than this was the considerable muzzle flash produced each time the weapon was fired making it easy for the Germans to spot it and have it shelled by artillery, bombed by their own trench mortars or bombarded with rifle grenades, none of which endeared the British mortarmen to the infantry who were nearby. The flash was accompanied by a loud report which also helped the Germans to locate the mortar. The noise and the flash were just as troublesome when the smallest charges were used to fire on targets that were considerably closer than 500 yd. It was not a weapon that was easy to conceal from the enemy. Equally worrying to the infantrymen was the propensity for the steel tail to be thrown back into the British line when the bomb exploded. Such a missile could cause much damage and injury. Casualties were common and this contributed to the unpopularity of the 2 in mortar with the infantry. Apart from this, the wastage of 'highly manufactured' steel was considerable.

For the Germans on the receiving end, British trench mortars were just as unnerving to them as theirs were to the British. Ernst Jünger, a lieutenant in the 73rd Hanoverian Fusilier Regiment, recalled that they made a 'whistling, whispering noise' and described them as 'treacherous . . . personally malignant. They're insidious beasts.' On one occasion, he was resting before a forthcoming night raid and

> was scared out of my wits by a terrific crash close to the dugout. The Englishmen were sending 'toffee-apples' over which, in spite of the moderate report they made when fired off, were of such weight that the splinters from them smashed the stout tree-trunk posts of the revetment clean through.

Clambering out of the dugout he saw 'one of these black fellows describe his circular course through the air'. Retaliation tended to be swift so that 'for every toffee-apple that came over we returned a Lanz'. The Lanz was a stopgap type of light mortar, produced in the early years of the war to satisfy the increasing demand. It was smooth-bored with a calibre of 3.6 in and threw a 9 lb shell about 350 yd, much the same as the toffee-apple except that the toffee-apple packed a far greater punch.

There were a fair number of British duds. Jünger recounted an incident when a NCO attempted to take off the fuse of a dud toffee-apple 'and observing that the powder was smouldering he put the end of his cigarette into the opening'. This suicidal act caused the toffee-apple to explode and kill him. A fellow lieutenant stored a collection of duds in a dugout which everyone else was very careful to avoid. This officer spent his spare time unscrewing the fuses and examining them. This dangerous fascination with duds and their fuses was not confined to the Germans, of course, and there were numerous accidents on both sides as a result. There was no reciprocal attraction for dumps of unfired

Right: *A 91.5 mm Lanz light mortar. This was a stopgap weapon with a smooth bore of 1915–16 and had a range of about 350 yd. Note the wooden bed with handles, and ramrods.* (ILN) Below left: *a Lanz removed from its bed.* Below right: *a 75 mm light mortar ready for action. Like the medium mortar, this has a recoil system.* (ILN)

Troops carrying the heads of toffee-apple bombs from a bomb store. Note the blocks to prevent them rolling around in transit. (ILN)

mortar bombs which, on the contrary, were treated with respect and given a wide berth. Perhaps it was partly due to what such dumps represented – impending assault on the German trenches. Edmund Blunden noticed the appearance of mounds of plum puddings 'steely and shining' behind the lines prior to the Somme and felt that they were 'serious and immediate omens of ordeal'. But such dumps became a familiar sight throughout the war, irrespective of an impending offensive.

Wyn Griffith, also in the Royal Welch Fusiliers, described watching a toffee-apple mortar battery firing. The mortars had been set up at night to avoid detection by the Germans in an abandoned trench 20 yd behind the line. A small dump of 'heavy globes of iron with a little cylindrical projection like a broken handle' was ready for the morning's shoot. In preparation for this, Griffith prudently moved his men away from the front-line trenches that lay between the mortars and the German line.

> A pop, and then a black ball went soaring up, spinning round as it went through the air slowly; more pops and more queer birds against the sky. A stutter of terrific detonations seemed to shake the air and the ground, sandbags and bits of timber sailed up slowly and fell in a calm deliberate way. In the silence that followed the explosions, an angry voice called out in English, across No Man's Land, 'YOU BLOODY WELSH MURDERERS.'

The 2 in mortar had other problems, specifically to do with the bomb fuse. When it first entered service the bombs were fitted with the time fuse used on artillery shells. Unfortunately, they suffered from a high percentage of blinds. Moreover, the craters the bombs made when fitted with this fuse became a problem when the mortars were used to cut barbed wire entanglements, a role for which the mortar was used more and more from 1915 onwards. Although the wire was cut by the exploding bombs, the resulting crater presented a new and equally difficult obstacle to impede the infantry as it crossed No Man's Land. Newton came up with an answer which was so successful that, perversely, it was deemed necessary to restrict its use until the Somme offensive so that the ability to cut wire with trench mortars without forming craters in the process could be concealed from the Germans.

Newton's answer was simple – substitute the Newton 107 fuse for the service one. This fuse had been originally designed for the Newton Pippin rifle grenade, another of Newton's inventions. Not surprisingly, the restriction on the use of the fuse also extended to the rifle grenade, itself a very useful munition. This did nothing to ease the shortage of rifle grenades. The fuse detonated the bomb before it penetrated the ground so that the explosive effect was directed outwards into the entanglement. Moreover, it was a fraction of the cost of the service fuse.

However, the bomb was not ideally shaped to get the maximum effect of the explosive. A bomb should perform one of three functions: provide shrapnel to incapacitate personnel, destroy wire entanglements, or bury itself before detonating for the demolition of structures like dugouts. It was found that when the bomb was detonated with the Newton fuse to destroy wire, only about 10 per cent of the explosive force was effective, the rest being expended harmlessly. This corresponded to a band of explosive that

Newton's diagram showing angle of impact and direction of explosive force of different mortar bombs. Top: *toffee-apple fitted with the Newton fuse; the shaded band represents the 10 per cent of explosive that is effective against personnel, assuming the fragments travel at 2,000 ft per second.* Middle: *6 in Newton bomb showing the direction of maximum blast is away from the mortar.* Bottom: *less than 10 per cent of the Stokes mortar bomb breaks up into effective anti-personnel fragments.* (MUN 5/383/1600/14)

Left: *a French 58 mm mortar, September 1915. The steel tail fitted inside the barrel with the bomb's three fins well clear of the barrel. The simple elevating mechanism can be clearly seen. Note the long fuse projecting from the nose of the bomb.* Right: *a store of finned bombs which were often known as aerial torpedoes. The fuses have yet to be fitted.* (ILN)

Making aerial torpedoes in a French factory, spring 1916. These workmen are welding the tails on to projectiles similar to the 58 mm torpedo. (ILN)

was more or less horizontal with the ground when the bomb exploded. During later comparative trials with a 6 in mortar of Newton's design it was found that 'Whereas Belgian farm houses in the proximity to the bursting bombs were unaffected for a long period in which 2" bombs were fired, when 6" bombs were fired complaints that missiles [shrapnel] reached them came from the Farmers'. This was one reason why Newton designed a streamlined bomb for the 6 in mortar; it not only went further but more of the explosive effect was directed sideways.

The 3.7 in and 4 in mortars were classed as light mortars while the 2 in mortar was classed as a medium and by 1916 each division was equipped with twenty-four of these types. During 1915, a heavy trench mortar of 9.45 in calibre was also introduced to British service. This was not a British design but a French one. The French were in much the same boat as the British at the start of the war as far as trench mortars were concerned and like the British they worked hard to devise suitable weapons. One of these was the 9.45 in weapon which had a separate firing chamber in the breech and had been designed by the Société de Construction de Batignolles. The chamber was to prove to be something of a mixed blessing. It was supposed to ensure that the pressure in the barrel was the same each time the weapon was fired. The company filed a patent application in Britain on 2 July 1915 and this subsequently became UK patent 16,869/15. The UK patent meant that the British government had to pay the French company royalties if it wanted to make the mortar and on 20 December 1915 the Treasury authorized payment of royalties amounting to £15,000 in respect of the government's use of the patent.

The 9.45 in was the only heavy mortar to enter British service during the war and by the end of 1918 it was being withdrawn because its weight made it unsuited to mobile warfare. The mortar was transported on horse-drawn carriages but lorries were needed for the heavy platforms. It needed a special platform – the building of which was labour intensive – to

Most of these 58 mm torpedoes have yet to have the tails fitted. (ILN)

Australians loading a 9.45 in mortar located in a chalk pit near Pozières on the Somme, August 1916. They are using a special cradle clamped to the muzzle to insert the flying pig. The soldier on the left is gripping the elevating gear handle to make sure the barrel is not moved. (IWM)

prevent it sinking into the ground, which it tended to do with each successive shot unless the ground was very firm. The Mk I had only a short barrel which restricted its range to 1,100 yd so the barrel was lengthened in 1916 in the Mk III to extend the range to 2,400 yd. However, the increased recoil necessitated the use of a sub-bed to prevent the base sinking into even hard ground. The model of sub-bed used by the French Army was used at first but this was a heavy, cumbersome wooden affair which made setting up the mortar much more difficult. Armstrong Whitworth was asked to come up with something to replace 'the wood bed and the sub-bed and greatly lighten the equipment, while giving sufficient surface to prevent sinking on soft ground'. However, the war ended before the metal platform they designed could be trialled.

The British version of the mortar used the same Lee Enfield system to fire it but this was susceptible to damage and jamming. Investigated by the Trench Warfare Committee in 1917, they elected to replace it with a simple mechanism invented by Major Hudson, who at the time was the commanding officer of the Third Army Trench Mortar School. It was first made at the base workshops in France and subsequently approved for use with the 2 in mortar as well as the 9.45 in. The means by which the mortar was laid was crude and not particularly accurate: it was a simple plumb line. Strangely, this was not improved on until 1917 when it was replaced by a simple mirror sight designed by Sergeant Wooderson, Royal Artillery,

This shot of a 9.45 in mortar shows the elevating gear (the curved pieces at the back) and the circular base. (ILN)

attached to the First Army Trench Mortar School. The elevating gear on the original mortar was a poor design which allowed the barrel to drop slightly on every shot unless the gear was firmly locked, which was difficult as there was no adequate mechanism to accomplish this. The solution was supplied by a Mr Heap who designed a self-locking arrangement (UK patent 126,324, application filed 12 December 1916). This not only kept the barrel in its laid position but as a consequence increased the rate of fire because the mortar was now much easier to lay and load.

The accuracy of the mortar was not all the British troops would have liked. For one thing, it had a tendency to drop its bombs short. Edmund Blunden experienced this unpleasant behaviour during the Somme battles of 1916 when it 'hurled its shells as much into our area as the opposite trenches'. The 9.45 in fired a short-tailed bomb which was often erratic in flight so a longer tail with the front part of the vanes cut away was trialled by the Trench Warfare Committee. However, this proved to be worse than the Mk I bomb and was very inaccurate. A simple answer was found – the back corners of the vanes were given a slight twist to impart spin to the bomb. Trials showed that the Mk IV bomb was very accurate, but subsequent trials using bombs from a different batch were not so encouraging.

The fall-off in accuracy was found to be down to the use of inferior metal for the vanes. No doubt someone somewhere had thought that money could be saved by using something cheaper which was perhaps also more readily available. By mid-1917 when these trials were under way, it was too late to do much about the problems of erratic flight and inaccuracy with the older types of bomb simply because so many of them had been manufactured in Britain and shipped out to France. These would have to be used up.

The 9.45 in trench mortar in Italian service. (The Times History of the War)

The bombs had other problems besides those already mentioned. They were especially prone to premature detonation. This again was entirely due to inferior materials being used in their manufacture. Throughout 1917 experiments and trials continued to try to improve them but until better materials were used in the factories in Britain it was somewhat unproductive.

The propellant for the Mk I bomb was 14 oz of cordite primed with black powder which was loaded in the mortar via the muzzle and positioned in the firing chamber in the breech. This was ignited by a specially adapted small arms ammunition cartridge which originally contained cordite but later black powder was used. The trouble was that the charge did not always get completely burned, nor did it burn at a consistent rate, and this tended to cause rounds to fall short, known by the mortarmen as fizzles. It was discovered that the fault lay with the breech chamber, the distinguishing feature of the mortar. Quite simply, the charge was too loose a fit. At the suggestion of Captain Alsop, who commanded a 9.45 in Trench Mortar Battery in France, the charge was increased to 17 oz which completely filled the chamber. Alsop had tried this both in the line and at the First Army school and it seemed to significantly reduce the number of fizzles but the evidence was not conclusive.

The Trench Warfare Committee decided to try a different tack and adapted the charges used with the 6 in mortar, another of the products from the Second Army Workshop. These charges were fitted into the recesses cut in the back of the vanes so that the chamber did not have to be used at all. This not only solved the problem of short rounds but had the added advantage of increasing the rate of fire because fewer loading actions were required to operate the mortar.

The 9.45 in mortar could pack quite a punch. Its bombs, looking for all the world like flying dustbins with wings, worried the Germans just as much as their big mortar bombs worried the British. Ernst Jünger called the big ‘cylinder bombs’ fired from the larger-calibre British mortars ‘clothes baskets’. Yet, despite their size and the fear they caused, a barrage of such bombs in which ‘it often looked as though the sky was raining baskets’ might actually achieve very little. Jünger noted that after such a bombardment, which lasted about half an hour, his company lost only one man killed and one man wounded, although considerable damage was done to the trenches and the dugouts.

A German mortar that fired a round which was less easy to spot began to appear at the front during 1915. This was the *Granatenwerfer* known to the Germans as the Priest mortar.

As the designation suggested, the bomb was more akin to a finned rifle grenade in both appearance and size than the shells fired by other mortars. It was popular with the German troops because it was simple to use and only weighed about 90 lb which made it easy to move from place to place. The bombs weighed between 4 lb and 5.5 lb and could be thrown from about 275 yd to about 330 yd depending on the model and the bomb. The mortar was a form of spigot mortar, the hollow tail of the bomb fitting over the spigot. A cartridge at the top of the hollow tail was fired by pulling a lanyard to release the firing pin.

Variation on a theme of Heath Robinson. Another form of aerial torpedo-thrower, summer 1915. It seems improbable that the flimsy mounting would have withstood more than one or two firings. (ILN)

The British dubbed it the pineapple because the segmented casing resembled one. They also called it the blue pigeon although it no more resembled a bird than a pig. Edmund Blunden recorded that they arrived so suddenly, without any apparent warning, that there was no time to be afraid of them, but Lieutenant Edwin Campion Vaughan was less sanguine about them. He described their discharge as a 'faint "pop" in the distance' and their flight as a 'rapid whistle'. They detonated with a 'sharp crack and

A French 80 mm mortar of 1915 loaded with a 130 lb bomb which is little more than a drum filled with explosive. A tail fitted down the barrel. The weapon could fire an even bigger bomb that weighed 236 lb. It is unlikely that any of these men posing with their gun for this picture would have remained quite so close when it came to firing it. Note how the barrel is supported by a wedge. (ILN)

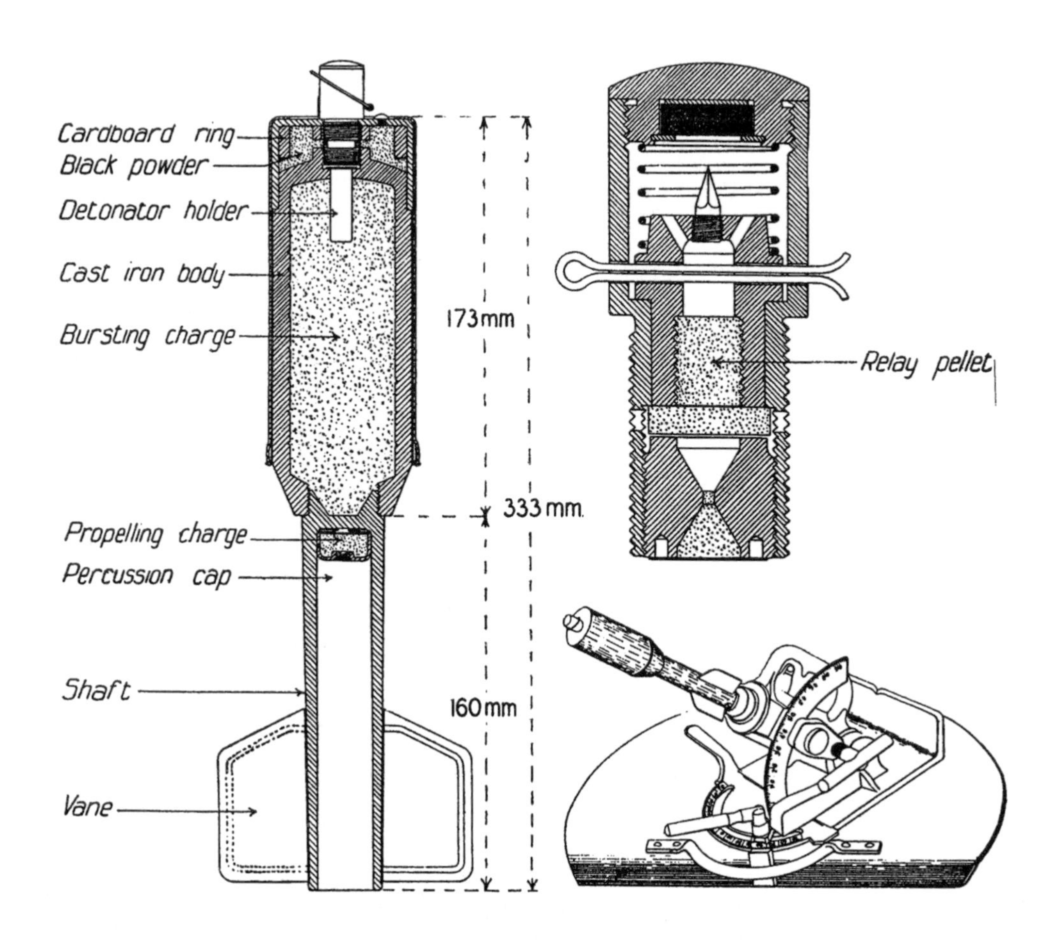

'New type of bomb for Granatwerfer'. This is the rebounding bomb which was just over 14 in long and weighed 5.5 lb. Drawing from SS 641 issued by GHQ in April 1918. Bottom right: *the* Granatenwerfer *showing the bomb in position on the spigot. Note traversing and elevating scales. Its maximum range was approximately 275 yd.* (MUN 4/3590)

a flash'. Captain Hitchcock recalled in late 1916 how 'little puffs of white smoke circled up from our front line. These I was told were rifle grenades and "aerial darts" which the enemy showed particular activity with in this sector.' They were something of a nuisance. One 'dart' destroyed a store of small arms ammunition with a direct hit and '50,000 rounds of ammunition and 10 boxes of Mills bombs went sky-high'.

A novel development of this weapon which appeared in 1918 was the so-called rebounding bomb which was designed to hit the ground and be relaunched into the air before exploding. The cast-iron body was fitted with a steel sleeve that was closed at one end in which there was a firing chamber containing a charge of black powder. When the fuse was activated by striking the ground the black powder charge was also fired so that the body was propelled out of the steel sleeve which acted as a mortar tube.

CHAPTER 3

Rubber Bands and Springs – Catapults 1914–15

The catapult is an ancient weapon. The use of torsion-powered artillery was a Greek invention and widely used by the Romans from at least the time of the Punic Wars 264–241 BC. There were two sorts of weapon that used this form of propulsion: weapons that fired arrows in a straight trajectory, a form of crossbow; and stone-throwers that used a rotating arm to propel a projectile in a vertical arc. They were quite sophisticated and effective pieces of equipment for their day. Reconstructions in the early years of this century by academics showed that they worked every bit as well as the fourth-century AD accounts of Vegetius suggested. Twisted ropes made of materials with elastic properties, such as animal sinew and horsehair, an art that has been lost, provided the torsional energy. By the twentieth century, of course, the elastic properties of natural rubber were well known even to small boys familiar with the simple catapult made from a Y-shaped twig and a piece of elastic stretched between the arms. Catapults and stone-throwers belonged to another age and mischievous boys.

They made a remarkable comeback in 1914 and 1915, like ageing stars who still had a thing or two to show the youngsters, and made a small but significant contribution to trench warfare. That they were treated seriously by the Army is perhaps a little surprising but severe shortages of trench mortars meant that it had to take what it could get. The need for bomb-throwing ordnance was not being satisfied by the trickle of trench mortars reaching the front during late 1914 and servicemen and civilians alike searched for alternatives. By mid-1915 there were about 750 catapults and bomb-throwers in France. Although it may seem obvious with the benefit of hindsight, there was nothing obvious about returning to the ancients for inspiration. Making a catapult or a bomb-thrower that used some form of mechanical action to hurl a bomb a reasonable distance with some degree of accuracy is not as simple as it sounds. In some ways, it is much more difficult to make a catapult that will hurl a bomb accurately over a given distance, and do so consistently, than it is to make a mortar to do the same thing. That a few emerged as effective engines of modern war was a remarkable achievement for their inventors and designers. Irrespective of the qualities of Roman artillery, they were not expected to perform with the accuracy and precision of a piece of twentieth-century ordnance.

Simply copying what the Romans had done 2,000 years earlier was no guarantee of success. Considering the reconstructions of Roman artillery undertaken around the time of the First World War it is not surprising that someone in academia should put two and two together and suggest a Roman catapult as a suitable weapon with which to bombard the Germans in their trenches. A Cambridge history professor prepared drawings and copious notes which he sent to the commanding officer of a battalion of the Cambridgeshire Regiment, stationed at Ploegsteert Wood, Ypres. They were acquaintances and the professor thought he was doing the battalion a favour. The commander was sufficiently impressed to be persuaded to have a catapult built according to the instructions he was sent. This was no simple matter as suitable timber of the right size had to be found, but it was done and the catapult was dug in at a suitable location in readiness. It was evidently 7 ft long and weighed more than a quarter of a ton.

When they came to fire this thing, all their labours of several days and nights came to nothing. The bombs they tried to fling at the Germans either failed to travel any distance, and certainly not as far as the German trenches, or the bombs went straight up in the air and dropped back on to the catapult operators. Although this may have been partly due to the inexperience of the operators, faulty construction or faulty plans, this was to become a common drawback of all bomb-throwers and catapults. Simple, catapults may have looked, but simple to use they were not. The professor's catapult was evidently torn up for firewood.

This amateur attempt at constructing a workable catapult was neither the first nor the last time a catapult was contemplated by the Army as a viable engine of war. A much better machine was brought to Louis Jackson in October 1914. Unlike the Cambridgeshires' Roman copy, this one was a version of the device so well known to small boys, only bigger and more powerful. A gentleman by the name of Claude Pemberton Leach of South Kensington brought the catapult to Jackson for his approval. Leach claimed that it could throw a golf ball 200 yd, which was not much of a recommendation since a bomb weighed more than a golf ball and 200 yd was no distance at all. However, Jackson saw potential in the device and suggested that Leach strengthen it and carry out endurance trials with the rubber springs which powered the catapult. Leach did what he could and succeeded in getting the contraption to throw a 2 lb weight 200 yd with a remarkable degree of accuracy.

Leach evidently also took his catapult to Gamage's department store, 'Cycling, Sports and General Outfitters', and together they applied for a patent on 22 May 1915 which was

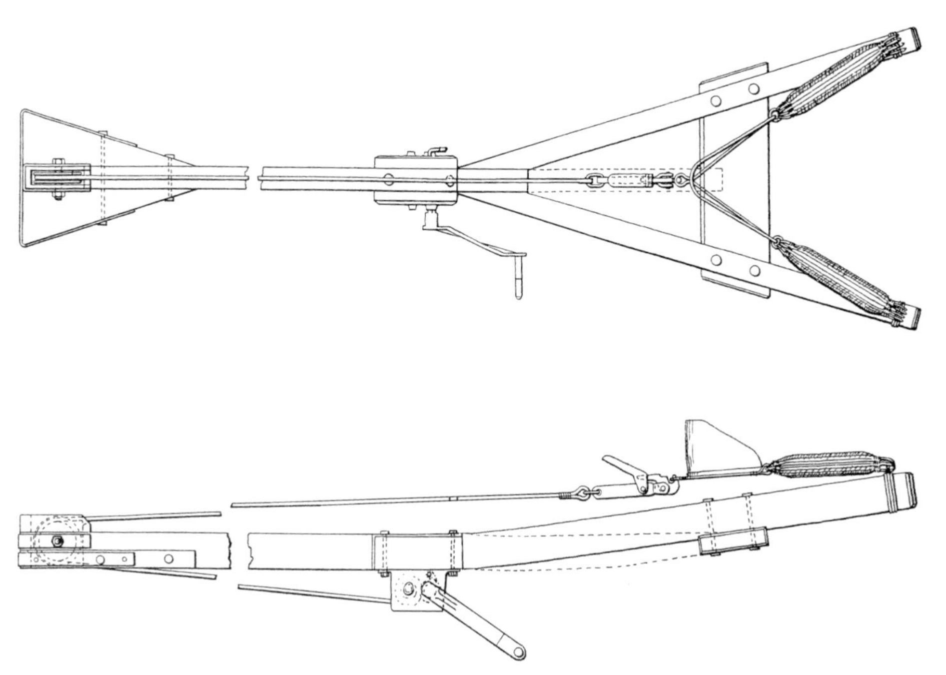

The Leach/Gamage catapult from UK patent 7,710/15. Note the pawl on the winding box in the top drawing. This was used to lock the winding gears. Note also the trigger mechanism behind the pouch.

subsequently granted as 7,710/15 one year later. That there was a delay of about eight months between Leach taking his catapult to Jackson and the patent application being filed, together with the fact that Gamage's was co-patentee, strongly suggests that his catapult was significantly developed by Gamage's. There is a very close resemblance between the patent drawings and the devices used in France. However, it is clear that the catapult was being used in France some time before the patent application (although this, in itself, signifies very little since the patent laws of that time would have permitted the device to be used outside the UK without prejudicing any future application in this country). Since the catapult was built by Gamage's factory, there was no question of the government having to pay royalties. The catapult was also used in the Dardanelles; these were not built by Gamage's but by the engineers of the No. 2 Field Company, Royal Naval Division. Since the catapults are so alike, No. 2 Field Company must have been supplied with drawings; the devices are not locally made improvisations.

The Leach or Gamage catapult with double winding handles and a steel stand. Although it is not easy to see, the stand has four legs. The stand allows the catapult to be angled upwards. The rubber strands, pouch and tensioning wire can all be seen. (IWM)

According to the complete specification of the patent, the catapult was 'light and readily transported and capable of being set by hand to throw a bomb, grenade or the like by mechanical means without the aid of any charge or explosive'. Basically, it was an enlarged Y-shaped catapult familiar to all boys, with an elongated 'handle' or central beam and a bracing arrangement between the forked arms, all of which was constructed in wood. The specification recommended ash. Rubber springs attached to the extremities of the arms were joined together at the centre line of the beam via a canvas pouch for the missile. On the back of the pouch was a loop to engage a hook on the end of a tensioning wire that extended rearwards over the central beam to a pulley at the rear of the catapult. It went round this and back up the underside of the beam to a winding gearbox with a handle. Inside the gearbox was a drum around which the tensioning wire was wound by turning the handle. When the required tension in the rubber springs was achieved, a pawl in the gearbox was used to engage the teeth on one of the gears to prevent the drum from unwinding the wire. The hook was part of a simple trigger mechanism which when operated released the pouch which was then pulled rapidly forwards by the springs and the bomb was hurled away.

Although Leach had first taken his catapult to Jackson, the Experimental Section at Hythe also conducted trials with it. Captain Todhunter, the Experimental Officer, visited Gamage's works department in the late spring of 1915 to discuss the canvas pocket which was not

This photograph taken in the Dardanelles in 1915 shows a number of weapons and devices made by the engineers of the No. 2 Field Company, Royal Naval Division. In the centre is a catapult based on the Leach design. Two more are behind the man on the right. On the extreme left and extreme right are two mortars which were probably made from lengths of pipe. The one of the right has a Lee Enfield firing mechanism. What appears to be an improvised grenade is at the foot of the catapult stand on the left. In the centre is a sniperscope with an auxiliary stock for firing the SMLE from behind cover. The man on the left is armed with a rifled loaded with a No. 20 rifle grenade; the rifle has a pendulum sight just to the left of his right hand. (IWM)

performing well. A new design was produced and Todhunter reported that 'good results have been obtained' and recommended that the new pattern should be shipped out to France for use on all the catapults already in service. When twelve strands of rubber were used in each spring and the catapult was angled at 35°, four shots with an 18 oz bomb travelled 160 yd, give or take a yard, every time. Not that this was much of a distance.

Todhunter also recommended that the pouches should be printed with a range scale and that full instructions on how to use the catapult should accompany all new devices, which begs the question of why full instructions were not issued in the first place. In May the works department manager prepared a set of instructions which were subsequently sent out as CDS 20. These included such caveats as 'The rubber springs should be fixed so that no twists in the rubber springs exist' and 'the tail of the machine should be firmly fixed or butted against some hard substance, so as to avoid . . . any recoil from the time the trigger is released until the grenade has left the pocket'. He also advised that to decrease the range, rubber strands should be removed rather than reducing the extension of them because accuracy could only be obtained with a full extension. He also pointed out that the angle at which the catapult should be set was 41.5° (rather too precise for the trenches) and that in

Operating the Leach catapult. The man crouched on the right is lighting the fuse. Note the muddy conditions. (ILN)

The same catapult has just fired the bomb, which can be seen in flight. The top of the catapult is very visible above the parapet. (ILN)

order to prolong the life of the rubber strands the springs should not be kept in tension for any longer than was necessary. From this, it is clear that there was plenty of room for error when operating the catapult and it is not surprising that things did not always go as planned.

One of the problems with any catapult that relied on pure natural rubber to provide the propulsive force was the degradable nature of unstabilized or unmodified rubber when exposed to the elements. In short, it perished. It was quickly discovered that the rubber soon lost its elasticity and acquired a permanent stretch which upset the optimum performance of the catapult. Moreover, the strands tended to break at inconvenient moments. The machine was fairly accurate when the rubbers were new but performance dropped off alarmingly quickly. Various 'preparations', a distinctly medieval sounding term, were developed to preserve the rubbers but none of them was really effective. The only solution to the problem would have been to use rubber that was at least partially vulcanized. The process of vulcanization produces chemical crosslinks between the coiled long-chain rubber molecules which not only hardens the material but helps to preserve its elastic properties by preventing the molecules from becoming uncoiled and from being cut up into shorter segments by the action of ultra violet radiation. The way in which the springs deteriorated and the fact that they did so quickly suggests that the rubber was not vulcanized. It is rather surprising that vulcanized rubber was not used since most rubber has always been cured in this way before use and the process was well known by the time of the First World War. Moreover, the works manager warned that 'it is essential that the rubbers . . . should be kept absolutely free from oil or grease of any description'; only unmodified rubber would be susceptible to deterioration by these materials.

When the catapult was producing its optimum performance, a bomb took 4.25 seconds to travel 75 yd. According to the works manager, the greatest distance one had hurled a bomb was 300 yd, the time of flight being a mere 5 seconds, the duration of a time fuse on a grenade and the ultimate factor in determining range. Generally, though, the catapults produced long flight times for short distances and gave the Germans ample time to spot a bomb in the air. However, the catapult had one advantage that no trench mortar could match: it was silent.

Although the heyday of the trench catapult was 1915, many remained in France long after they had been superseded by mortars. In the summer of 1916, Edmund Blunden came across a Gamage's catapult and since he had time on his hands to please himself to some extent he whiled 'away a foolhardy hour with a trench catapult ("Gamage's"), which . . . I discovered, would readily toss a Mills bomb far enough to burst as shrapnel over the huge crater in front of the German line'. This was a more foolhardy exercise than perhaps he realized, although he must have been aware that timing the release of the Mills' lever with the release of the catapult trigger, even with two people working together, was critical if a potentially fatal accident was to be avoided. In the days of 1915 when it had been used in earnest, the catapult had thrown bombs with safety fuses that had to be lit, a far more straightforward procedure when combined with firing a catapult than arming a Mills in its pouch just as it was about to be released, although special pouches to accommodate Mills grenades were supplied. Nevertheless, irrespective of the type of grenade fired by the catapult, a certain amount of coordination and practice was required if all was to go well. Blunden seems to have succeeded, however.

In May 1916, long after the catapult had ceased to be a front-line weapon in France, 300 Leach catapults were issued by the Trench Warfare Department for home use. This was a rather curious act since no catapult could substitute for a trench mortar for training purposes and the range of the catapult was so limited that it is hard to imagine who the enemy at home

This French catapult had a very short range of about 90 yd. The soldier on the right appears to be about to fire it. (ILN)

A similar catapult loaded with a grenade. Note the winding handle on the right and what appears to be a seat. The man on the right has a basket of grenades. (ILN)

might be. The catapults could have served no useful purpose. In France, they had only ever been convenient substitutes for trench mortars until the supply of the latter increased. Even in July 1915 the catapult was already becoming obsolete. The Royal Welch Fusiliers came upon a Leach catapult at Red Lamp Corner where the German trenches were only 80–100 yd away, well within the range of the catapult. But instead of throwing bombs it was now 'used mainly for hurling abusive messages wrapped in clay'. Evidently, their predecessors in the line had been on friendly terms with the enemy.

The Leach or Gamage catapult was the only one to see British service, although other improvised contraptions appeared locally from time to time. Although the Leach catapult was light, it still needed two men to operate it so the Trench Warfare Department decided to experiment with a smaller version. This was designed by Captain Wicks and became known as the Wicks Baby Catapult. This would have been a good opportunity to have dealt with the problem of deterioration of the rubber bands by using more suitable material but they stuck with the same unmodified rubber and the problems remained. As a result, the Baby Catapult never saw service in France. How much use it would have been, however, is open to question since it had a range of only 100 yd.

The British were not the only ones to make use of catapults. Both the Germans and the French used them as well. These all appear to have been locally made improvisations, rather than officially adopted devices, on the lines of a Leach catapult but one type of French catapult must have been an official piece of equipment since the Trench Warfare Supply Department was asked to carry out trials with it at the request of GHQ, France. Some French contraptions bear a similarity to the Leach and may have been inspired by it although they

Two more French catapults from 1915. These use bicycle gears, chains and pedals for winding. They appear sturdier than other French devices and are probably improvised. From the casual appearance of the men, this must have been a demonstration well behind the lines. (The Times History of the War)

A French leaf spring catapult from 1915. Note the size of the pit needed by this device. (The Times History of the War)

appear to have been cruder; e.g. one was basically an upright double A-frame made of wood with a firing ramp between. It appeared to use bicycle gears and chain with a single pedal to wind back the rubber with a tensioning wire attached to the rear of the bomb pouch, the wire being wound on a spindle at the back of the machine.

Another French machine appeared to use half of a lorry leaf spring with some sort of mechanical winding gear to pull it back. This was about 5 ft long. It is difficult to see how this could have thrown a bomb into the air as from its construction it appears more likely to throw it at the feet of the operators, since the spring would end up horizontal without some sort of stop or buffer, which seems to be absent or located in the wrong place. A similar but smaller device was improvised by the British. This was a balk of timber with a piece of springy metal (part of a steel spring from a railway truck) held in a slot by hammered-in wedges. The short spring was no more than about 18 in long. It was pulled back by a rope loop and secured in a trigger. This was simply a length of wood with a notch in it to take the end of the bent back spring, held in another slot with more wedges. The timber balk was laid up against the parapet to get an angle but it is doubtful that the device could throw a bomb very far. Apart from the obvious size difference between this and the French leaf spring

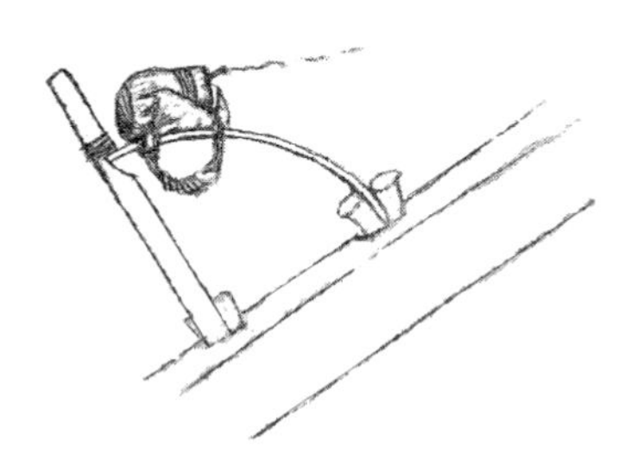

An improvised catapult made from a balk of timber and a length of spring steel. It is loaded with a Jam-Tin grenade. The upright stick was pulled back to launch it. The range was not much greater than a man could throw it unaided.

catapult, the most significant difference was the fact that the spring of the British one was secured vertically so that the spring formed a convex curve when in tension, whereas the French one was secured horizontally and formed a concave curve when in tension.

Only one other true catapult was patented in Britain but this was a much more complex machine than the Leach device which it resembled. This was UK patent 10,662/15, applied for on 22 July 1915. Unfortunately for the inventor, R.T. Glascodine, catapults were old news by then. The inventor had clearly attempted to devise an effective and portable machine that was less susceptible to the drawbacks that plagued the Leach machine but although it was made of tubular steel rather than wood it appears to have been much less robust than the Leach and less able to withstand the rough treatment it would have received in the trenches.

There was one other machine that used rubber as the motive force to propel a projectile: John Robertson's device, for which the inventor filed a patent application on 26 August 1915. This was subsequently granted on 28 August 1916 as UK patent 12,298/15. Like Glascodine, he had missed the boat. The motive behind the device was laudable. Robertson was a gunsmith who owned a business called Boss & Co. He wanted to produce a robust and compact catapult that would throw a bomb further and more accurately than previous catapults. He had thought about the problems of recoil and provided the device with springs or buffers to absorb the impact of the bomb-carrier as it reached the end of its travel when propelling a bomb. It was a more solid-looking device than Glascodine's but like Glascodine's it was far more complex than the Leach.

Altogether there were about eighteen patents granted to inventors of various sorts of catapult, including those discussed above, most of which were applied for in 1915.

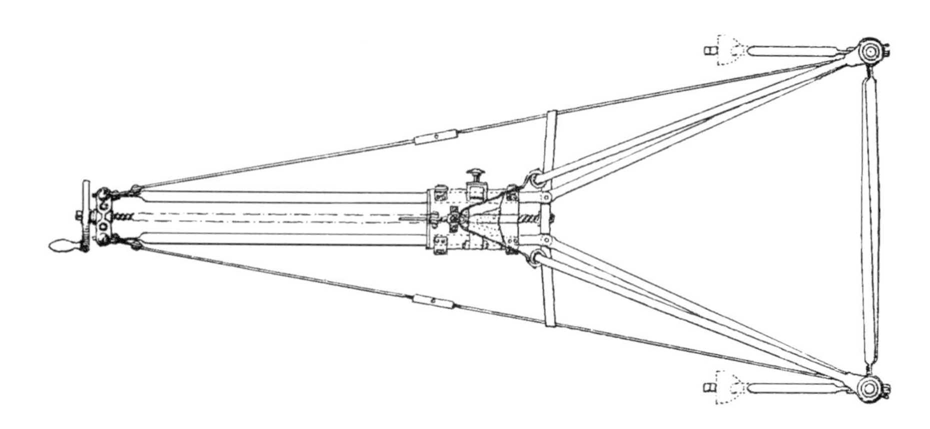

Yet another patented rubber-spring operated catapult, this one made of tubular steel (Glascodine's patent 10,662/15). Note the anchors at the front and very long screw (dotted lines) between the winding handle and the bomb-carrier.

Specifications continued to be filed throughout the war, indicating that inventors were not always on top of current trends. The majority were mechanical 'spring guns', although the term gun was something of a misnomer since such contraptions were no more guns than the Leach catapult was a mortar. The only spring gun to enter service was the West Spring Gun which was under development at the same time as the Leach/Gamage catapult. The West Spring Gun was named after its inventor, a Captain West. This was a version of a Roman stone-throwing engine.

About the same number of West's device saw service in France as the Leach catapult. Guy Chapman was one of the unfortunate few who came into contact with one when his unit's bombing officer proposed using it to respond to German light mortar fire in late 1915. Chapman was more than a little sceptical of its value:

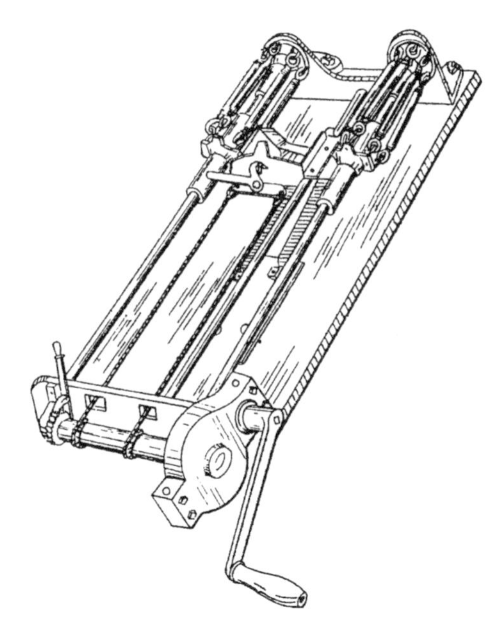

Robertson's catapult from UK patent 12,298/15. This worked on a similar principal to the Leach catapult. Note the banks of rubber springs.

The West Spring Gun being demonstrated somewhere in England. The helmets suggest that this shot was taken in 1916 when the Spring Gun was no longer in service in France. The device is on a duckboard weighted down with sandbags. Note that it takes three men to pull back the throwing arm. Some of the springs can be seen at the front of the device. (IWM)

> It was supposed to hurl a hand grenade with much force and accuracy into the enemy's lines. In practice, it was much more apt to shoot the missile straight up into the air to return on the marksman's head, supposing he still possessed one; for the machine was also calculated to decapitate the engineer if he was clumsy enough to stand in front of its whirling arm.

He was not sorry to see it disappear into the mud produced by the winter rains. Edmund Blunden's unit contemplated resurrecting a West Spring Gun in 1916 which had long lain unused in a dump 'a legacy of the ingenuity of 1915, but antiquity was respected, and our lives may have been saved'. They left it alone to rust in peace.

The postwar 'Development of Weapons used in Trench Warfare' by Lieutenant-Colonel Brothers described the operating procedure for the gun. It was evidently used in similar circumstances to those under which trench mortars were used but it was limited by its range of about 240 yd. It was used mostly 'as a support to "cutting out" operations, and was not used in general work'. The reason it remained in service was its great accuracy and its silence. It was heavy, bulky and inconvenient to move from place to place. Moreover, it required an emplacement 8–9 ft square which was considerably bigger than that required by a trench mortar, but worse than this was the fact that the cocking lever was often visible above the parapet. It is not altogether clear how the gun functioned other than by the combined action of twenty-four springs, distributed in banks of equal size, on a throwing arm. Setting up the gun was something of a rigmarole.

> The ground had to be as level as possible. Then by means of carrying rods, the gun was carried into position. The sandbag boards were then unstrapped and fixed in position on each side, 13 or 14 sandbags being placed upon each of them. The throwing arms were then put in with the straight side up. It is advisable not to tighten the holding shoes till the bomb cup is affixed.

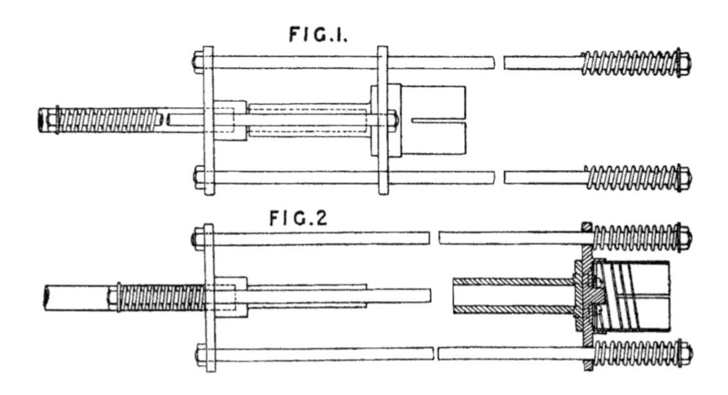

M.E. Brett's spring bomb-thrower (UK patent 10,165/15). This odd-looking object was attached to the muzzle of a rifle and the bomb was discharged by a blank which acted on a rod inside the barrel. The bomb-carrier is between the two guide rods fitted with compensating springs. The carrier also contains a spring to help the grenade on its way. The recoil would have been severe. Top: *normal position.* Bottom: *fired position.*

Although there were two types of cup, one for percussion grenades, the other for time-fused grenades, only the V-shaped cup for the latter was generally used. The V in the wooden block prevented the grenades from rolling off the machine – these were mostly spherical bombs – a serious hazard to the operators and anyone near by.

> There is also an elevating screw for varying the height of the trajectory. The screw acted almost in the same way as the fingers of a throwing hand, decreasing the height of the trajectory as it is lengthened and vice versa. The knuckle of this screw must be at right angles to the surface of the bomb.

There was a two-piece cocking lever. The gun could be ranged in three ways, the most common being the raising or lowering of the trigger 'that is, if the trigger is lowered, the throwing arm would have to come farther down, thus increasing the tension, and giving longer range'. The second method was to alter the height of the elevating screw on the bomb cup to give a higher or lower trajectory. In practice, the range was altered by a combination of these two methods. The third alternative was to remove or add springs but this was not a simple process. The gun could be traversed only slightly by slewing it round on its bed which required the securing bolts to be slacken off. Traverse was limited to 15 yd in every 100 yd.

Lieutenant-Colonel Brothers' report affords only a glimpse of the West Spring Gun and does not reveal its construction. There are several patented devices dating from late 1914 and early 1915 which resemble the West device but none of the inventors is named as West. An application filed on 25 November 1914 to become UK patent 23,044/14 on 2 September 1915 bears a strong resemblance to it although it differs in some important ways. The inventor was described in the document as an architect, one Matthew James Dawson. It operated on a similar principal to the West device except that whereas the Spring Gun relied on one set of the springs arranged in banks the Dawson device used two sets of springs so that when the apparatus was

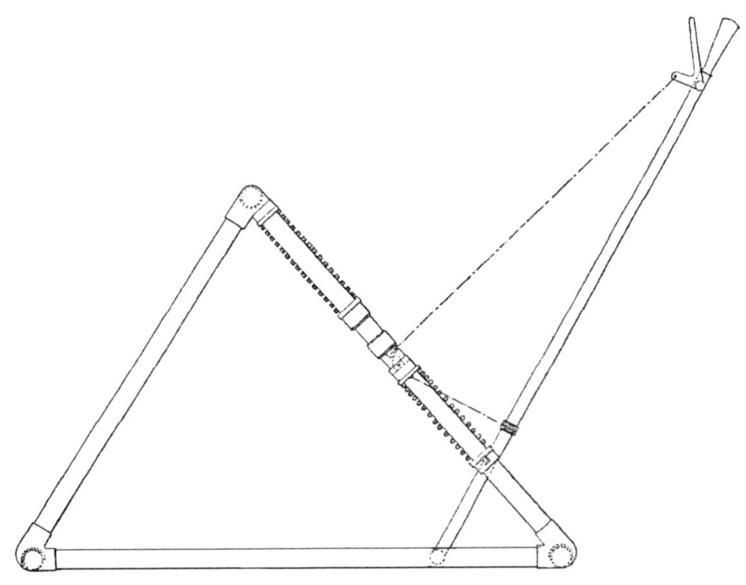

J.A. Hill's 'spring projector for bombs, grenades, and like missiles', UK patent 106,656. The device was supposed to be secured to the ground by 'anchoring-spades' (not shown).

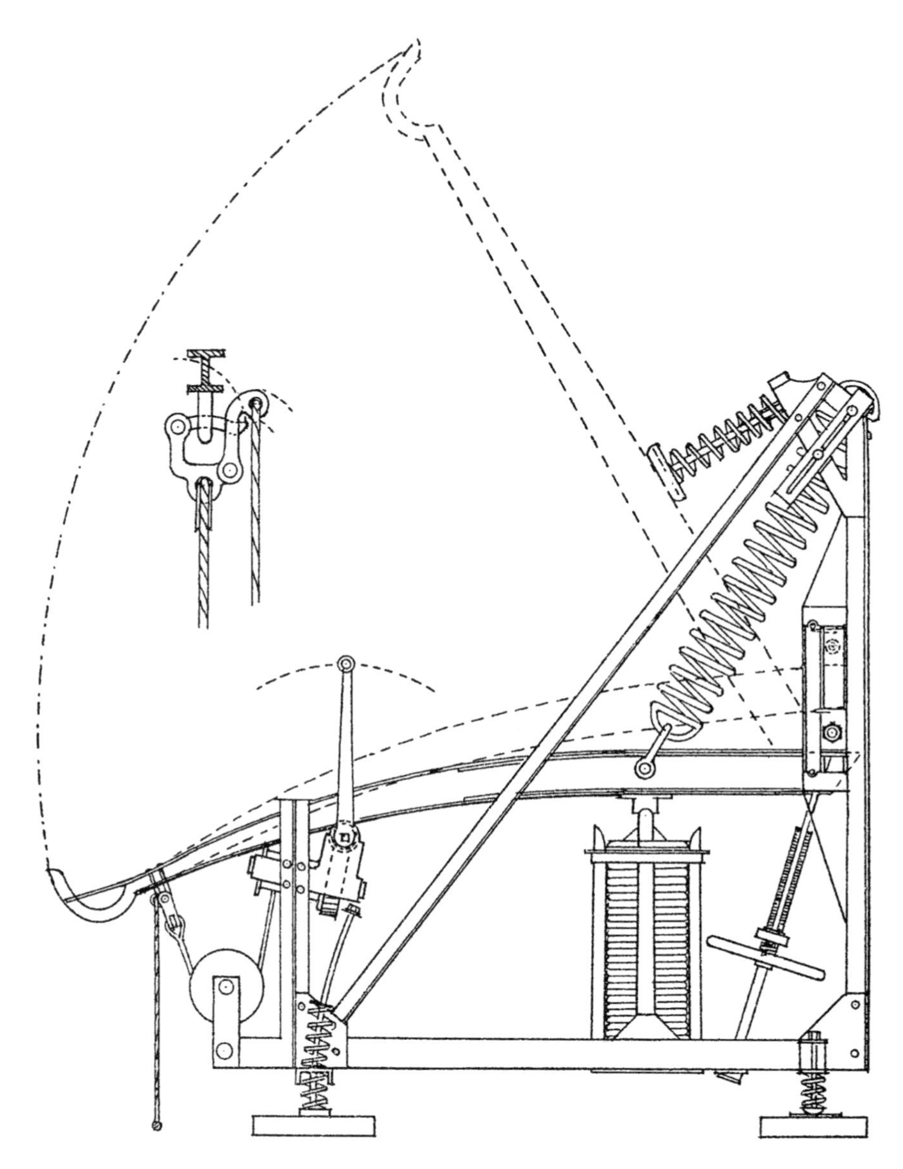

Dawson's spring projector made of steel with banks of springs above and below the throwing arm (UK patent 23,044/14). Note the buffer to arrest the forward movement of the arm. Details of the trigger located below the end of the arm are shown in the inset. Note that the arm was intended to be flexible and provide some of the throwing energy.

cocked one set was under compression while the other set was under tension. A similar approach was adopted by J.A. Hill in 1916 with his patented spring-operated bomb-thrower (106,656 and 107,045). Although this appears to be a robust, workable contraption, it is highly improbable that the Army would have been interested at that late date. A bomb-carrier was retracted along two inclined guideways against the action of propelling springs using a long lever. A trigger on the lever released the carrier and propelled the grenade into the air.

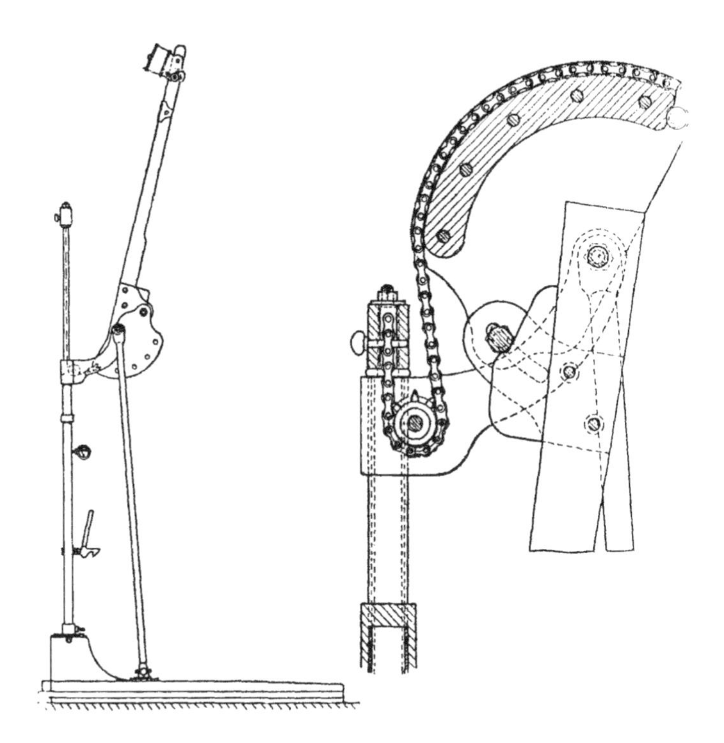

A pneumatic bomb-thrower with a difference – a bicycle chain. Drawings from UK patent 12,291/15 granted to A. and G. Wood. The cylinder and piston at the front form the pneumatic part. The piston is connected to the throwing arm by the chain. Note the pressure gauge midway down the cylinder and the catch below this to hold the cocked arm.

The West Spring Gun was manufactured by the Reason Manufacturing Company which also developed a grenade fuse although it does not appear to have been used. It filed for a patent on 19 October 1915 and this became UK patent 14,793/15. Another company, A. West & Co. of Brighton, also manufactured the Spring Gun but it is not clear whether this West was related to the inventor.

Special bombs were manufactured for catapults and Spring Guns, although sometimes the only difference between the hand-thrown variety and the catapult and Spring Gun variety was a longer fuse for the latter to ensure that it reached the target before the fuse burned down to the detonator. These bombs tended to be spherical although Jam-Tins and Lemons were often fired from them but mostly they were No. 15 Ball grenades with 9-second fuses. In August 1915 'Special Bombs' were ordered for the West Spring Gun from the manufacturer but Jackson complained that samples had been late in arriving for his department to test, which had delayed the placing of the order. 'The Company had been repeatedly pressed for a sample, but caused great delay by sending them unofficially to the front by Captain West.'

In November 1915 the Director General of Trench Warfare Supplies informed the Director of Artillery that although the supplies of grenades for catapults in France and Gallipoli were inadequate, a supply of 100,000 Ball grenades per week could now be guaranteed, a quarter of them going to Gallipoli, the rest to France. The supply of Ball grenades for hand throwing had been discontinued.

In addition to these, 40,000 D grenades per week could also be supplied, presumably in similar proportions as the Balls to the respective theatres. The D grenade was a 4 in diameter spherical bomb made of tin containing 19 oz of ammonal. Whereas the No. 15 was a fragmentation grenade the D was a blast grenade, producing very little shrapnel. There was also a small supply of E grenades (No. 33) which were, in effect, 3 in diameter versions of the D containing 8 oz of ammonal. The supply was shortly expected to rise to 40,000 a week. All these grenades had Brock igniters to overcome the problem of wet weather.

On 17 February 1916, 10,000 3.75 in diameter spherical R grenades were ordered for the West Spring Gun. Already, 150,000 were waiting to be filled with explosive and by March a total of 500,000 were on order. However, those already made but unfilled ended up being put into storage as GHQ was having second thoughts about the wisdom of supplying grenades for catapults and Spring Guns which were being phased out. On 14 March 1916 the requirement for catapult and Spring Gun ammunition was cancelled and Lieutenant-General Maxwell wrote to the Army Council to state that the 3 in Stokes would replace the catapults and bomb-throwers. On 13 July the Leach catapult and the West Spring Gun officially became history when they were dropped as service equipment by the War Office.

CHAPTER 4

Mills and Patent Hand Grenades 1915–16

From August 1914 to November 1918, more than a hundred patents were granted in respect of inventions related to hand grenades, thirty-nine of which were applied for in 1915 alone. Most of these were concerned with the fuse and firing and safety mechanisms as these were the fundamental parts of the bomb and determined not only how it worked but whether it would work at all. By far the majority sank without trace. Some were merely misguided attempts to come up with something that could solve the problems at the Front. Others were speculative forays into the field of military engineering and munitions in the hope that the government would place contracts for the grenade. Mostly, this was a forlorn hope and it did not happen because the Munitions Inventions Department or the Trench Warfare Department or some other department or committee, charged with sifting the potentially serviceable from the outright useless, did not regard it to be an improvement over what already existed. Mostly, they were right.

Many were simply unworkable or had some flaw unforeseen by the inventor. The granting of a patent did not mean that the invention actually worked. Even when something was adopted for trials, or events had progressed well beyond the trial stage, it was all too common for unexpected faults to show themselves as soon as the grenades came into contact with soldiers at the Front, who were apt to do things unimagined or overlooked by the inventor or anyone investigating its usefulness as a weapon of war. This was certainly true of the early Mills grenades. Sometimes the invention got to the trials stage but no further and, on occasions, a great deal of time and money were expended trying make a grenade work or in rectifying defects that caused accidents.

It was a rather complicated situation and a direct result of the sudden need for grenades when there were none. The design and supply of grenades tended to occur simultaneously because of the urgency. Inevitably, this meant that there was 'no time available for exhaustive experiments with a view to producing a perfected article'. Every new pattern of grenade that found its way to the Front in 1915 was flawed, including the Mills. Moreover, once the administrative machinery for meeting the demands had been put into operation for a particular pattern, from the placing of contracts to getting the grenades to the men at the Front, it was no simple matter to call a halt and start all over again with a different pattern. There were delays and dislocations with unavoidable shortages. This became a serious problem so there was no incentive whatsoever to take on a design of grenade which might, in time, turn out to be safe and effective. It had to be workable right from the start and offer tremendous advantages over what was already in service or in the pipeline. Consequently, it is not surprising that trench warfare departments tended to be lukewarm about new inventions brought to them by hopeful inventors. For many inventors the patenting of grenade inventions was a waste of time and effort.

It was further complicated by the necessity of training, something that was often overlooked by inventors. Under Major Claude Beddoes of the Gloucestershires, the first

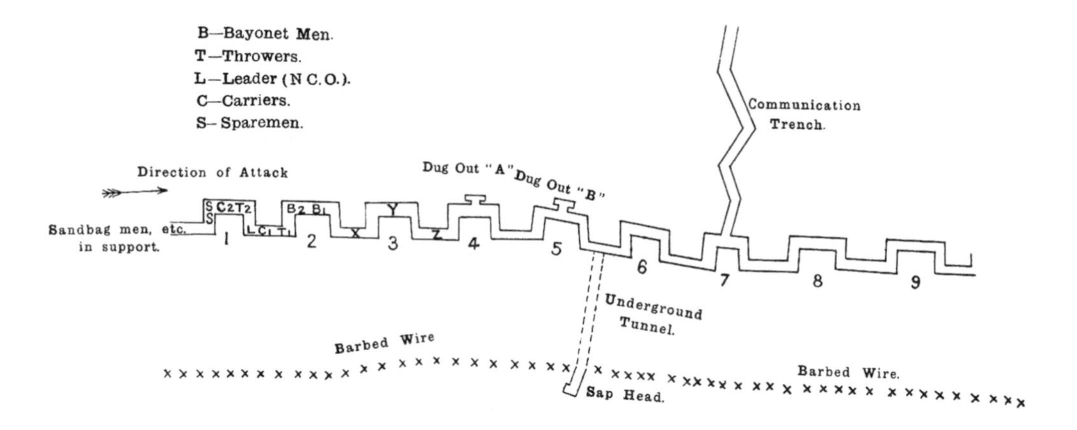

A diagram from The Training and Employment of Grenadiers *showing how to clear enemy trenches using grenades, as taught in late 1915. It was acknowledged that there was unlikely to be enough room in a trench for two bombers to stand side by side to throw their grenades. X, Y and Z are the bombers' targets from the positions shown. When the bayonet men report that the bombed areas are clear of enemy the whole party advances, the bayonet men taking up positions in traverse 3.*

school to train bombing instructors was set up at Clapham, south London, in the spring of 1915. In time, a bombing school was established in each Home Command and Major Beddoes was appointed as Inspector of Bombing Schools, GHQ Home Forces in January 1916. He became the Experimental Officer for Trench Stores to the Ministry of Munitions and during 1916 liaised with the Army in France. These schools made a considerable contribution to the reduction of accidents by providing proper training in the handling and use of grenades, each pattern of which required different procedures. Whenever a new pattern of grenade was adopted by the Army, new training programmes had to be instituted. It was a constant battle during 1915 to keep up when so many different patterns were being supplied to the Army. Once scientific training methods were introduced, standards rose and fatal accidents during training decreased to 10 in 74,000, the number of officer and NCO bombing instructors who successfully passed through the Home Training Schools. Discipline was, of course, a major factor and in these schools it was rigid. According to Lieutenant-Colonel Brothers after the war, 11,863,012 Mills grenades were fired from rifles or thrown during training at the schools.

Brothers explained that because of the grenade problem 'It became necessary . . . to balance the advantages offered by an improved Grenade, against the supply and training problem involved by its introduction to the Service'. None of this helped prospective inventors who believed that they had an even chance, at least, of getting a fair hearing. Although patenting their inventions was, perhaps, a logical thing to do to protect their interests, in the most part it was to no purpose because no one was going to make their grenades.

The curious thing about all these patents is that they were published during what was a time of war, as publication meant that anyone 'skilled in the art' could make use of the information either to manufacture grenades, provided they had the facilities, or to gain valuable information about how they worked. And that included the enemy. A patent has to contain sufficient information for a person to make the article, perform the process or carry out whatever the invention claimed to be. Patents could be made secret under the provisions of the 1907 Patents Act, however, and indeed at least one secret application was filed and granted as a patent. This was the application filed by Sir Ernest Moir, head of the Munitions Inventions Department; the subsequent patent was not published (secret patent No. 88). Simply because the patents were published in Great Britain, rather than worldwide, would not have precluded sight of them by unwanted eyes – those of the enemy.

This would only have mattered, of course, provided the invention was not only workable but practical. There is no evidence to suggest that the Germans did make use of the information in any UK patent to produce weapons although they may have gained useful information by studying them. Strangely, no one in Britain seems to have considered looking at German patents or British patents granted to German companies before the outbreak of war. (A case in point is flamethrowers. There was at least one British patent owned by a German company dating from 1910 but no one seems to have looked at it when the British were trying to develop flamethrowers in response to their use by the Germans in 1915.)

The alternative to a secret patent, of course, was to publish nothing about it at all. That way, the invention remained secret. To a large degree, the question of secrecy would only have arisen for patent applications related to inventions made by those in the military or a member of one of the government departments or committees concerned with the development of new weapons. There were certainly rules governing the patenting of inventions made by such people during the war but it was grey area. A civilian would not have been subject to the same rules. Nor is it likely that he would have been aware of the secrecy provisions in the Act. Neither would he have considered the advisability or otherwise of having his invention published in a form that could aid the enemy since most applicants were interested solely in protecting their property from unlicensed use. An invention is, after all, property and a patented one is afforded legal protection. On the other hand, an invention that remains secret is also protected simply because it is not known. Moreover, it was not necessarily the job of the patent examiners in the Patent Office to decide whether something should become a secret application although they might draw a likely candidate to the attention of the War Office. However, there is nothing to suggest that this ever occurred.

Nevertheless, it did worry some people – Captain James Leeming of the Trench Warfare Department for one. He was concerned that the publication of a grenade patent abridgement in the 22 December 1916 edition of the *Engineer* would provide useful information to the enemy (although it begs the question of why he was unaware of the patent until its appearance in the journal since it was only reproducing what had already been published by the Patent Office). A note written by Louis Jackson on 17 January 1917 stated, in a somewhat convoluted way, that 'we do not stop patents that are not likely to be taken up by ourselves or to be useful to the enemy'. By implication, this indicated that the Trench Warfare Supply Department, or indeed any other similar department or committee, would stop a patent that was going to be taken up by the British government or one that was potentially useful to the enemy. If an invention was passed (i.e. accepted) by the Trench Warfare Supply Department, publication of any patent related to it would have been considered likely to provide useful information, though there is no evidence to suggest that they ever stopped one. Indeed, the contrary seems to be the case as there are several instances of patented inventions being taken up, the most significant of which are the Mills grenade and Stokes mortar patents.

In any event, it appears that Leeming's concerns were misplaced. The patent in question was H.D. Black's grenade patent, 15,984/15, a feature of which was a safety device to prevent premature detonation if the grenade was accidentally dropped. The application had

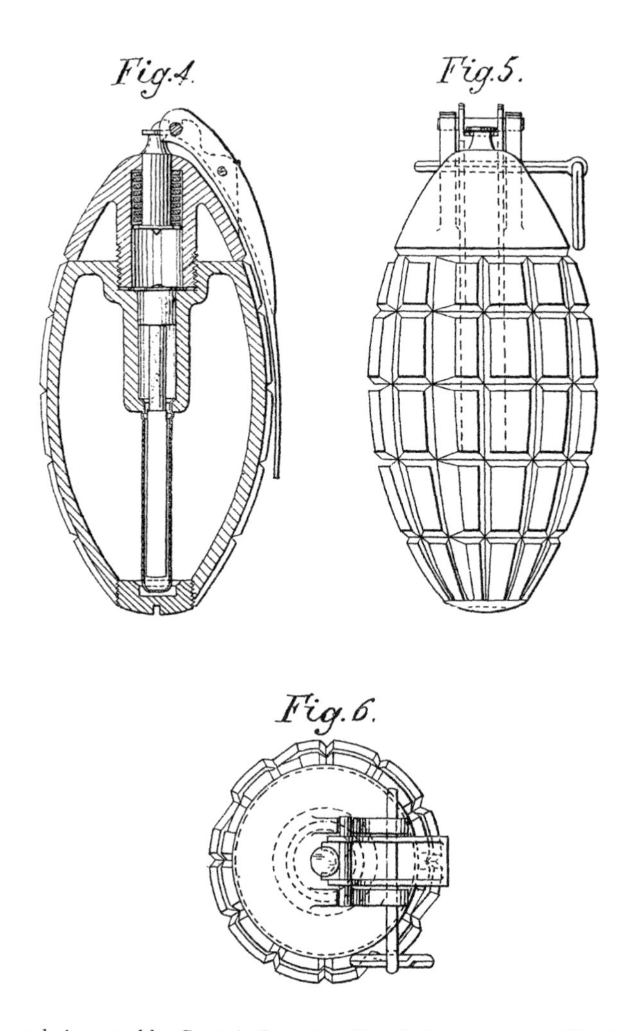

The time-fused grenade invented by Captain Leeming, Frank Brewerton and Frederick Fraser (UK patent 11,679/15). The head containing the firing mechanism is screwed into the body immediately prior to use. It has a lever mechanism similar to the Mills.

been filed on 12 November 1915. Black was one of three co-patentees, Frank Brewerton and Frederick Fraser being the other two. The grenade had been submitted to the Trench Warfare Department and Leeming was of the opinion that it was one of the best devices the department had seen and therefore the patent should not have been published. However, Louis Jackson, the Director General of Trench Warfare Supply, disagreed, pointing out that it was impractical and had been rejected. Needless to say, Black's grenade was not taken up.

There was, however, another side to this. Leeming, Brewerton and Fraser had been co-patentees on an earlier application for a grenade patent, subsequently granted as UK patent 11,679/15. This had been accepted by the Patent Office and published before publication of the offending abridgement in the *Engineer*. The later patent which named Black was a development of the earlier invention which was concerned with what was, in effect, a two-part device. One part constituted the body with explosive, detonator and fuse, the other 'head

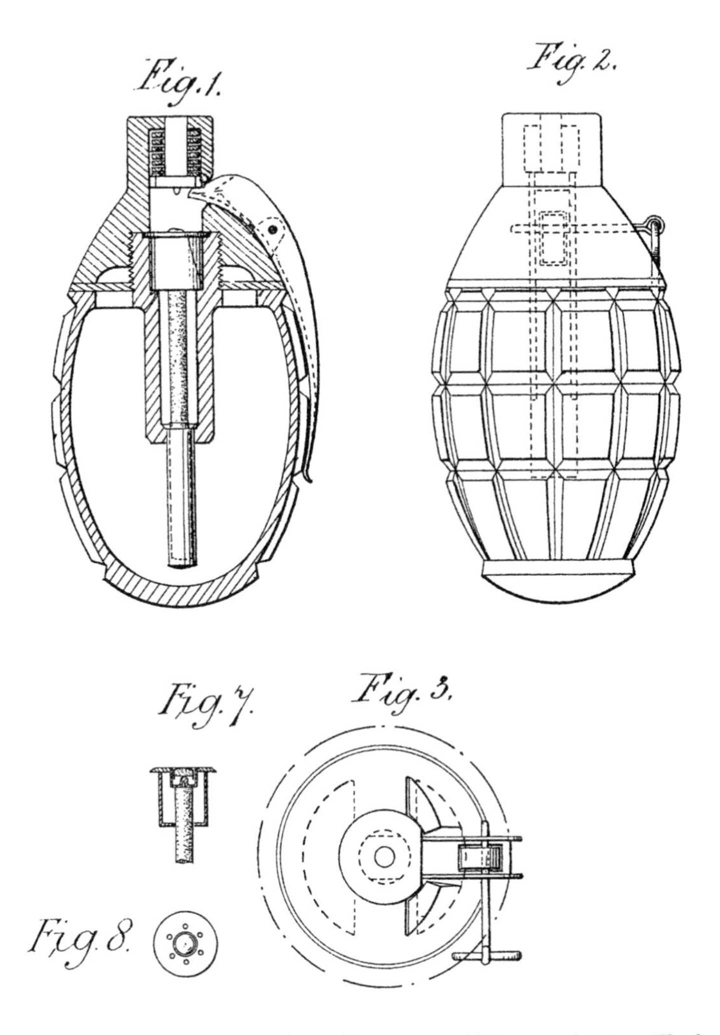

Another version of the Leeming grenade with a different sort of firing mechanism. The lever holds the bottom of the striker instead of the top.

part' containing the firing mechanism locked by a safety device in the 'inoperative position until the grenade is to be used'. The idea was to screw in the head immediately prior to use. The invention was a clever idea but it was not taken up. Passing over the fact that the earlier patent was published with Leeming's full knowledge, Leeming may have been under the impression that the Black grenade, and by association his own, had been accepted by the Trench Warfare Department. Maybe he was upset by the failure to get his own accepted.

Not all of the patents relate to British grenades, of course: some are French or Belgian inventions. Some of these were adopted by the French or Belgian armies. UK patent 11,551/15 granted to L.L. Billant (who filed several other applications for grenade patents during the war) was a percussion-fused hand grenade adopted by the French as Grenade P1. In September 1915 General Maxwell told the War Office that the BEF was considering the French P Modele 1915 made by a Paris firm because of the shortage of grenades being

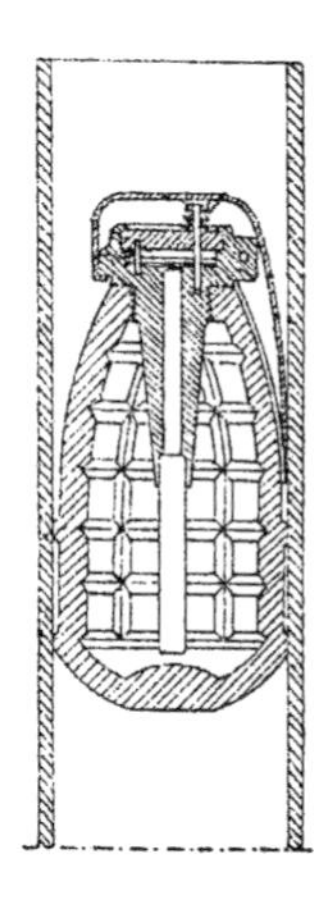

Drawings from L.L. Billant's patent, 127,279. In the plan view on the left, the striker is the flat spring going from left to right. The retaining pin (it is on the right at the top of the grenade in the left-hand figure) is held in place by another spring which is retained by the lever. The striker pivots about the short pin on the left (right-hand figure). The grenade is shown in a discharge tube but how to insert it so far down is not explained.

supplied to the BEF. It was probably the Billant grenade. In the end, considering did not turn into adopting and the grenade did not see British service. Then there was 11,747/15, filed at the UK Patent Office on 10 March 1915, which became the French Besozzi grenade, named after its inventor. This had a friction igniter similar to the matchhead types in British service at the time, the matchhead being protected from the wet by a brass cap. There were others.

Since the first hand grenades used by the British Army were stick grenades it is not surprising that, at first, inventors should follow this line of development and try to overcome the inherent hazard of percussion grenades. On 10 February 1915 the firm of W.M. Still & Sons filed an application for a stick grenade with the firing pin in the handle, activated by the act of throwing. It used a time fuse rather than an impact one although there was provision for an impact fuse when the grenade was adapted to be a rifle grenade. The mechanism was neither robust nor simple enough for field use and it is likely that manufacture would have been too

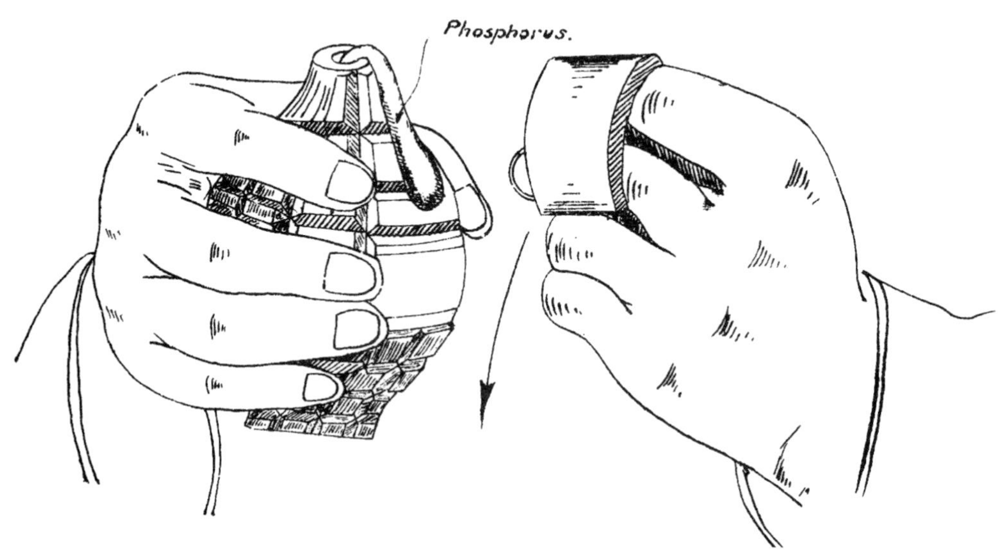

The Besozzi grenade and how to ignite it, as illustrated in The Training and Employment of Grenadiers *of October 1915. The fuse is about 2 in long and bent over and waxed to the body of the grenade and tipped with red phosphorus. The grenades came with the necessary accompaniment, a striker box or ring. It was essential that the phosphorus tip was struck with a downward motion of the striker box to prevent the fuse being pulled away and consequently failing to ignite.*

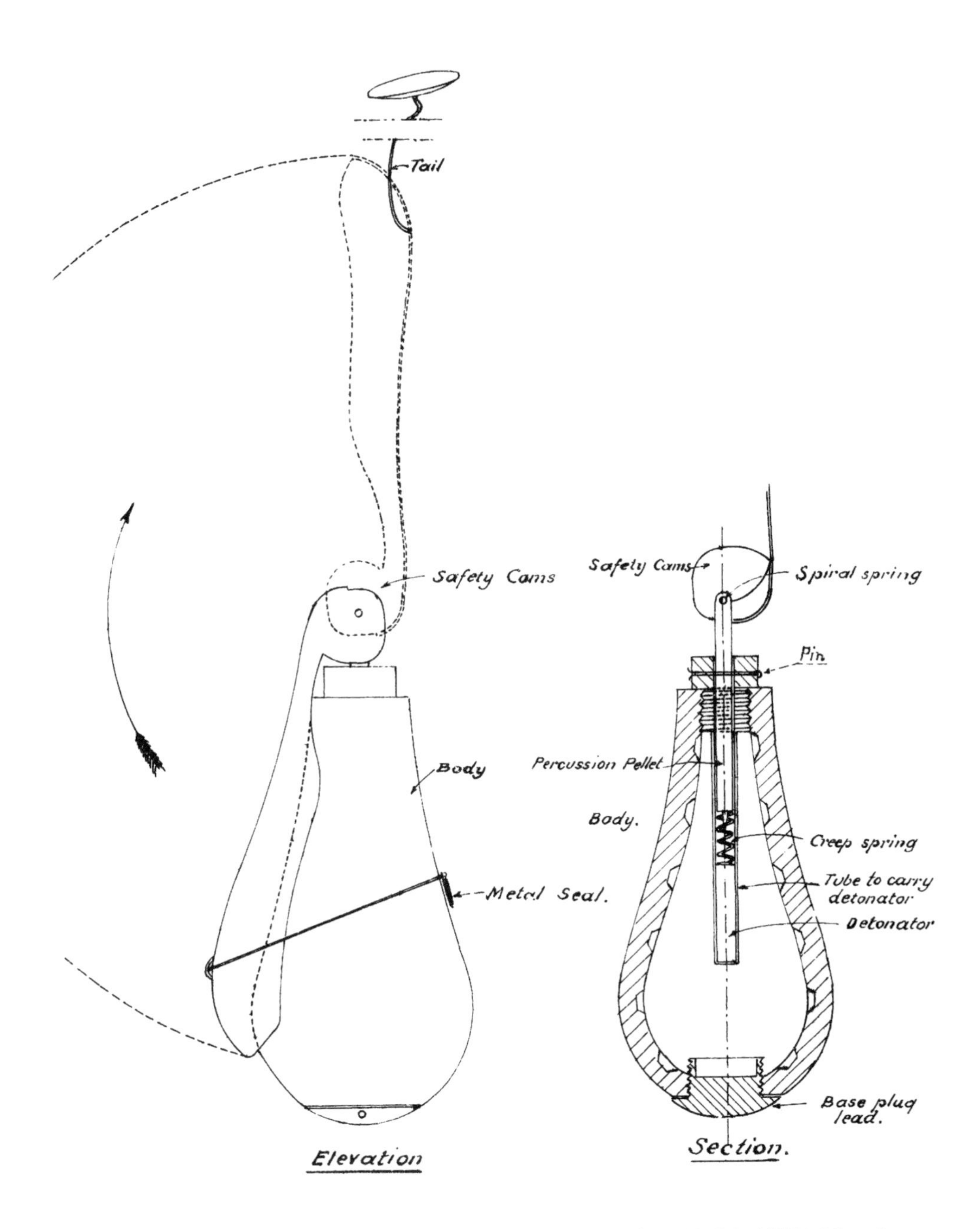

The French Pear percussion grenade of 1915. This may have been the P Modele 1915 (although, confusingly, Billant's grenade was called the P1). It was 3.5 in long with a maximum diameter of 2 in and contained 1 oz of explosive. The aluminium lever was secured to the body with a string fastened with a metal seal. An 18 in streamer or tail with a small metal 'steadying plate' was attached to the lever and folded beneath it. The cams on the top of lever held the striker until the grenade was thrown. When the lever flew up, the cams were freed from the grenade neck, freeing the striker. Like the Mills, the grenade was held with the lever against the palm and immediately before throwing the seal was twisted off. (The Training and Employment of Grenadiers)

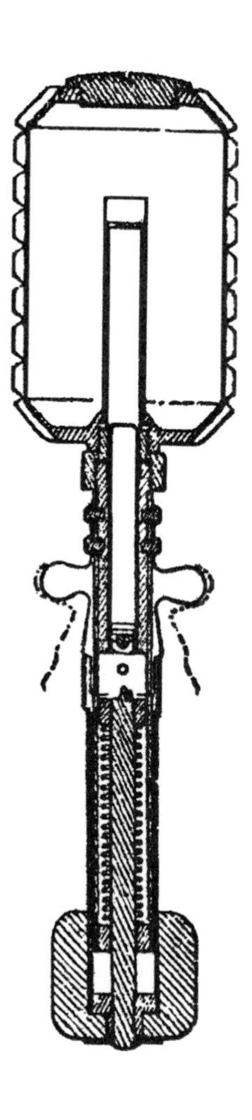

The side projections are leaf springs which hold the firing pin until the grenade is thrown. The dotted lines show the springs after being released by inertia of the central shank. Still's patent 2,139/15.

complex for quick production. It was not adopted. A few days after Still & Sons filed their application, Frederick Marten Hale filed an application for a similar device, a development of his patented grenade (4,925/11) of 1911. This was another complex design that would have been far too complicated for quick production. Moreover, it was a prime candidate for accidental detonation due to rough handling because of the way the striker was released, achieved by the act of throwing.

Arthur Cardwell Roodhouse took a different approach. He was an 'explosives merchant' who lived in Wigan and he invented a hand grenade of two concentric spheres and a firing mechanism. His application, filed on 20 March 1915, became UK patent 4,392/15. His complete specification stated:

> Heretofore it has been proposed to make spherical bombs of solid, thick, metal, with zonal grooves at intervals so that part of the force of the explosion shall be exerted in breaking the bomb into rings corresponding to these zonal grooves. It has also been proposed to make cylindrical bombs formed of two casings with hemispherical ends, the inner casing containing picric acid, and the space between the cylindrical as well as the hemispherical parts of the two casings being filled with steel balls.

His invention was intended to take 'all the advantages obtained from both' and provide a grenade with additional 'advantages not found in either'. This suggests that Roodhouse was aware of the current developments in service grenades, the Lemon and the Jam-Tin in particular, when he invented his but that was not the case. Moreover, his understanding (or perhaps that of his patent agent) of fragmentation was clearly not based on sound knowledge. He believed that because the grenade was spherical, blast would inevitably be radial and equal in all directions. It is highly improbable this would have happened in practice.

The grenade consisted of an outer sphere made from two hemispheres of 'Swedish tinned sheet iron . . . soldered, brazed, welded' together to form an airtight container. Inside this and attached to it was a second similar sphere. Roodhouse was aware of the problems caused by damp and made it clear that all the openings in the outer sphere – such as for the explosive filling tube and for the detonator and firing mechanism – were covered by airtight and watertight closures. The inner sphere contained the explosive and the space between them

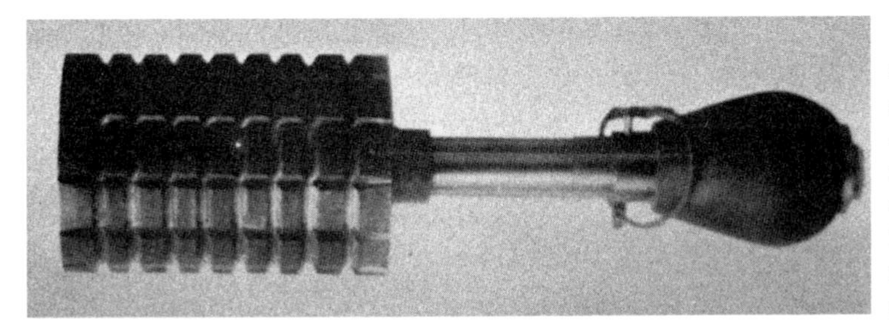

Hale's patent safety grenade (UK patent 3,091/15), photographed in the summer of 1915. Hale claimed it would produce 200 fragments. Compare this with the patent drawing below. (ILN)

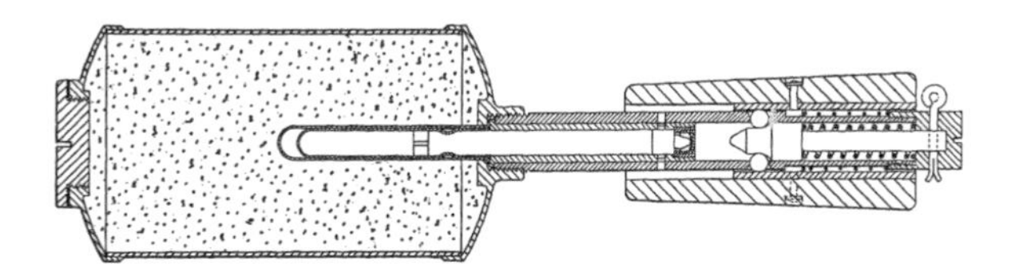

Hale's hand grenade in which the firing pin is released by inertia during the act of throwing after the pin has been removed.

was filled with shrapnel. The firing mechanism was a neat device, resembling that used in the Mills, using a striker to hit a percussion cap which ignited the time fuse which in turn ignited the detonator. It had a trigger and a safety catch of wire to prevent the trigger activating the striker until the bomber was ready to throw it.

All in all, this was a neat and potentially safe and effective grenade. It sufficiently impressed one of the trench warfare departments that it went into limited production so that trials could be conducted. Unfortunately for Roodhouse it did not pass and was rejected, most likely because the Mills was superior, although the safety may have presented problems as it had the potential to be accidentally moved off the trigger without its unlucky user noticing.

Although the time fuse quickly supplanted the percussion fuse for hand grenades, inventors endeavoured to overcome the inherent problems and develop a safe 'all-ways' fuse that would detonate the grenade irrespective of the angle of impact. James Frank Buckingham developed several fuses of this type. UK patent 4,407/15 described a mechanism that used a vibrator with an eccentric weight on the vibrator stem, while 5,553/15 described a development of this in which the vibrator was located in a grenade at a position distant from the grenade's centre of gravity and at an angle to it. Buckingham was the owner of an engineering company in Coventry and was already working on incendiary bullets. The Buckingham incendiary was

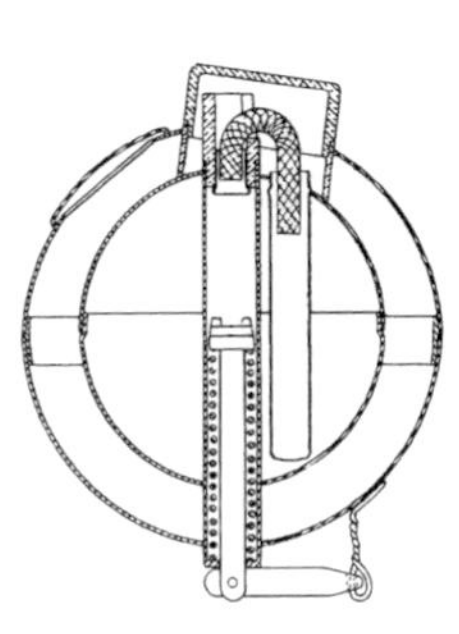

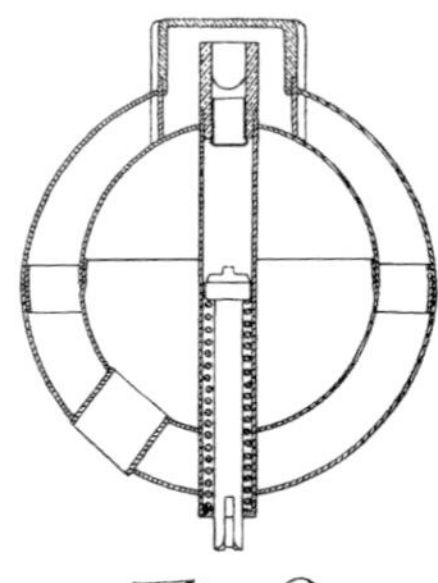

Arthur Roodhouse's hand grenade (UK patent 4,392/15). In fig. 2, the grenade is turned through 90° to fig. 1. From these drawings, the flimsiness of the safety device is readily apparent.

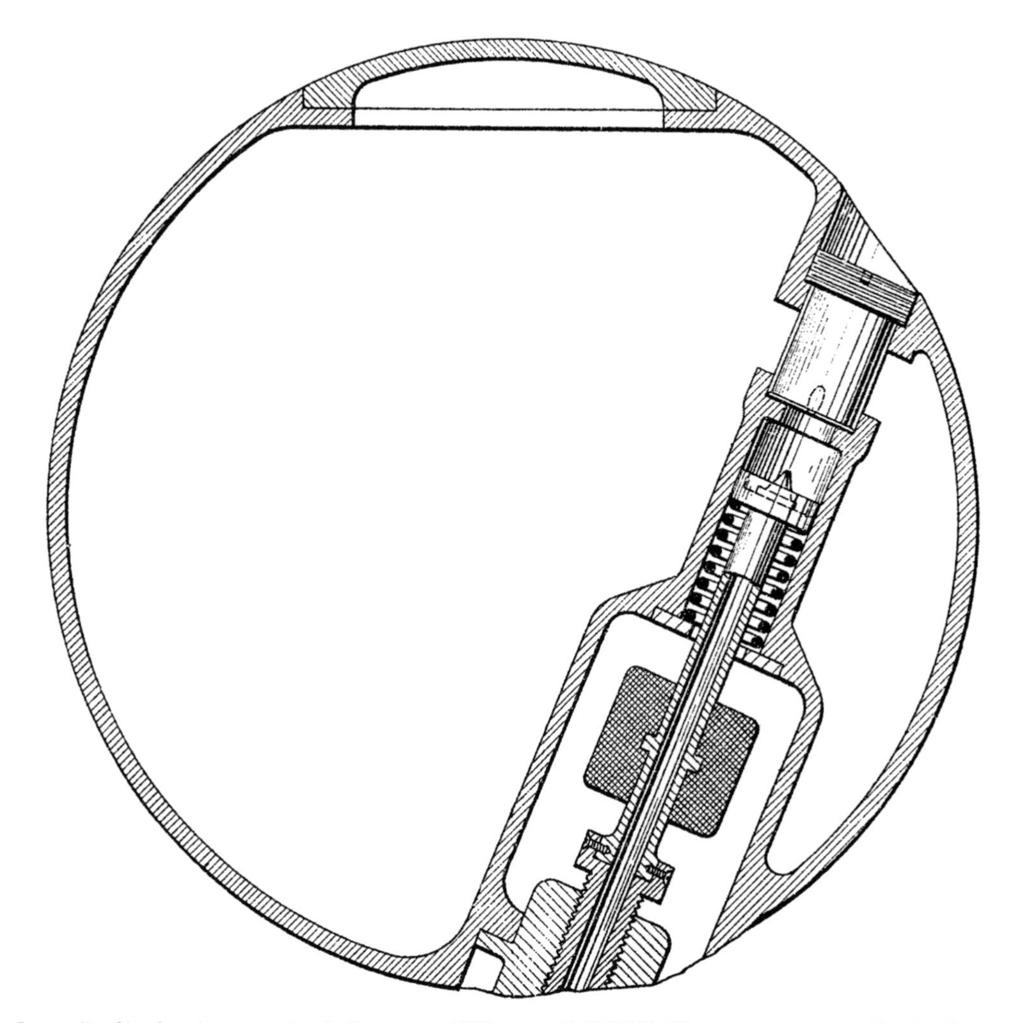

James Buckingham's percussion ball grenade (UK patent 5,553/15). The narrow stem leading back from the firing pin is broken on impact by the weight in the chamber, thereby freeing the firing pin to strike the detonator.

subsequently used by the Royal Naval Air Service and the Royal Flying Corps. However, his impact fuses did not find favour.

One of the oddest grenade inventions was J.A. Armstrong's. He filed an application on 8 September 1915 for a wheel-shaped grenade which, although it could be thrown, was intended to be rolled along the ground at the enemy. Just how this was to be done in the trenches and under fire was not explained. It became UK patent 12,889 and languished in obscurity. Other oddities included Senior's grenade (105,400, filed in April 1916) which had knife edges to alter the flight path of the grenade when 'thrown in a particular manner'. It was intended to go round corners like a boomerang. Then there was Marks's grenade (136,857, filed in June 1917), a disc-shaped bomb constructed in two conical sections joined to form an object that resembled a discus. One section contained the explosive, the other section contained the bullets, the idea being that on detonation the bullets were sprayed out.

It was not clear how the grenade was supposed to align itself so that the bullets sprayed in the direction of the Germans rather than the British. It was hardly practical although Shaw Grenades Ltd who owned the patent seemed to think it was. Neither was accepted for service use.

It is possible that these were all inspired by the German *Diskusgranate* which was in service in 1915. It had four metal tubes leading to the centre, each of which contained a percussion cap. At the centre of the grenade was a star-shaped striker. A large tube at the top of the grenade contained a brass pellet which covered the striker until the grenade was thrown. A lower tube contained the detonator which was fired by whichever percussion cap was struck when the grenade landed. However, the German troops which used these were not altogether happy with them because of the ease with which they could be accidentally detonated, and treated them with suspicion.

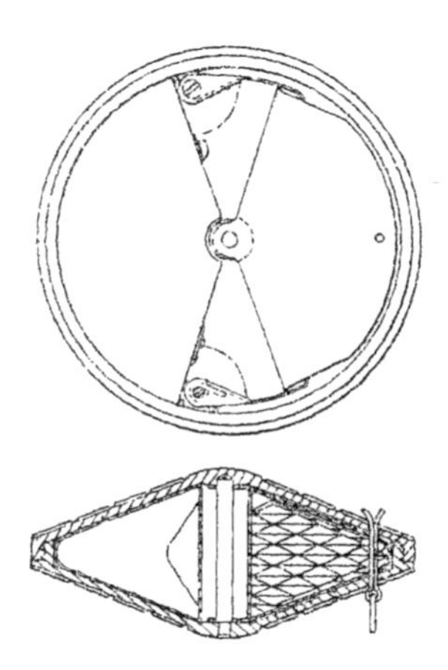

One of the war's oddities, the discus grenade invented by E.C.R. Marks of Shaw Grenades Ltd. Half of the body contains bullets which, on impact, is supposed to rotate about the central spindle to release spring-activated rotating strikers (the top and bottom triangular pieces in the upper drawing) to hit the detonators as indicated by the dotted curves.

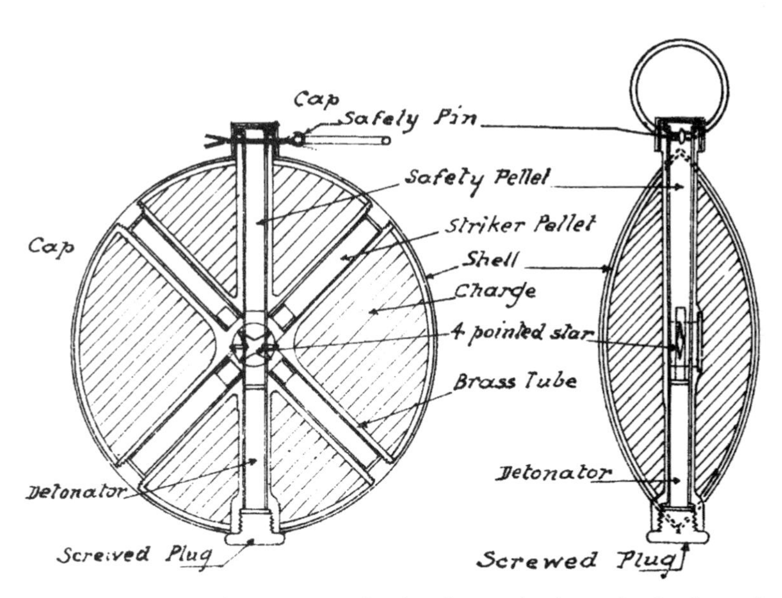

The Diskusgranate *in section, showing its mechanism. It contained two circular bags of explosive, each holding 2 oz. To use the grenade, it was held in the right hand with the safety pin upwards and the pin was pulled with the left. The cap was removed and the safety pellet was held in position with the right forefinger (if necessary the pin could be replaced). When throwing, it was important to ensure that it went as high as possible with the edge vertical. Each box of grenades included a wrist strap with which the grenade could be thrown and the fuse fired but this required a lot of practice. In flight, the grenade spun like a wheel, releasing the safety pellet, which flew out. On detonation, fragmentation was lateral. This grenade clearly inspired British inventors.* (The Training and Employment of Grenadiers)

Some patents represent milestones in the development of the hand grenade; the inventions were major advances and had a profound impact on grenade technology. The prime example of this was the Mills. Other patents represented significant refinements on existing patterns, usually the Mills, and often to its central section that housed the fuse, detonator and firing mechanism. Of all the grenade patents granted during the First World War, those granted to William Mills and to others who developed the grenade are the most important; nine were granted to Mills in 1915.

When the Mills appeared on the scene, the heavier types of grenade were dropped from departmental development programmes. This was mainly because their weight precluded soldiers from carrying many of them at a time and the high explosive charges they contained made them dangerous to friendly troops. The Mills was vastly superior to what had gone before and what was in development. Frank Richards was not alone in his opinion that the Mills was the best grenade of the war on either side. The Mills changed everything about British hand grenades for decades.

William Mills was born in 1856 and educated in Sunderland where his father was a shipbuilder. Eventually, almost inevitably, he was apprenticed as a marine engineer and went to sea. He was an accomplished engineer with a distinguished career behind him before the outbreak of war (he was fifty-eight in 1914) and well used to solving problems. He established the first aluminium foundry in Britain and was a pioneer of research into alloys of aluminium, an important material in the blossoming aircraft industry of the second decade of the twentieth century. By the end of the war, the consumption of aluminium in the aircraft industry was huge and his companies in Sunderland and Birmingham had produced an enormous quantity of aluminium castings for the leading manufacturers in the aircraft industry. Before the grenade that was to make him world famous and turn his name into a household word, he already possessed a number of patents in the fields of foundrywork and metal moulding.

Mills had no experience of munitions, however, and that he came to invent a hand grenade was down to a chance meeting. A Belgian engineer called Albert Dewandre and his colleague Captain Leon Roland, an officer in the Belgian Army and working for Compagnie Belge des Munitions Militaires, had devised a grenade which contained an automatic fuse ignition and detonation system which overcame the problems of accidents associated with impact fuses and the ingress of moisture common with safety fuse grenades. The grenade did away with the need to use a cigarette or portfire to light a length of safety fuse. In short, it was a breakthrough in grenade design. The problem was that it was far from perfect and Captain Roland was no longer available to develop the device because he had become a prisoner of the Germans in 1914. There were serious flaws in the design that needed to be resolved before the grenade could be manufactured and used with confidence. Fortunately, Dewandre happened to meet William Mills in 1914 and they talked about the grenade.

Mills was very much taken with it and believed that between them they could come up with a design that worked and which could be manufactured without a lot of complex machining. In the end, Mills so altered the original Belgian idea that there was a gulf of difference between them, and what Mills produced can be fairly said to be his and not merely someone else's idea slightly modified. Mills turned a good idea into something that worked.

Mills and Dewandre took the grenade to the Inventions Branch of the Directorate of Artillery, yet another inventions investigation department, in late January 1915. The Inventions Branch expressed considerable interest in it and gave the go ahead for immediate trials. At this first meeting, Mills must have told them that he was about to file patent applications in respect of the grenade because on 10 February he filed two, one for the fuse assembly, the other for the lever and striker mechanism. These applications were subsequently

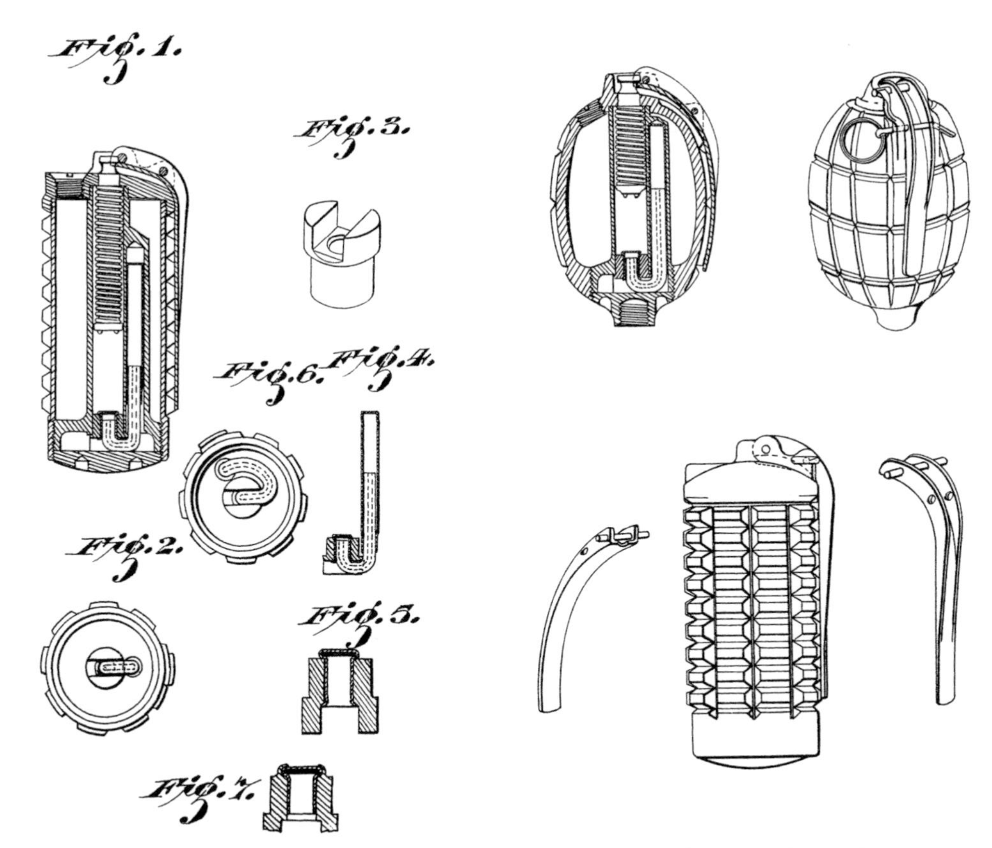

Drawings from Mills's first grenade patent, 2,111/15, showing the arrangement of the fuse, striker and lever. Fig. 3 is a perspective view of the cap holder, while figs 5 and 7 show holders with caps in place. Fig. 4 shows the cap and fuse assembly as it 'may be . . . introduced into . . . the grenade'.

Drawings from Mills's second grenade patent, 7,636/15, with the familiar Mills shape. The base plug has a screw thread for a rod to enable the grenade to be fired from a rifle. The design of the centre-piece is clear from the top left-hand drawing. Note the design of the lever head. This patent mentions a grenade cup attached to the rifle to retain the lever.

granted as 2,111/15 and 7,636/15 respectively, both within eight months of the application date. He filed another application six days after the first two. This, when combined with yet another filed shortly after that, became UK patent 2,468/15 and related to the venting of gases from the percussion cap as it detonated. It was also concerned with preventing the fuse from being pushed home incorrectly to ensure that there was a space between the fuse and the cap. This represented a strong portfolio of patents for the grenade and more were to come.

The Mills grenade was first issued as the No. 5 Mk I in the late spring of 1915, but it was still considered to be new a year later because some battalions had hardly seen it in all that time. In appearance, all subsequent versions of the Mills remained essentially unchanged. The barrel-shaped casing was made of cast iron and segmented to aid fragmentation. The explosive filling hole was near the top, closed by a brass screw which was carefully cemented in place after filling. Fixed centrally inside the casing was an aluminium centre-piece. This was a fairly complicated structure but fundamental to the grenade. It consisted of three parts: an open-ended tube; next to it another smaller-bore tube, one end of which was closed and the other open; and a base which took the two tubes and screwed into the bottom of the grenade. A base plug was screwed in after it. At the bottom of the open-ended tube was a rimfire percussion cap that sat in a holder, into which fitted the end of a 5-second fuse which curved away under the main tube and into its smaller neighbour which contained the detonator (the No. 6). The fuse resembled a letter J, the shorter part being under the cap.

The centre-piece was often made as one part although it was also made in three sections which were then soldered together. In September 1916 G.C. Salsbury filed an application for a patent concerned with the centre-piece in which the main tube had slots which engaged with lugs in the base before being soldered to it to make a firmer join that would 'take up torsional and longitudinal stresses'. This may have been directly related to the forces on the grenade when it was discharged from a rifle. Several other similar patents concerned with the centre piece were granted in respect of the method of manufacturing it, all of them designed to make production easier (e.g. C.W. Findlay, 17,397/15, filed 11 December 1915; S.R. Parkes, 17,898/15, filed 22 December 1915; J. Walker, 102,173, filed 21 January 1916; Oritur Manufacturing Co. and J.W.G. Starkey, 106,555, filed 8 July 1916; A.B. Gibbons, 114,122, filed 20 November 1917). The bottom of the centre-piece made a 'firm base to receive the shock of the striker when released'.

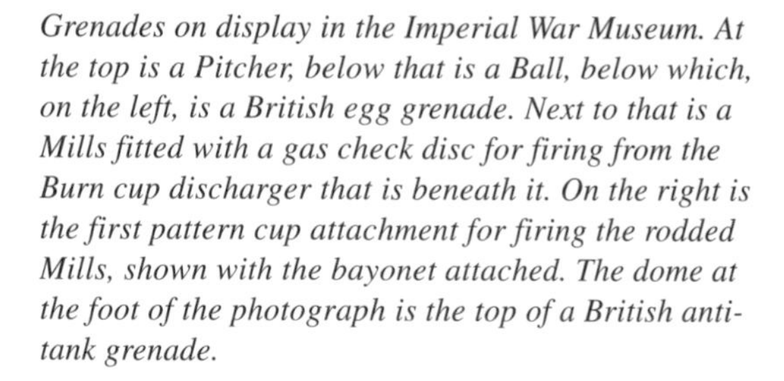

Grenades on display in the Imperial War Museum. At the top is a Pitcher, below that is a Ball, below which, on the left, is a British egg grenade. Next to that is a Mills fitted with a gas check disc for firing from the Burn cup discharger that is beneath it. On the right is the first pattern cup attachment for firing the rodded Mills, shown with the bayonet attached. The dome at the foot of the photograph is the top of a British anti-tank grenade.

The centre-piece of the Mills designed by Salsbury (UK patent 102,364). The detonator holder is not shown. The notches in the cylinder engage the lugs in the base which has an external screw thread.

The spring-operated striker, which when released exerted an impact force of 30 lb, was secured at the top of the main tube by a lever. The top of the striker was narrowed and topped by a flange and the end of the curved lever fitted into the narrowed part and under the flange. The top of the lever had a pair of short trunnions to act as a pivot which sat in grooves in parallel projections on the top of the casing and either side of the lever. The lever was held in place by a safety pin that went through holes in the projections and through the lever, holding it against the casing. So long as the pin retained the lever against the casing, the striker remained where it was above the cap and the grenade was safe but once the pin was removed and the lever released, the striker would hit the cap which would ignite the fuse. The thrower then had 5 seconds to get rid of it, preferably in the direction of the enemy. As long as the thrower gripped the whole grenade, pressing the lever against the casing, the pin could be removed without danger – in theory, at least. This was the first grenade to use this method of a spring-operated striker and lever. It was the first service grenade anywhere to have an effective automatic ignition system. The match and the glowing cigarette end were redundant.

The two Mills patents give some idea of how the original Roland grenade worked. In 2,111/15, the complete specification explained that

> In grenades of this type heretofore proposed, the arrangement is such that the proper assemblage of the time fuse is a matter of considerable difficulty. The separable part . . . which carries the percussion cap is first screwed into the grenade. Then the time fuse has to be assembled and in this operation the end of the time fuse has to be inserted into the already assembled separable part. The relationship between the percussion cap and the time fuse is a vital matter in the working of the grenade and with improper assemblage the firing of the time fuse by the percussion cap is liable to fail.

It then goes on to explain what the invention is.

> According to the present invention the separable part in relation to which the percussion cap and time fuse are assembled is adapted to be assembled in the grenade without being screwed therein; thus the percussion cap and time fuse can separately from the grenade be combined with said separable part in a unit and disposed in the form and arrangement which they assume when in the grenade and be afterwards so assembled in relation to the grenade as to render it unnecessary in such assemblage to alter or disturb the form and arrangement of the parts of which the unit is composed. The unit can be transported separately from the grenade and can, when the latter is ready for use, be assembled with extreme simplicity and accuracy.

Perhaps it should be pointed out that the 'statement of invention' of a patent must consist of a single sentence, no matter how unwieldy it becomes.

The second patent, 7,636/15, dealt with the lever. Again, it provides an insight into the original Roland grenade.

> In grenades of this type heretofore proposed the external lever has been adapted to rock on the edge of the opening of the grenade body from which the striker projects; this arrangement I have found unsatisfactory in action and the lever is liable to fail to release the striker. My present invention has for its purpose to provide for a free and particularly effective and certain operation of the lever and with this object in view the

> external member is mounted with a pivot advantageously constituted by trunnions adapted to work in bearings provided upon or in connection with the body of the grenade.

The complete specification went on to explain that

> during the operation of releasing the lever . . . [it] can be grasped by the hand, whereby in this grasping operation the greatest possible leverage is obtained which reduces the possibility of the lever being accidentally released by the hand.

Almost as soon as the No. 5 Mills was adopted as a service grenade there were problems. Difficulties experienced with its manufacture kept the numbers low until the middle of the summer of 1915. The Trench Warfare Department took over responsibility for the contracts at the beginning of July when only 16,000 had been delivered; the War Office had ordered 5,000,000. By mid-August, on the instructions of the Trench Warfare Department, orders had been nearly doubled but production was still proceeding at a snail's pace and by 4 September deliveries from the contractors amounted to less than 10 per cent of the quantity ordered. In an effort to increase the rate of supply, the department arranged for a number of explosive filling stations to be set up in different parts of the country as well as making 'very extensive arrangements for inspection, assembling, packing and despatch'. It was partly because of these production difficulties that improved ways of making the centre-piece were devised as its manufacture was one of the main causes of the delays. By October output had exceeded the '120,000 per week, asked for by the Field Marshal'. In fact, it was now in excess of 300,000 a week and was soon to reach 400,000 a week.

More than twenty contractors were involved, including the company already owned by Mills, William Mills Ltd, and a new one set up for the sole purpose of manufacturing the grenade, Mills Munitions Ltd, both of which were in Birmingham. Each unfilled grenade cost 3–5*s*; filled ones were costed at between 5*s* 3*d* and 6*s* 9½*d* (about 26–34p). Among the other contractors were Vickery's Patents Ltd and Dover Ltd, both of which developed new types of lever. In late 1917 Dover filed a patent application (which became 117,734), while Vickery's seems to have been set up specifically to make munitions. It is unlikely that Vickery's was a patentee but obtained licences to use other people's patents – hence the name – although Vickery's certainly made some significant contribution to the lever which in 1921 led to a claim being submitted to the Royal Commission on Awards to Inventors in respect of the improvement in safety which it conferred on the Mills.

The production difficulties were not helped by the need to change the cap due to a rash of accidents. And blinds were rather too common. In June 1916 the Royal Welch Fusiliers amused themselves by 'lobbing blinds . . . a good average throw was 20 yards'. There were several causes of accidents according to Major Beddoes when he gave evidence as an expert witness at a hearing for the Royal Commission on Awards to Inventors in January 1921 in respect of the claim made by Vickery. Among them were faulty fuses due to their being poorly made, prematures caused by soldiers interfering with the fuse, and poor design of the top of the striker and the way the lever engaged it. In addition, prematures were caused by inadequate venting of the gases from the detonated cap which adversely affected the fuse. Then there were problems with the head of the striker which had two raised points on it to detonate the cap; sometimes the points failed to hit the rim of the cap properly so that the cap failed to detonate. The number of accidents was running at one for every 3,000 grenades, which was far too high.

The problem with the striker and lever arrangement was a serious defect as it went to the very heart of the grenade and the way it worked. It was found quite early on that if the bomber relaxed his grip on the lever while holding the grenade, even only slightly – something that was very easy to do without realizing it – the striker was released, even though the lever was still held firmly against the casing of the grenade. The lever movement was supposed to have an allowance of 1.25 in before the striker was released but sometimes a very much shorter movement released it. This was a common occurrence in the early days of the grenade and Beddoes gave evidence that there were hundreds of accidents due to this happening. With a similar root cause, accidents also happened when the grenades were carried in the canvas buckets or bags used to bring the grenades to the Front from the supply dumps. The lever of one would catch the pin of another and pull it out because of the jolting and bouncing around of the grenades inside the bucket. This kind of thing was common knowledge. With the Mills it was essential to make sure that the ends of the pins were properly split (grenade pins were always malleable split pins) and bent back to prevent them being accidentally pulled out. They were kept like this until they were needed and then someone had the onerous task of straightening them again, usually on the fire-step of the front-line trench.

Dewandre, meanwhile, continued along a different line of development derived from the original Roland grenade and, with J. de Laminne as co-patentee, filed four patent applications in Britain on 15 June 1916 for his new grenade, which used a weak percussion cap in a holder made of an elastic material (UK patents 141,743 and 141,744) which may have been a plastics or rubber compound (which would make this one of the earliest uses of plastics in ammunition). The weak cap was presumably intended to overcome the problems associated with poor venting of the cap gases in the Mills. Internally, it resembled the Mills but was more complex and included a ribbed main tube to help guide the striker and help the venting of gases (UK patent 141,741). The second of the four, UK patent 141,742, was concerned with a lever made of an elastic material which by virtue of being bent round the casing exerted an outward force against the safety pin helping to keep in it firmly in place and preventing accidental removal. Again, 'elastic' suggests that the lever was intended to be made of a plastics material, an innovative departure from the metal lever of the Mills. A plastics material would certainly have been tough enough and resilient enough for the job. Plastics did not become a common material in grenade construction until the 1970s, however, although the British No. 69 of the Second World War was almost entirely made of a phenolic plastic (Bakelite) and the No. 74 Sticky Bomb also made use of phenolic components.

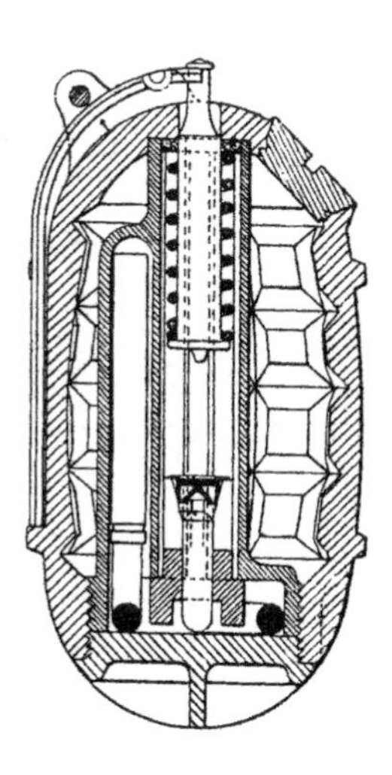

Dewandre's development of the original Belgian grenade that inspired the Mills. The similarities with the Mills are outweighed by the many differences. The detonator is on the left. The fuse descends to the base plug and runs round to the opening of the central tube. The black circles are sections through the fuse cord and the short, central, parallel-sided oval is the fuse as it passes through the holder to the percussion cap.

To begin with, there were great difficulties in training bombers with the No. 5, the 'ordinary Mills', because of the problems with the lever. Beddoes also pointed out that no one was ever taught to release the lever and count to three before throwing the grenade, which only had a 5-second fuse. However, that did not stop this from happening. Charles Carrington cited an example of this when a Mills exploded in the face of a German before it hit the ground which he put down to the thrower, a Lance-Corporal Matthews who 'knew nothing of the technique of bombing', having held the grenade after releasing the lever, before throwing it. This was not a safe thing to do. The 'ordinary Mills' did not have a good reputation.

Clearly, these problems had to be addressed as soon as possible. Mills devoted much time and effort to their resolution. He was aided by William Morgan, a professor of automotive engineering at Bristol University and later by F.J. Gibbons a manufacturer of locks, altogether an odd collection of people to solve munitions problems, but solve them they did, along with Vickery. Whereas Vickery never obtained a patent, Mills and Morgan as co-patentees obtained two fuse patents related to the Mills (10,925/15 and 14,665/15), while Gibbons successfully applied for two, one related to the fuse, the other to the lever and striker (110,068 and 111,949).

The No. 23 Mk II version of the Mills, introduced in 1916, incorporated some of the solutions to these problems as embodied in 10,925/15 and 14,665/15. To some extent, better training in the newly established bombing schools helped to prevent some of the accidents. The problem with premature release of the striker was largely overcome by teaching bombers

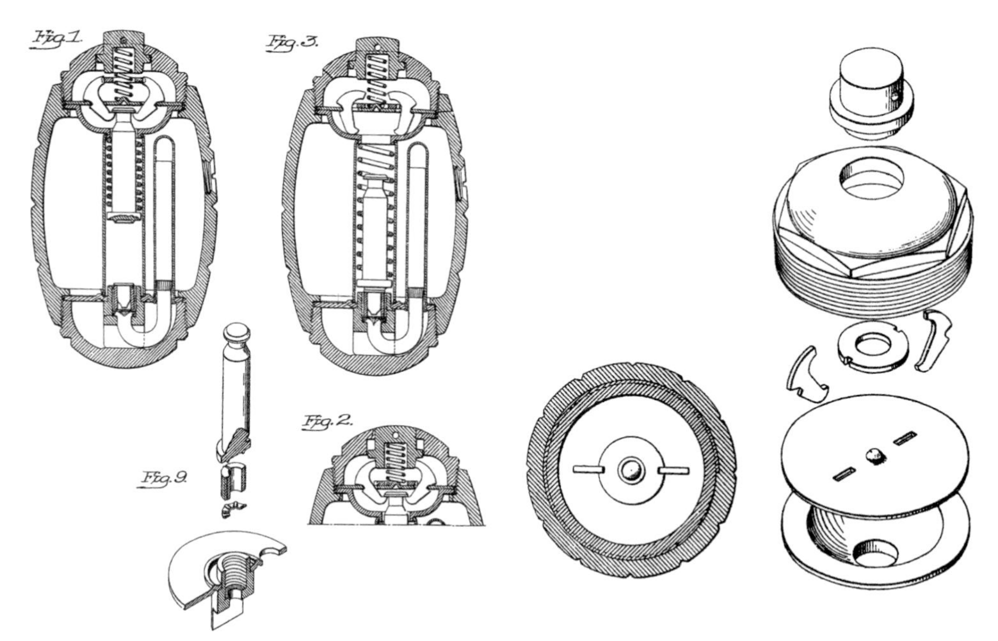

Drawings from one of two patents granted to American Harry Asbury in March 1917 (filed in March 1916). These are from 104,542 and illustrate a different kind of mechanism. The striker is held above the percussion cap by latches. These are disengaged by pressing and releasing the button. This is demonstrated by figs 1–3. Such a design would have made it awkward to hold the grenade.

Drawings from the same Asbury patent illustrating the button and latch system. The spring is not shown. The striker fits through the hole in the lower dished plate. The latches fit through the slots in the disc.

to grip the grenade with the lever against the palm of the hand rather than by pressing it against the grenade with the fingers. However, irrespective of how much better training had become, this did not deal with the basic problem of the striker being released too readily and before the bomber chose to release it. Nevertheless, the No. 23 Mk II was more reliable than the No. 5. The striker head in the No. 23 Mk II was redesigned with a diagonal slot cut into it (when viewed from the side) which extended right through it and along the side of the striker body for about ⅛ in. This adequately vented the cap gases and prevented premature ignition of the detonator. The twin points of the striker head were discarded and replaced by a sharp ridge that ran round the perimeter of its face. This prevented misfires by ensuring that the rim of the percussion cap was always struck squarely.

Mid-1917 saw a complete redesign of the Mills grenade, including improvements to the firing mechanism, and it eventually emerged as the No. 23 Mk III and the No. 36 which were essentially the same thing. The most important change was to the head of the striker and the lever. The striker was no longer narrowed and flanged at the top but of equal diameter all along its length, with a deep slot cut into the top to engage the new lever. With this system it was practically impossible for the bomber to inadvertently release the lever and therefore accidents of that sort stopped. Moreover, there were far fewer bucket-type accidents. The Munitions Invention Department trialled a new lever with 'an improved method of pivoting and weighting' in mid-1918, designed to prevent accidental detonation when a Mills was dropped after the pin was removed. It is not clear whether this was the Gibbons/Vickery lever. Because the Mills was now much safer and more reliable, bombers had greater confidence in it. However, it seems that Mills himself was not in favour of some these changes to the striker and lever and told Newton in the Trench Warfare Department that they were unnecessary. Clearly, he was overruled.

Generally, opinion of the Mills was high. The front-line soldier had come to expect grenades to be more dangerous to their own side than to the enemy, a somewhat pessimistic view based on experience, largely due to the high number of accidents with early grenades. Because the Mills came to be the epitome of reliability and safety, its early dangers were often overlooked by memoirists after the war. But not everyone was enamoured of it. For some, the Mills at 3.75 inches in length and 2.3 inches in diameter was too big to get a good grip, while at between 1 lb 7 oz (No. 5) and 1 lb 9 oz (Nos 23 and 36) it was too heavy to throw as far as the German potato-masher (Frank Richards likened it to a 'swede-smasher'). This was a genuine concern (although Brothers was of the opinion that on the whole the British bombers could always out-throw German bombers) and when the Germans introduced the light egg grenade which could be thrown much further than the heavier Mills it became a real headache.

According to Richards, a Mills could be thrown between 20 and 30 yd although some could throw them even further, but he admitted that many could not throw them even 20 yd. On the other hand, Carrington thought that 30–40 yd was possible if 'bowled like a cricket ball with a full pitch'. The Mills, and indeed all hand grenades, was a short-range weapon and the troops were not encouraged to rely on them to stop an attack, although this tended to happen. Richards was not alone in his opinion that 'Mills bombs were wonderful for throwing into shell holes, trenches and dug-outs, but were absolutely useless for holding up attacks'. In 1917 Haig sent out a notice about not relying on the grenade to stop attacks but to make full use of the rifle, quoting the examples of Le Cateau and First Ypres in which German assaults had been halted by rifle fire alone. Excessive reliance on the grenade was blamed for losses of ground during German counter-attacks. What he failed to mention was that there were not only no hand grenades then but that the regulars who fought those battles

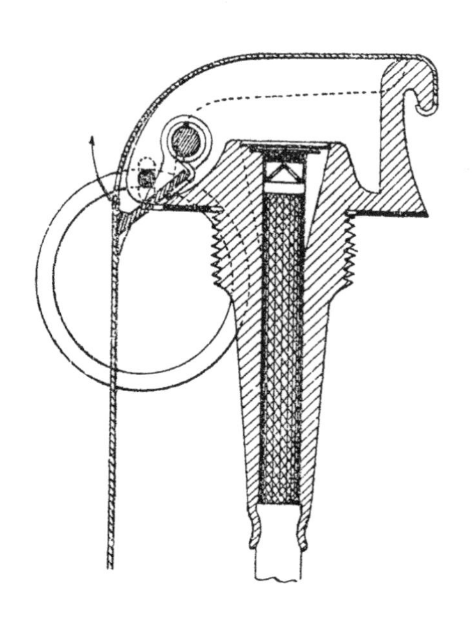

A French lever and rotating striker 'mousetrap' mechanism. Leblanc filed his application in August 1916 which was granted as UK patent 127,293. The dotted line represents one of two side walls through which passes the spindle of the striker. The whole unit screws into the body of the grenade. This was used on the French OF (offensive-fusante) *grenade.*

were well trained in pre-war musketry and were highly skilled at aimed rapid fire which the new arrivals in 1917 certainly were not. According to Richards, new recruits hardly knew how to load a rifle.

But in trench work the bomb was king – provided the bomber remembered to pull the pin first. Charles Carrington related an incident on the Somme when a bomber forgot to remove it before throwing. It was immediately returned by a German, this time without the pin. Sassoon described a bombing attack along a German trench in 1917 in which he commanded a section of twenty-five men that included fifteen bombers each armed with ten Mills, four men armed with rifle grenade dischargers each with five grenades, five grenade carriers who acted as bayonet men, and a sergeant. His objective was to clear 500 yd of trench. Alone, he came upon a Cameronian corporal with a bag of grenades in the trench, a survivor of an earlier attack. Together they advanced, throwing bombs as they went without a word passing between them. The corporal 'who was obviously much more artful and efficient than I was . . . dodged up the saps at the side' each time he threw a Mills. They reached their objective without seeing a German, only retaliatory bombs.

Charles Carrington described bombing as 'a scurry . . . in which parties of men rushed up and down the trenches throwing bombs at one another, a most unsatisfactory employment, exceedingly unpleasant and rarely leading to decisive victory for either party'. He explained that the reason that grenades had to be used in trenches was because of the 'tortuous plan on which trenches were always dug'. Straight trenches could be enfiladed so bays were separated by traverses every 5–10 yd in a castellated pattern. It was 'like walking in a maze', there were so many corners which made it difficult to maintain a sense of direction. To move along a trench was very tiring 'squeezing past people at narrow bends, paddling through mud and water, climbing over obstructions made by shell-fire and being caught under the chin or across the ankles by trailing telephone wires', all made worse when it had to be done at night.

When a position had been fought over, the difficulties were magnified by the debris and destruction. The trenches of the Somme battlefield 'became a labyrinth', weaving in all directions in a chaotic web, with bomb-stops erected at intervals to separate friend from foe and prevent the enemy from bombing his way along them. Under such circumstances, it was hardly surprising that the bomb and the Mills in particular came to such prominence. The stress of bombing along trenches was enormous. Grenades could have a deeply psychological effect. The Germans called this *Granatfieber*, grenade fever, a form of war neurosis.

CHAPTER 5

Timed Eggs and the Elusive Percussion Grenade 1916–18

In some ways, the popularity of the Mills grenade turned out to be a bit of a millstone. Although its shortcomings were eventually resolved, the Trench Warfare Department wanted to provide the Army with a safer grenade that had none of the defects of the Mills. Unfortunately, this was no easy matter as there was considerable resistance to change. As far as most bombing officers were concerned, the Mills worked perfectly well and some even turned one of its recognized defects into a desirable quality by suggesting that all future grenades should have a lever that needed to be firmly gripped against the casing after the pin had been pulled. Its popularity, together with the dislocation to supplies that would inevitably ensue if it were to be replaced, along with the difficulties of introducing a new training programme for a new grenade, all proved to be strong arguments against change. Indeed, no subsequent service pattern of grenade supplanted the Mills as the principal type.

The only other time-fused grenade to be used in any numbers was the No. 34 Egg grenade, which appeared at the Front in the spring of 1917. It was designed in France in response to a recognized need for a lighter hand grenade that could be thrown further than the Mills. The Germans had introduced the *Eierhandgranate*, a light egg grenade, and with it were out-throwing the British bombers armed with the Mills. While on the Somme in 1916, Charles Carrington experienced at first hand one of the new German *Eierhandgranate*. 'Suddenly I saw lying in the middle of the trench a small black object, about the shape and size of a large duck's egg. There was a red band round it and a tube fixed in one end of it.' The tube was the striker assembly. Although he had never seen one before he realized immediately that it was a grenade, but he was trapped in a corner of the trench with the object no more than 3 ft away. It exploded, but apart from a minor wound, shock and being showered in dirt, he was unharmed. Carrington believed that this was the first recorded use of the *Eierhandgranate*.

Although the *Eierhandgranate* was supposed to be highly effective for trench work, Carrington's experience suggested otherwise. Sassoon's experience of the German egg grenade in April 1917 also suggested that it was ineffective. It was a blast grenade and produced very little shrapnel. In theory, blast in the confines of a trench should have been highly destructive to human beings but clearly there were circumstances under which it was not.

The British egg grenade, on the other hand, was a fragmentation bomb like the Mills. It may have been another of the designs to come out of the Second Army Workshop, although Newton was no longer there in 1917 having moved to the Trench Warfare Department as an assistant director in 1916. It was, at any rate, an Army invention designed in France and did not come out of any of the weapons inventions departments in the UK, although the Trench Warfare Department was involved in testing it. Samples of the new grenade were made in France and supplied to front-line units for trials. These went well and in the spring of 1917 GHQ asked for 500 of the grenades to be manufactured in Britain so that further trials could be conducted. GHQ wanted the trials to be comparative and asked that similar numbers of any like grenade should also be supplied.

Two types were eventually supplied for trial, one in the GHQ design which had 'an internal spring wire in a groove' to retain the striker, the other having a shear wire to retain it. The trials showed that the latter design was preferable but the shape and weight were not ideal. In 'Notes on Inventions and New Stores No. 1' (SS171) covering the months April, May and June 1917, another similar pattern of grenade was mentioned in relation to these although it is not clear what this was. It had recently been brought to France and had a shape that was better suited to throwing and weighed less than 10 oz whereas the GHQ pattern weighed 12.5–13 oz. GHQ wanted a supply of these for troop trials. The shear-wire pattern had a 5.5-second fuse and weighed 10–11 oz. These were all referred to as egg grenades and all were fragmentation types. Weight for weight, the shear-wire pattern produced 30 per cent more fragments than the Mills. This pattern had to be struck against a hard surface to break the wire and initiate the fuse. In practice, this was the side of a boot. The striker on all of them protruded from a short cylinder on the top of the grenade.

By midsummer 1917 trials with the egg grenades were well under way in England. These indicated that there was a danger of prematures caused by flash through but subsequent trials with 1,170 grenades fitted with a 5-second fuse revealed no such problem. In fact, the fuses were remarkably consistent in the length of time they took to burn, 97.5 per cent burning for at least 5 seconds and none burning for longer than 6 seconds. The shortest fuse was within half a second of the ideal. This was a far cry from the fuse problems a year or two earlier when some of them were so short as to be for all practical purposes instantaneous and deadly to the unfortunate thrower. Because of the success of the trials of the egg grenade, GHQ asked for 150,000 to be shipped out to France 'with a subsequent weekly supply of 25,000 a week'. Curiously, GHQ added a request that 'the first supplies might be fitted with 7-second igniter sets until the troops have become accustomed to handling these grenades'. Presumably GHQ believed that if the soldiers had to strike a hard surface to initiate the fuse before throwing the grenade they would either forget to strike it or hang on to it for too long afterwards.

At some point in the trial process the egg grenade became the No. 34 and the various types under trial were given mark numbers. The Mk I was the original GHQ design with the internal spring. The Mk II was the shear-wire model with a 7-second fuse while the Mk III had a more ovoid shape; Mks I and II had more bulbous bodies with narrowed necks so that they resembled pears with flattened sides. In addition, the location of the filling hole was different on the Mk I, being in one side of the curved base of the body, while on the other marks the filling holes were in the side. They were all just under 4 inches in length and fitted very neatly into the hand.

There was also a Mk IV version. This was essentially the same as the Mk III except that it had a ring cast round the middle of the ovoid at its greatest diameter. The purpose of this was to allow the grenade to be fired from a cup discharger without the need for a gas-check disc which had to be fitted to the Mills in order to fire it from a cup discharger. It made no difference to its effectiveness or use as a hand grenade. When this modification was proposed to the Army Council in the autumn of 1917, it was not keen to adopt the alteration to the shape. The manufacture of the Mk III was well advanced and any alteration to the design would 'entirely dislocate the current supply and is therefore very undesirable'. However, it was persuaded by the arguments of Major-General Richard Butler, one of Haig's staff. He pointed out any such change in the design should not be made immediately but gradually introduced 'as opportunity occurred' so that supply would not be disrupted. There were other arguments related to the inevitable necessity of adopting another cup discharger to fire the grenades as rifle grenades if the modification to the design was adopted. The question came down to resources both in terms of skilled labour and in terms of materials. Butler made it clear that in the balance of pros and cons, the pros won hands down. As these relate to rifle grenades rather than hand grenades this is dealt with more fully in Chapter 7.

Despite the effectiveness of the egg grenade in trench work, it never ousted the Mills as the main hand grenade in British service. The egg could be thrown further and because it was lighter more could be carried by one man than the Mills. It was also safer than the Mills; there was no rash of accidents as soon as it was given to troops. It was better designed in some respects, certainly simpler, having no lever and striker arrangement. The fuse was straight, not curved into a letter J, and the fuse burned for the stipulated time. The Mills made a big bang and was dangerous to anyone within a distance of more than 60 yd because the big fragments and the base plug had the momentum to travel a very long way and still cause fatal injuries.

In some ways the egg had more similarities with the expedient grenades of 1915 than it did with the Mills. Although greater experience meant that it was a better design by far than grenades like the Pitcher and the Lemon, nevertheless, it was still an underdeveloped munition as witnessed by the changes in its design that occurred in quick succession. The Mills was no more perfect than the egg but it was developed over a longer period into a very effective munition. And it filled a desperate need when there was nothing else comparable. Moreover, the Mills was an independent design that was not created as a response to the German grenade threat, whereas the egg was. Perhaps if the egg had come in 1915, it might have taken the place that the Mills assumed but it came too late to make much of a dent in the Mills's reputation and position.

The Mills effectively stifled all other grenade development. There was no incentive to change and, in fact, the converse was true. This was a major obstacle to the development of an effective and safe percussion grenade. Although 1915 saw the percussion grenade supplanted by its time-fused cousin, the desire for a percussion grenade never went away. The Trench Warfare Department was especially keen, its enthusiasm for the percussion grenade never diminishing. It put a lot of time and effort into searching for the ideal one. Such a grenade had to be safe and foolproof yet at the same time sensitive, a conflicting set of criteria that made the task far from easy. On top of that, it also had to be waterproof. Bitter experience had shown the havoc that bad weather could cause with grenades that were not waterproof. And if that were not enough, any new grenade was expected to be suitable for both throwing by hand and rifle launching (by late 1917, this meant capable of being fired from a cup discharger).

Lieutenant-Colonel Brothers claimed in 1919 that 'the advantages of a Percussion Grenade over the Time Fuze type have always been realised'. Whether percussion grenades were better than time-fused grenades was debatable. As a hand grenade, the percussion type has never been popular or common. The advantage of the time-fused variety is that the fuse itself forms part of the safety system, whereas the percussion fuse is inherently dangerous. The Trench Warfare Department wanted a percussion grenade that was actually safer than time-fused grenades, a rather lofty and unattainable goal. Brothers conceded that until this was in sight it would be ill-advised to 'disturb the position of the Mills'. He had to admit that the department had not succeeded in providing a suitable percussion grenade because the trials were 'more severe and searching than have been applied hitherto to any type of Grenade accepted for the Service' and nothing had been passed. It is not inconceivable that had the Mills been subjected to these tests it would have failed.

Nevertheless, in the context of the trenches and shell-pocked landscape of the battlefields of the First World War the percussion grenade did possess certain advantages

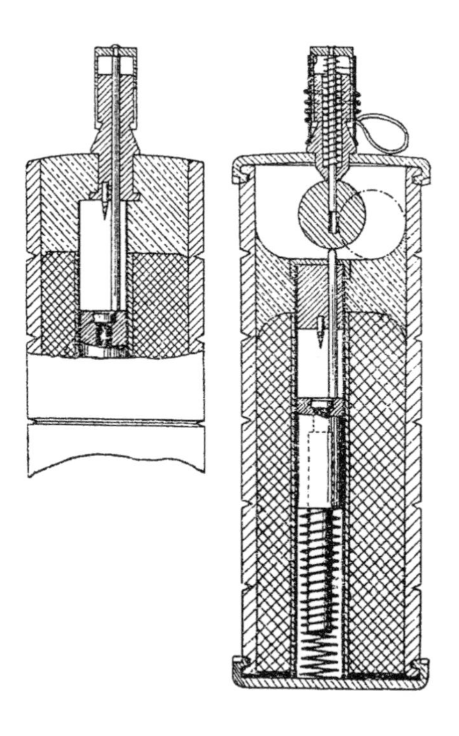

Percussion hand grenade invented by H. Siegwart and illustrated in UK patent 102,332. It includes a safety device to prevent accidental detonation. The firing pin is held away from the cap by a rod and ball which are released by pressing down the split sleeve on the upper projection. The sleeve is held safely by waterproof fabric bound with wire (as indicated by the loop). Only the cross-hatched section is explosive. It is doubtful if this would have worked in the trenches.

over the time-fused sort. Principal among these was the fact that a safe and reliable percussion grenade that could also be used as a rifle grenade would reduce the number of types of service grenade, in itself a good enough reason to keep up the search. The Munitions Inventions Department had been actively searching for a percussion grenade since the early days of the war. Whereas the Trench Warfare Department tended to deal with in-house ideas or ideas that had originated in the armies in France, the Munitions Inventions Department sifted ideas submitted to it from other sources, including the public.

A percussion grenade had to satisfy stringent criteria which were set out in a Munitions Inventions Department report in 1918 and in Brothers' 'Development of Weapons used in Trench Warfare'. A percussion grenade should be capable of clearing a shell hole or a trench bay (the Mills was too powerful while the egg grenade was not powerful enough; a 1 lb percussion grenade was deemed to be about right). It should be usable as a hand grenade that could be thrown at least 15 yd and capable of being fired from a discharger, without having to use adapters of any sort, to distances of 450 yd. The percussion fuse should detonate the grenade on any surface, hard or soft, and irrespective of the angle of impact but leave the grenade safe if it failed to detonate and yet not be so sensitive that it exploded prematurely in flight. Moreover, it should not explode if the bomber accidentally hit something with it or dropped it after it was armed and it should withstand rough handling. It should not be affected by water or mud and be cheap and easy to make in large numbers, as well as easy to assemble correctly but impossible to assemble incorrectly, and easy to inspect. The fact that the simpler the grenade was to manufacture the safer and more reliable it was likely to be was not lost on the designers. Moreover, the undesirability of streamers tied to a handle was well understood. The concept of what constituted a good grenade had come a long way in four years.

One of the Trench Warfare Department's first attempts at a percussion grenade was an improvement on the No. 1 and No. 2 patterns and resulted in the No. 19 but this was far from ideal as it was a stick grenade over 11 in long. In early 1916 GHQ complained that the handle had a poor grip and that the grenade was too sensitive, like the No. 1 Mk III. Nevertheless, it asked for a supply of 12,000 for troop trials. It was not an unqualified success. Although the

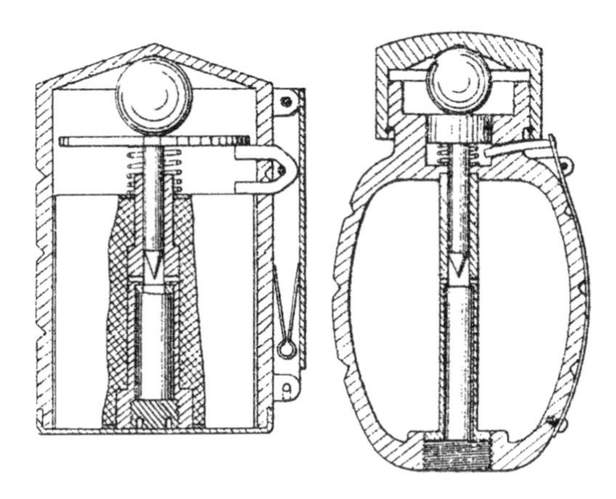

Billinghurst's patent safety percussion grenade with all-ways fuse operated by inertia of a weighted ball (UK patent 102,390).

fuse functioned well enough, it was hardly any more safe than the earlier percussion types and had to be handled with far more care than a Mills. In the meantime, a different line of approach led to the Woolwich Arsenal developing a percussion fuse adapted from that used on German trench mortar bombs. Its sensitivity had to be increased by using a new method of ignition. In addition, a new delay device acting as a safety mechanism was also devised. The new fuse was fitted to a Ball grenade and trials were conducted in March 1916.

While this was going on, the Trench Warfare Committee imposed additional requirements for percussion grenades and the modified Ball went back to the drawing board. In 1916, while the development of the percussion Ball continued, a number of other percussion grenades were brought to the attention of the Munitions Inventions Department and GHQ. Among these were the Charmier (for some reason spelt Chamier in the departmental reports) and DG grenades, both of which were patented inventions (125,436 and 124,837 respectively). Both appeared to be quite promising. However, tests with the Charmier were ultimately unsatisfactory and in 1917 work with it was discontinued, although SS 171/4, the fourth inventions newsletter, indicated that GHQ was expecting a supply of the Charmier for troop trials in March 1918. The discrepancy may be due to both the Trench Warfare Department and the Munitions Inventions Department undertaking trials of the Charmier independently of each other, although it may have more to do with the political pressure that was brought to bear over the DG grenade.

The DG grenade, also known as the DG Patent Safety Grenade, got its name from the initial letters of the surnames of its two inventors Leslie Daniels and Charles Gardiner who took the grenade to the Munitions Inventions Department in early February 1916. The company that made the grenade was Trench Warfare & Armaments Ltd which may well have been set up during the war to manufacture munitions, if not the DG specifically, because the two inventors were in the boat business; Daniels was an associate member of the Institute of Naval Architects while Gardiner was a master mariner. The department was sufficiently interested in it to want to undertake trials, provided some modifications were made. These were duly carried out and trials started. By June 1917 a total of 6,730 DG grenades had been

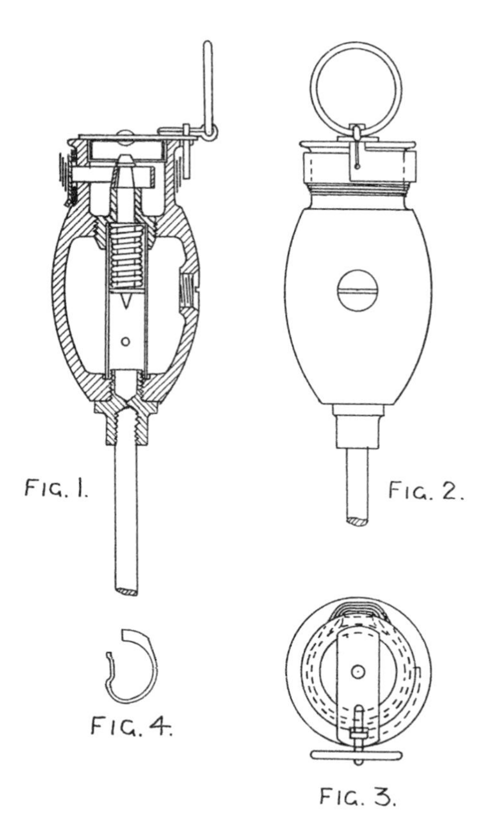

The DG grenade (UK patent 124,837). Fig. 4 shows the retaining catch, a stiff metal blade that goes round the head of the striker. The white bar on the left in fig. 1 is the safety pin. Fig. 3 is a plan view of the top of the grenade, illustrating the tape and the metal weight on its end (the dotted line on the lower right, extending east to south.

thrown without a single accident. However, the grenade had evidently gone through numerous modifications of various sorts because by December 1917 it had become the Mk VIII. By this time, rifle-launched trials had also been conducted and in December the Munitions Inventions Department reported that the trials, with a new ballistite blank cartridge to fire the grenade from a cup discharger, had also been successful, without any prematures in flight. However, it is evident that by May 1917 the Munitions Inventions Department had decided to drop the grenade as unsuitable.

Enter W. O'Malley. It is not clear who he was but it seems likely that he was a former colonel of the Indian Army. In a forceful letter dated 21 May 1917 written to Sir Worthington Evans, MP, the Parliamentary Secretary, Ministry of Munitions, he expressed his dissatisfaction with the handling of the trials and decisions taken and demanded that something be done to rectify the situation. Evidently, the letter to Evans was prompted by a lack of response to a similar letter written some months earlier to Dr Addison, head of the Trench Warfare Department. O'Malley complained that all he got for his trouble was 'one of those stereotyped replies which are so characteristic of Government Departments'. Dr Addison had told him that he was in no position to interfere with the decisions taken by the Design Department which had taken over responsibility for the development of the grenade.

O'Malley's account of the history of the DG grenade is no doubt accurate, if somewhat biased, as he was trying to bring pressure to bear and needed to get his facts right. After the initial modifications to the grenade following its first appraisal by the Munitions Inventions Department, Lord Ardee (who was a grenade expert), Captain Godwin Smith and Major Colley were more than happy with it and 'declared it "perfect"'. A year later and the grenade had still not been adopted, which O'Malley put down to political manoeuvring and gerrymandering. At much the same time, the Design Department became involved and General Bingham, its head, freely confessed that he knew nothing whatsoever about grenades and relied on what his 'expert' told him. This was a Captain Ley. According to O'Malley, Ley 'took out a patent, in May last year [1916], for a device in connection with the grenade and he evidently was determined to have a grenade of his own rather than that recommended by the M.I.D.'. This is a curious statement.

In the first place, no grenade patent was ever granted to a Ley in May or any other month in 1916, nor indeed at any time during the war. However, Daniel and Gardiner applied for a patent for their grenade on 3 May 1916 and this may have been the patent to which O'Malley alluded. A possible explanation is that Ley acted on behalf of Daniel and Gardiner to get their invention patented, in which case his name would not have appeared on the patent as he was not one of the inventors, although this does not explain why this should have upset O'Malley. Indeed, O'Malley was gunning for Ley. The grenade that was favoured by the Design Department over the DG was one called the Humphries (O'Malley called it the Humphrey) which had evolved from the percussion Ball experiments to meet the Trench Warfare Committee requirements. Since there is no Ley patent, the implication is that the Humphries was his design, except that someone called Humphries was more probably the designer.

Although there were similarities between all percussion grenades, which became more alike as they were developed to overcome problems and satisfy the changing requirements, the DG and the Humphries had quite different mechanisms. The DG had a striker in a central tube, at the bottom of which was the detonator. The striker was held above the detonator by a spring and a safety device that was designed to prevent the grenade from exploding if accidentally dropped but which would arm the grenade once it had left the thrower's hand. The top of the striker was narrowed (or grooved) so that it had a flanged head round which was a safety catch made of 'a stiff blade of metal'; one end was held between the flanged head and a central plug through which the striker projected by the pressure of the striker spring, while the other end was weighted. The idea was that an impact displaced the weighted end by inertia so that the catch came away from its retaining position and released the striker. A safety pin held the catch in place which in turn was held by a tape wound several times round the top of the grenade. The free end of the tape had a metal plate fixed to it and this was held against the grenade by the safety pin. Before throwing the grenade, the pin was removed and the act of throwing unwound the tape which freed the safety catch in flight, so that when the grenade hit the ground the safety catch was displaced and the striker hit the detonator and exploded the grenade.

The Humphries' mechanism used two pellets with curved ends which were kept apart by a spring. One carried the striker while the other carried the cap which was opposite the mouth of the detonator tube. The pellets were in a chamber of larger diameter than the pellets and its ends were also curved to accommodate the pellets. They were brought together by an impact, causing the cap to be fired. A pin was used to keep them apart and render the grenade safe. A tape was attached to the pin and wound round the top of the grenade and held by a cap that locked in place. Before throwing the grenade the cap was removed and the tape unwound in flight, releasing the pin and arming the grenade.

On the recommendation of Ley, who evidently had never thrown the DG, Bingham pronounced the DG grenade to be dangerous and wanted it dropped forthwith. On the other hand, the Munitions Inventions Department had by then thrown several thousand over a period of sixteen months. Indeed, although Bingham had turned down the DG, the Munitions Inventions Department was continuing to test the grenade, a situation which O'Malley described as an expensive 'farce' as it had spent £3,000 on trials. To muddy the waters further, O'Malley claimed that Bingham had told him that GHQ did not want a percussion grenade whereas Sir William Robertson, Chief of Imperial General Staff, had told O'Malley that it did.

While the Design Department remained unimpressed, the Trench Warfare Department was more than happy with it. Following trials at the Lyndhurst Bombing School in January 1917, a report by Dr Addison described the mechanism as 'perfect'. This was the complete opposite of what the Design Department claimed. There was even a report from independent experts, Messrs McAlpine, that showed that the DG was superior to the Humphries. O'Malley could not understand why Addison had capitulated so readily to Bingham when his opinion of the grenade seemed to be very high. He was firmly of the opinion that 'departmental etiquette is infinitely more important than providing the Army with the grenade they require'. He wanted Evans to look into 'this most important matter' so that he would 'set aside the prejudiced and stupid decision of the Designs Department' to adopt the Humphries instead of the DG, a course of action he believed was 'wrong and ill-advised'. He also wanted Evans to investigate why an order for 25,000 DG grenades to be sent to France had been cancelled because a fair trial at the Front would, he was convinced, settle the matter once and for all.

Whatever the outcome of O'Malley's lobbying, trials were conducted in France in 1918 with 1,000 modified Mk VIII DG grenades. However, for all his efforts the grenade never got beyond this stage. It had been under consideration and development since at least early 1916. Its great rival, the Humphries, had a similarly chequered history. It underwent trials in 1917 and was rejected because the percussion mechanism was unreliable, mainly due to an unacceptably high proportion of blinds, only to resurface again in 1918 when it emerged as one of the leading contenders in comparative trials with several other percussion grenades. However, the Humphries had undergone a number of modifications since its rejection in 1917, including development of a more sensitive fuse. These later trials were rather different from the early ones. As already mentioned, the criteria were tougher and the candidates had to perform well as both hand and rifle grenades because the idea now was to find a single, multi-purpose grenade.

One of the problems facing designers of percussion grenades was the uncertain requirements of the troops at the Front. They were imprecise and rather vague so that developments tended to elicit negative responses rather than constructive comments. Part of the trouble was the lack of will to replace the Mills. However, it became apparent to researchers that an all-ways fuse was needed to ensure that a percussion grenade would explode irrespective of the angle at which it struck the ground. In July 1918 an exhaustive set of trials of all types of percussion grenade was conducted. The contenders were subsequently reduced to four: the Bellamy, the Coles, the Vickery and the Humphries. It is not known what the first three were. Both the DG and the Charmier had failed to make the shortlist. When the war ended, no decision had been reached and the Army was still without a percussion grenade.

CHAPTER 6

Rods and Phosphorus – Rifle Grenades and Chemical Grenades 1914–18

For about the first two years of the war, the development of rifle grenades followed much the same pattern as that of hand grenades; in other words it was piecemeal, with the overriding necessity of expedience governing supply. Moreover, their development progressed independently of hand grenades for much of the time despite the introduction of a rifle-launched version of the Mills and a growing realization that a grenade was needed that could be thrown as well as rifle launched without the need to convert it with attachments. Rather than becoming more streamlined from then on, the development of rifle grenades grew more complex because there were now several lines of enquiry which were followed by several different departments which did not always confer or cooperate.

The first rifle grenades were rodded, the rod being inserted down the barrel of the service rifle. With the continued development of the Mills, it was found that by fitting it with a rod it too could be fired from a rifle. However, in order to do this a means of retaining the lever after the pin had been removed had to be devised and this resulted in the first grenade cup attachment. This led to the development of cup dischargers which obviated the need for rods altogether but, rather than superseding rodded grenades entirely, both sorts remained in service and rodded grenades were still being developed when the war ended. To complicate things further, the cups themselves had to be developed; then there was the percussion fuse; and finally the development of an entirely new sort of grenade discharger or gun was also pursued. This last weapon was a radical departure from the standard munitions, being something that could be fired from the shoulder and dedicated solely to grenades – small arms ammunition could not be fired from it.

There was much to be said for the rodded rifle grenade, most of it concerned with its simplicity, although in terms of its construction the earlier ones were far from simple. However, the basic means by which they were fired from the rifle was. This simplicity dominated thinking about rifle grenades for a long time despite the fact that their disadvantages were considerable. For one thing, the rods were inconvenient for the rifle grenadiers. The rods were additional weight that had to be carried and because they were long they tended to snag on things. Worse than this, they were very bad for the barrel which tended to bulge and eventually split. The propellant gases hit the end of the rod at extremely high velocity and were reflected back down the barrel. This caused a reflected pressure wave. The shorter the rod, the greater the velocity of the gases because they travelled further up the barrel before meeting the end of the rod, and the greater the pressure of the reflected wave. The increase in pressure in the barrel was enormous and it could only stand just so much before the metal failed. Burst barrels were a common hazard. There was also the danger that the rod could jam in the barrel.

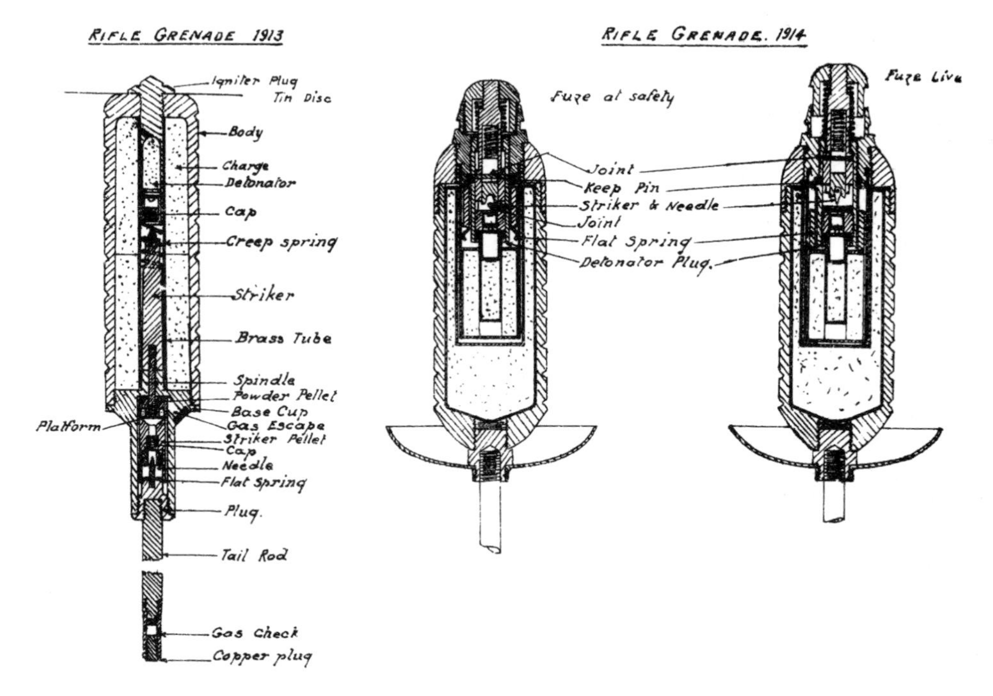

German rifle grenades from the early part of the war. The 1914 model contained less explosive than the 1913 model and its live condition was more easily recognizable, which was fortunate because the fuse was extremely sensitive. In The Training and Employment of Grenadiers *of October 1915 it was noted that damp rods should be dried prior to use and if a rod did not slide easily into the barrel on no account was force to be used; the rod should be discarded if it did not fit. Such caveats applied equally to British rifle grenades.*

If that were not bad enough, the whole rifle could shake itself apart with the recoil which tended to be far greater than when normal small arms ball ammunition was fired. When a rifle grenade was fired, the butt of the rifle was held against the ground which resisted the recoil. Whereas short rods caused the barrel to split sooner than long rods, long rods allowed the gas pressure to be exerted on them for longer because it took them longer to clear the muzzle. Although this increased the velocity of the rodded grenade and therefore extended the range it also had the disadvantage of increasing the recoil. In a relatively short time, the rifle could break up because it was stressed beyond its limits. Of course, when the war started none of this was known.

Unlike the Germans, the British only adopted a rifle grenade after the outbreak of war when it became apparent that such things were a necessary evil. In 1914 the German Army was equipped with the *Gewehrgranate* 1913 and 1914 models. These, like all early rifle grenades, were rodded. The 1914 model had a complex percussion mechanism which was armed by inertia when the grenade was fired from the barrel. A special cradle or frame was used to support the rifle, turning it, in effect, into a mini trench mortar. Complexity was also a common problem with the first British rifle grenades. The No. 3 Mk I Hale rifle grenade was a complicated piece of precision engineering and as a consequence was very expensive to manufacture. When there was an urgent need for as many rifle grenades as possible, this was a distinct disadvantage that reduced the supply.

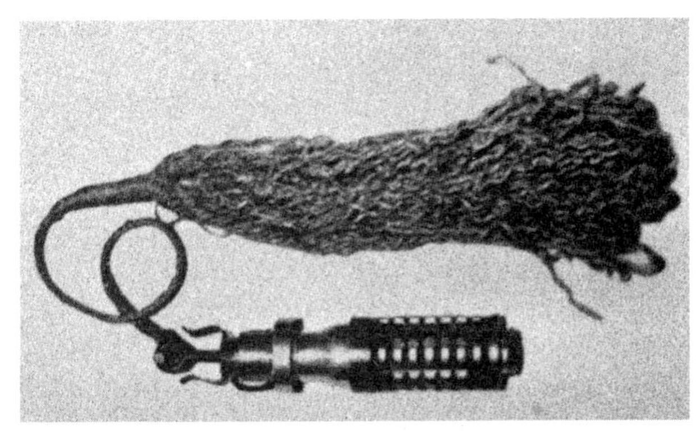

A No. 3 rifle grenade adapted to be thrown by swinging the rope handle. (ILN)

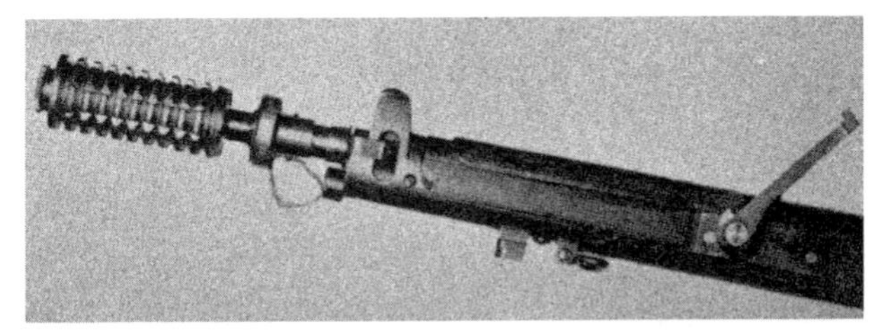

A No. 3 fitted in the barrel of an SMLE with the clip round the muzzle, summer 1915. The pin is still in place. Note the special sight attached to the side of the fore-end. (ILN)

Its predecessor, the No. 2, was an interim measure supplied from the Cotton Powder Company contracts for Mexico. Because of its origins it was also known as the 7 mm or Mexican pattern. This was essentially the same as the hand-thrown version except that it had a steel rod attached to the base and a two-pronged clip or clutch which engaged the muzzle and held the grenade in the barrel. It was fired by a blank cartridge. As well as commandeering the grenades already in stock, an order was placed for more in August 1914. By September 1915 Roburite & Ammonal were also involved in making the grenade. A slightly different model intended to be fired from 8 mm rifles was also supplied from the existing stock. These had no clip, presumably because the rod was a tight fit in the barrel whereas the 7 mm model was a loose fit and needed a clip to make sure that the grenade did not slip out. Clearly, as stopgap measures they were better than nothing but they left a great deal to be desired.

Nevertheless, the No. 2 remained in service well into 1915. The problem of securing an adequate supply of detonators for this and the No. 3 has been discussed elsewhere (*see* Chapter 1) and in an effort to resolve this the Trench Warfare Department and the Woolwich Arsenal started to look at new designs. Even in late 1915, the possibility of redesigning the grenade so that it could use a different detonator was looked on as an undesirable course of action. This was partly because the process would take too long to solve the immediate problem. On 27 August 1915 Field Marshal French had asked for 112,000 rifle grenades a week but by October the supply was still only 19,000 a week (mostly No. 3s), although output was increasing because of the pressure the Trench Warfare Department brought to bear on the contractors.

A proposal to use a different explosive, Tonite, in the No. 3, put to the Chief Inspector at Woolwich to increase production was eventually accepted (the grenade was then designated the Mk II). The Trench Warfare Department predicted that this would increase production by 75 per cent. However, it was not unusual for a platoon to be issued with no more than six No. 3 grenades for an entire tour of trench duty. Considering that the Germans were amply supplied and using them in considerably larger numbers than this, six per platoon was pitiful. Fortunately, the situation changed. By the time of the Somme in July 1916, there were enough for the Royal Welch Fusiliers to expend thousands in a matter of a few hours during a retaliatory raid by two reinforced companies on German positions.

The No. 3, also known as the J pattern and the Hale pattern, was the first wartime design. It was similar to the No. 2 and although it quickly followed the latter into service, trials continued well into 1915 to improve on it and find the most suitable length of rod. Eventually, the grenade went through several changes resulting in a total of eight different marks (No. 3 Mks I, I*, II, II*, III and No. 3A Mks I, I*, II). The differences were minor for the most part, the most significant being more streamlined contours and different explosive fillings.

The body of the No. 3 was machined from a solid steel cylinder and had the customary 'serrations' for fragmentation. A brass base piece was bored out to take the striker (a sharply pointed steel needle) in the top and was screwed into the body. The bottom of the base piece was machined to take a circular wind vane and, below the boss of the vane, a check was also machined on it. Over this was fitted a safety socket that had been machined so that it was a tight fit over the check and was flush with the boss. This prevented the vane from unscrewing and held the striker retaining bolts in place (these extended radially into the striker and prevented it from moving forward). A plug was screwed into the bottom of the base piece, machined with a screw thread to take the steel rod. The detonator and a three-grain

This shot allegedly shows rifle grenade practice but it is posed for the camera. To fire the grenade, the butt of the rifle had to be held firmly against the ground because of the recoil. It would be highly dangerous to fire a grenade while holding a rifle in both hands like this. Moreover, because of the possibility of a premature at the muzzle, everyone in the photograph is taking his life in his hands if they propose to fire the grenades. (ILN)

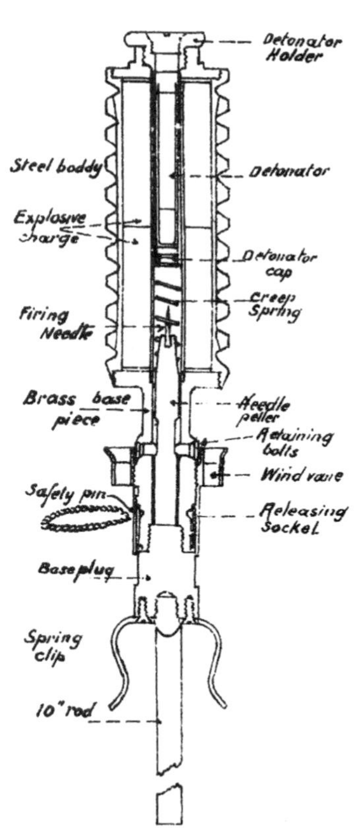

The No. 3 rifle grenade. Grenadiers were warned not to launch the grenade with a bulleted round because this would burst the barrel. It was a safe grenade to handle as it was only armed in flight by the vane. (The Training and Employment of Grenadiers)

percussion cap were in the top of a central tube inside which the striker moved (from the bottom to the top). This tube was screwed into the top of the grenade and a brass retaining plug screwed over it.

Before the striker was inserted it was important to make sure that it was properly held by the retaining bolts. It was, unfortunately, quite possible to assemble the grenade with the striker in front of the bolts. If this happened, the act of inserting the detonator would be an act of suicide as the striker would immediately penetrate the cap. A simple way to check that everything was as it should be was to insert a pencil into the tube and see how far it went before touching the tip of the striker, then to compare that with the length of the detonator. There was supposed to be a clearance of 0.33–0.50 in. It was a foolish man who did not carry out this crude test. The cap was, itself, a potential hazard as it was powerful enough to cause serious injury, so it had to be handled with great care.

A report from May 1915 of a trial of the long rifle version of the grenade (the No. 11 which was essentially the same as the No. 3, except that it was intended to be fired from the older Lee Enfield and Lee Metford rifles) set down the correct procedure for loading and firing and stressed the importance of abiding by it.

1. Fit rod and secure it with the small securing screw.
2. Gauge with plug and fit detonator.
3. Insert rod in rifle and rest the butt on firm ground at the angle necessary for range.
4. Remove safety pin and pull back the safety pin collar [safety socket] to disengage it from the vane wheel.
5. Insert a round of special blank.
6. Fire.

It also stressed that all the rods should be tried in the barrel to make sure they fitted, before screwing them to the grenades to avoid potentially dangerous jams. It was possible that nickel fouling from firing small arms ammunition or a defective rod could cause a jam.

On firing the blank, the grenade was propelled from the barrel and the shock of discharge forced the safety collar back over the check, allowing the vane to be turned by the wind. This unscrewed, releasing the retaining bolts from the striker which was now free to move forward and hit the percussion cap when the grenade struck the ground.

It soon became apparent that the grenade had several weaknesses, not the least of them being the precision with which the components had to be made. This meant that production in quantity was practically impossible. Moreover, the vane was particularly troublesome as it was very difficult to align correctly and strong winds, rain or a single particle of dust could prevent the vane from working properly. The consequence of this defect in the design was a very large number of failures.

The obvious solution was to do away with the vane and make the safety socket longer so that it held the bolts in place until the shock of discharge forced it back, allowing the bolts simply to fall out. Not only was this a workable solution but it reduced the number of components. The first grenades to use the extended safety collar in place of the vane were converted No. 3s. The No. 20 vaneless grenade was the fruit of this evolution. It is not clear when the converted No. 3s and the No. 20 entered service but it was probably sometime in 1916. They suffered far fewer failures than the No. 3 Mks I and II. However, the No. 20 had a problem with the explosive filling. Neither pressed Tonite nor TNT pellets, used in No. 3, were readily available for the No. 20, so ammonal was initially used in their stead. This would have been a perfectly acceptable alternative but for the fact that it was a powder that produced dust which got into the working parts of the grenade no matter what precautions were taken to prevent this happening when the explosive was loaded into the body. The ammonal powder corroded all the brass parts it touched. This, not surprisingly, affected the grenade's performance, defeating the improved mechanism and striker of the grenade. Like the No. 3, the body of the No. 20 was machined from a solid steel cylinder, the Mk I having the usual segmentation, while the Mk II was made from weldless steel tube and made do with milled circumferential grooves.

The next development along this evolutionary road was the No. 24 Mk I. This was intended, among other things, to solve the problem of prematures with the No. 3 and the No. 20 due to the powerful and sensitive percussion cap; it did not take much to set it off in flight. Sometimes, the grenade did not even manage to leave the rifle. Edmund Blunden came close to injury at the Harfleur Bull Ring when he first went out to France because of a premature at the muzzle. There was a 'strange hideous clang' as it exploded, killing the instructor and several others. A less sensitive and weaker cap was needed.

A waxed-paper container for the powdered ammonal was designed to overcome the dust problem. It was loaded with explosive in a building dedicated to just this purpose and the charged container was placed into the grenade body in another building. In this way, contamination was avoided but it was a tiresome additional step in the manufacturing process.

Ammonal is a mixture of ammonium nitrate and powdered aluminium – hence the name – and ammonium nitrate is sensitive to moisture, which in a European environment is a considerable nuisance since the humidity is such that there is nearly always moisture in the air. However, experiments showed that by warming the explosive to a particular temperature on special heating tables, it was effectively dried and the sealed waxed-paper container was found to be sufficiently moisture resistant to prevent the ammonal becoming recontaminated once it was inside the grenade. When it was contaminated by moisture it expanded, but now that a way had been found to prevent contamination, the expansion space was reduced which meant that the central tube which held the detonator and striker could be shortened to the minimum length. This not only reduced the manufacturing costs but improved the detonation of the grenade. Moreover, a less sensitive and less powerful cap could now be used and in combination with a blunter striker the problem of prematures was solved.

Further improvements were made with the adoption of cast iron for the grenade body instead of weldless steel tube. Cast iron had better fragmentation characteristics. The Mk II was made from cast iron without the circumferential grooves. This was not the end of the evolution process of the No. 3 as the No. 24 was developed into the No. 35, the final manifestation of the original No. 3. This was essentially the same as the No. 24 except that the detonator holder was a shortened small arms ammunition cartridge case and it had a slightly different base piece and a shorter striker. By the time the No. 35 entered service, it was 1918. The No. 3 percussion rifle grenade had been developed over four years from an expensive and unreliable munition into a much simpler and dependable weapon. For all that, it had been more a case of digging the same hole deeper than digging different holes in a search for water. Others took quite different routes to solving the rifle grenade problem and set about digging different holes.

Soon after Captain Newton set up the Second Army Workshop at Armentières, he designed a rifle grenade that was simple to make and much more reliable than the troublesome No. 3. His first grenade was a hand-thrown device but very little is known about it. The rifle grenade is documented much more fully. Confusingly, both are referred to as the Newton Pippin so it is possible that the rifle grenade was a development of the earlier hand grenade, or was simply the hand grenade with a rod. Production started in about June 1915 and eventually about three million were produced. After his visit to the workshop, Todhunter reported that although it satisfied the demand for rifle grenades when the No. 3 was in short supply, it was not a device that was suitable for storage because of its firing mechanism, but noted that it could still be made in Britain if it was subsequently filled at the workshop. This suggestion was going to be taken up but when the grenade was compared with the improved rifle grenades of the No. 3 family it was considered to be inferior and production never started. So in the end, all Newton Pippins (designated the No. 22) were made in France. Some, apparently, were made in another workshop in Hazebrouck which seems to have been an outstation of the main one at Armentières.

The body of the grenade was a cone-shaped cast-iron cylinder with the 1.75 in diameter blunt end uppermost. The rod was screwed into the base which had a thread machined into it. Todhunter's report described it as having the sharper end uppermost and the rod being cast integrally. Although photographs do not support this description, it is unlikely that he was mistaken as he had discussed the grenade with Newton and had seen it being made. Since the grenade had not yet entered serious production, Todhunter may have seen a pre-production model that was subsequently modified. The rod was 15 inches in length and had a copper gas check on the end which was supposed to spread and seal the propellant gases behind the rod when the launching blank was fired. The gas check did not always perform as it was supposed to. Some were too stiff to spread while others were too fragile and broke, causing range discrepancies.

The grenade contained 2.25 oz of explosive which was fired by a shortened commercial No. 8 detonator inside a holder made from a standard 0.303 cartridge. The detonator sleeve was made from cardboard. Four lugs were cast on the outside of the body near the top. A

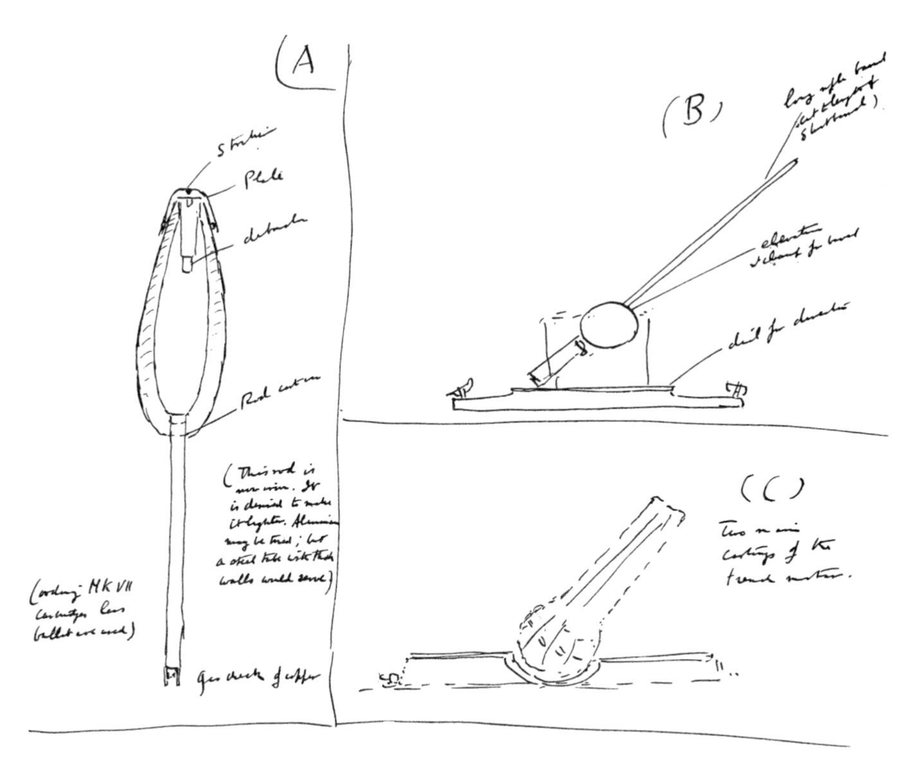

Captain Todhunter's rough sketches following his visit to the Second Army Workshop in 1915. 'A' is the Newton Pippin rifle grenade, 'B' is the rifle grenade launcher (see *Chapter 7*) *and 'C' is Newton's experimental 3.7 in mortar.* (WO 140/14)

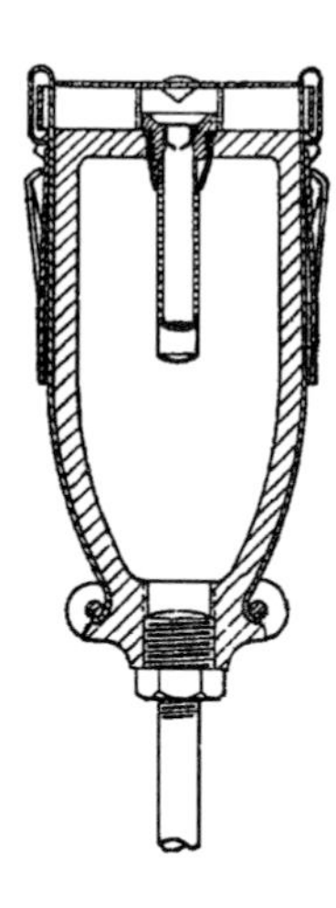

Another Mills patent (109,066). This appears to be a development of the Newton Pippin. The white blocks above the body and beneath the cap are 'distance-pieces' to keep the striker away from the percussion cap, held in place by spring arms which pivot at the base of the body. These are held by a ring which is set back on discharge to free the arms which fall away, removing the distance-pieces.

loosely fitting cover made of plate steel with four side straps had a fixed striker riveted to the centre of it; the side straps snap-fitted over the lugs. Because the weight of the grenade was distributed well forward it always fell head first and the cover was driven back causing the striker to hit the cap. This surprisingly simple, almost home-made, rifle grenade was cheap, extremely effective and reliable although there was a problem with prematures at first due to the launching shock. A slight modification to the cover reduced the risk, however. Nevertheless, rifle grenadiers were instructed to fire the grenade from cover with the aid of a lanyard, standing about 6 ft away.

About 2 per cent of launchings resulted in the grenade exploding in the barrel although it had 'very little effect on the gun, beyond chipping the wood where the fragments strike'. The same could not be said for the grenadier if he was too close. Two possible explanations were mooted: the rod was driven through the grenade so that the detonator was forced into the striker; or the inertia of the cap and striker was enough to drive the latter into the detonator. Certainly, the casings were thin in the base area so the former was a distinct possibility, especially if a thin casing was combined with a badly made rod. However, tests to establish the primary cause of prematures was inconclusive. Newton believed that the prematures were caused by the inertia of the cap. He also blamed the use of safety pins which were imposed on the grenade by the Ordnance Board but he stopped using them and substituted a more closely fitting cap which seemed to resolve the problem.

An unexpected bonus was the fact that the grenade did not make a large crater when it exploded (it was about 18 inches in diameter and 6 inches deep in 'good stiffish clay' leaving the rod intact but for its screw thread). This was because of the instantaneous fuse which detonated the grenade before it had time to bury itself. This also meant that the grenade tended to explode even when it struck marshy ground. When it was fired at barbed wired entanglements it was found to destroy the wire without leaving a crater behind, one of the problems of shooting high-explosive artillery shells at wire; these were not fitted with instantaneous fuses, buried themselves on impact and produced craters that the infantry found difficult to cross in an attack. The fuse was subsequently adapted by the Second Army Workshop for use on the trench mortar bombs produced at the workshop so that the mortar rounds could be used for cutting wire. Sometimes, however, the grenade failed to detonate. This was often due to human error, such as failing to remove the safety pin first, rather than a defective design.

The Newton Pippin had a range of 250–300 yd when the rifle was elevated at around 45°, although a poor gas check could reduce the range to 220 yd while a very good one could extend it to 350 yd. This was about double that obtained with the No. 3. Because the muzzle velocity was about 200 ft per second, the flight of the grenade was easy to follow once it had been spotted, according to a memo about the grenade, especially if the observer was 'about 100 yards away in a direction at right angles to the plane of the trajectory'. (Spotting a rifle grenade in the first place was, however, the tricky bit and for the most part the observer was more or less in a direct line of flight, not at right angles to it. Frank Richards and Robert Graves both agreed that they were hard to see. This was because they rose to a considerable height before descending and were practically silent.)

The grenade rotated slightly in flight and usually lay tangential to the trajectory but sometimes it slewed at right angles. This was attributed to the rod whipping as it left the barrel so that it oscillated about the line of the trajectory. However, it invariably recovered to a tangential flight, the oscillations reducing in amplitude but when a grenade oscillated it had a much shorter range. The Newton Pippin made a distinctive whistling noise immediately after leaving the barrel when its speed was greatest. When the grenade exploded, fragments were observed to be dangerous at 50 yd but at 75 yd they were harmless. Tests showed that fragments no bigger than a pea embedded themselves in board at a distance of 6 ft.

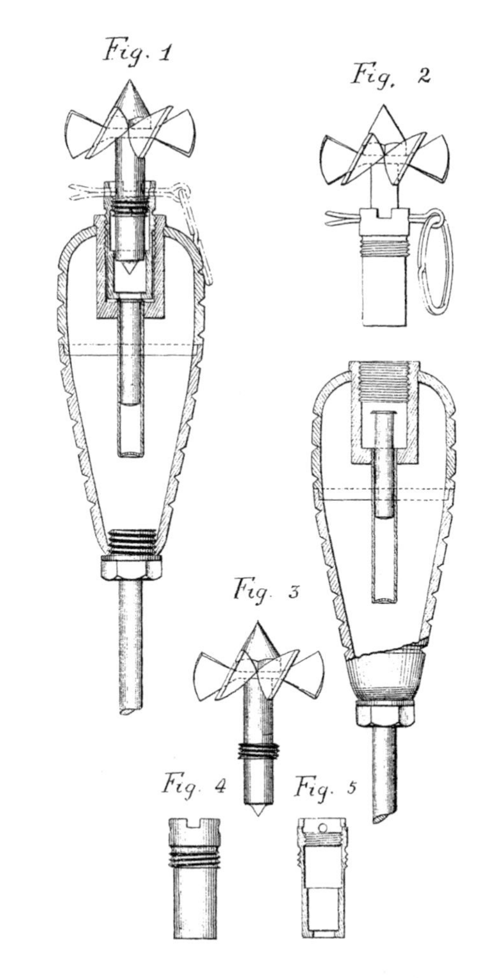

The drawings from Charles Sangster's rifle grenade patent, 107,893, illustrating its construction.

An ingenious design of rifle grenade was submitted by Charles Sangster who had designed the Pitcher grenade. As with the Pitcher, he patented his invention, obtaining two patents, 107,893 and 124,775, which he applied for in October 1916. The idea behind the grenade was to provide a safe way of arming it in flight that obviated the drawbacks of existing percussion grenades fired from rifles. The body was a streamlined pear shape which ensured that it had a good range. The striker was mounted at the bottom of a thin cylinder on top of which was a propeller-like wind vane. The cylinder had a male screw thread that engaged a female thread in a tube inside the grenade above a percussion cap on the detonator. It was held in a safe position by the ubiquitous pin. When this was removed and the grenade was fired, the passage of air through the blades of the vane turned it so that it unscrewed and the cylinder descended in the tube until it rested on an internal rim just above the cap. When the grenade hit the ground the striker was forced into the cap.

The Sangster underwent troop trials, being designated the No. 25 grenade, but was dropped afterwards, not because it failed to work but because it was not a commercial proposition. To function correctly, the grenade needed to be manufactured within very high tolerances and this was not feasible for something that would have to be manufactured quickly in large numbers.

There were other rifle grenades of the percussion type that failed to make the grade. The No. 17 was one. It was designed by the Royal Laboratory and nicknamed the opera hat grenade because of the appearance of the striker which was topped by a steel disc. The Humphries was another (*see* Chapter 5). The only other rodded percussion-fused rifle grenade to emerge from the war was the No. 39 Stewart pattern (sometimes spelled Steuart). It was first proposed by the Trench Warfare Department in 1917 and underwent severe trials well into 1918 before being finally accepted after some modifications suggested by the Munitions Inventions Department. The No. 39 was too late to be used in anger. It was of a quite different design from other percussion rifle grenades and was intended to overcome the drawbacks of the No. 3 family.

These relied on forward movement of the striker to detonate the grenades so that if they struck muddy or soft ground, there was a slight delay before detonation which allowed their momentum to bury them before they exploded. This severely restricted their effectiveness. As much as half of the fragmentation effect was dissipated in the ground and inevitably a large crater was the result. Moreover, the damage caused to the brass components by the exudation from the explosive when it got damp sometimes made the grenades unsafe to handle. The problem was that the working parts were hidden inside the body so it was impossible to tell what state the grenade was in. The No. 39 had all the mechanism outside the body of the grenade in a cylinder that gave it the appearance of a bottle on a stick. It had an instantaneous fuse and because the mechanism was in the neck of the bottle shape the explosive effect was practically guaranteed to be above ground even if the neck buried itself first.

The rifle grenade was an extremely effective weapon and was often used to suppress German trench mortars. Todhunter reported in 1915 that unless rifle grenades were available for this purpose, some front-line trenches became untenable because of mortar bombardments. They were also useful in eliminating snipers; when one was spotted he might be subjected to a volley, especially from 1916 onwards when rifle grenades were more plentiful than in the early days of the war. All soldiers tended to have a healthy respect for rifle grenades. Germans captured by the French at Ypres in January 1916 told them that 'English rifle grenades do great execution, but the precision of their flight is very much influenced by the elements'. Sometimes batteries of several grenade rifles were rigged up to fire barrages like the one witnessed by Edmund Blunden in 1916, 'sending over by one pull of a cord volleys of half a dozen, which cooed somehow like pigeons as they soared over to do mischief'.

Although all rifle grenades, whether German, French or British, were designed to land head first they did not always do so. Robert Graves had a lucky escape when one landed tail first only feet away from him. It was a chance in a million. Mostly, they were deadly. Frank Richards described an incident when one fell in a bay and killed three of the five men there and wounded the other two. He complained that the British rifle grenade then in service (probably the No. 3) was very poor in comparison.

The rods were usually 15 in or 10 in long, depending on the grenade (although the rodded Mills had one that was only 5.5 in long). For example, the No. 22 and No. 35 had 15 in rods, while the No. 3 and No. 20 had 10 in rods. Range was determined by angle but getting it right was always something of a problem. Experiments with rods of different lengths for the same grenade were not entirely satisfactory. If range was to be determined by rods of specific lengths, the rifle grenadier would inevitably be burdened with extra weight to carry as he would need adequate supplies of rods of each length to give him the full range of options. This was not practical.

Someone had the bright idea of using tightly fitting rubber rings to act as stops so that the rod would only go so far into the barrel before the ring encountered the muzzle and prevented further travel. Preliminary experiments in the summer of 1917 were very promising and arrangements were made to issue a number of rings and range strips to front-line units for trials with 15 in rodded grenades. The results were encouraging and there was a suggestion that the idea could be extended to the 10 in rodded grenades. By late 1917 the rubber ring solution had been adopted. Twenty-five rings were issued for every twenty 15 in rodded grenades. To help grenadiers adjust the rings to the correct position for the desired range, eight range rods were also supplied to each platoon which worked at one per grenadier as there were at that time eight rifle grenadiers per platoon.

Rodded rifle grenades were used for purposes other than dropping high explosive on the enemy's head. There were also smoke and signal grenades and by the end of the war anti-tank grenades as well. There were even occasions when rifle grenades were used to send messages across No Man's Land as recorded by Robert Graves, presumably with the explosive and detonator removed first.

Smoke grenades did not appear until 1916. The smoke was generated by white phosphorus although this also had an incendiary effect. White phosphorus is a pyrophoric incendiary, that is, it spontaneously ignites in the presence of atmospheric moisture. If it touches the skin it can cause serious burns that are difficult to treat because of this property. Since the First World War, its pyrophoric nature has been utilized to ignite other more destructive incendiaries, for example, those based on petroleum products (commonly called napalms although the original napalm was a thickening agent not the thickened fuel itself). The first grenades to use white phosphorus were the No. 26 and the No. 27. The former was a crude device much like the Jam-Tin in appearance being made from a tin cylinder with a time fuse and was intended for the West Spring Gun.

The No. 27 was both a rodded percussion rifle grenade and a hand grenade with a tin body that contained 13.5 oz of white phosphorus. The striker mechanism was brass, including the sleeve and striker which was held in a safe position by a shear wire. Like the egg grenade, the hand-thrown version had to be struck on a hard surface to ignite the fuse before throwing it but when discharged from a rifle the shock of launching it forced back the striker and sheared the wire. Eventually, a Mk II version was produced without a rod, for launching from a cup discharger. The grenade produced an effective smokescreen and was also used to produce air bursts to shower the enemy with white phosphorus. Because of the pyrophoric nature of the white phosphorus, transportation was something of a problem; the bursters, grenades, rods and cartridges all had to be carried in separate boxes.

In 1917 the No. 27 was superseded by the No. 37 which was similar to its predecessor but, as it was intended to be fired from a cup discharger, a steel gas check disc formed the base of the cylindrical grenade. The striker in the first models of the No. 27 were flimsy so for the No. 37 it was redesigned to be machined from solid brass making the latter more reliable and safer.

The smoke grenades were not the first chemical grenades of the war. The patterns of the earliest ones are not clear as they are referred to as No. 1 and No. 2 grenades but it is unlikely that they were modified versions of the explosive percussion grenades with the same numbers. More likely, they were designated as chemical grenades and because they were the first were given the numbers 1 and 2, later to be redesignated because of the inevitable confusion this would cause. Hence, the No. 1 and the No. 2 are most probably the No. 28 Mk I and the No. 28 Mk II (or possibly the No. 29). These were spherical and looked very much like the No. 15 Ball grenade, especially the No. 28 Mk I as this had a similar igniter. It is the similarity of the igniters, suggesting a safety fuse that had to be lit by a match, that points to this having been introduced in 1915 before the development of automatic igniters like those in the No. 34 Egg grenade. The Mk II had a fuse mechanism that protruded from the top of the grenade like that on the No. 31 signal grenade (they were, in fact, essentially the same). A photograph in the Public Record Office clearly shows a No. 28 Mk I with the date 1915 moulded in the casing.

Chemical grenades contained tear gas such as ethyl iodoacetate or stannic chloride and were mainly used for clearing dugouts. The only other tear gas grenade was the No. 29 which resembled the No. 16 Oval pattern. Whereas the No. 28 started out with a match igniter, the No. 29 had a fuse mechanism like that on the No. 28 Mk II. Designed by the Trench Warfare Department, it was probably a chemical variant of the No. 16.

Signal grenades fired from rifles were introduced in late 1916 with the idea that they might replace mortar signal shells if they proved effective. The grenades, similar to the No. 27, having many interchangeable parts, were the No. 31 day signal grenade and the No. 32 and No. 38 night signal grenades. They were essentially the same except for the fillings. The body consisted of a 7-inch tin cylinder 2.25 inches in diameter which was originally made in two pieces and connected by a bayonet joint. Later, the body was made in one piece with a removable base of stamped tin for filling the grenade. No detonator was used, only a percussion cap and a short length of safety fuse, originally of 2.5 seconds duration but later extended to 3 seconds. The grenades were fired perpendicularly so that they went straight up, the shock of discharge forcing the striker into the cap.

The No. 31 contained a coloured smoke composition. Different colours represented different messages. The No. 32 and No. 38 grenades produced a string of three stars suspended from a parachute, the only difference between them being the colour of the stars. The colours of the No. 32 stars remained the same as they burned whereas the stars in the No. 38 changed colour. Troop trials with star grenades in the summer of 1917 indicated that the grenades might be better if they reached a greater height but were otherwise satisfactory. Nevertheless, 50,000 were ordered in addition to the 50,000 already asked for. A supply of 6,000 a week was also requested. Initially, there were three colour combinations of stars, reading from the top: red, red, red; red, green, red; green, red, green. However, the colour combinations had to be changed periodically as the Germans tended to copy them and sent up fake messages to create confusion.

These rodded signal grenades were replaced in 1918 by similar munitions designed to be fired from discharger cups: the No. 42, No. 43 and No. 45 respectively. These were launched to a height of 350 ft where they were burst by a time fuse. Unlike their predecessors which were made of tin, the grenades were rolled brown-paper cylinders with tin lids held in place with adhesive tape. Each had a wooden base with a tin closure which were pierced by two holes to allow the flash from the launching cartridge to ignite the 3.5-second fuse. When the No. 42 burst, a parachute was dispensed from the paper cylinder, from which a coloured smoke candle was suspended via an asbestos string. The other two grenades used stars instead of the candle.

The anti-tank grenade was an unexpected consequence of the invention of the tank. Although the Germans introduced a big-bore anti-tank rifle firing armour-piercing ammunition to kill the crew, the British went for a more explosive answer to German armour. The anti-tank grenade proved to be more effective, and more durable, than the anti-tank rifle although the British Army was still equipped with one at the outbreak of the Second World War. Many of the German tanks were captured British models which were built with hard steel. The German design, the A7V, was a clumsy monster built with mild steel. The British, therefore, decided to develop a grenade that was capable of destroying their own tanks and came up with one that was little more than a large tin containing more than 11 oz of alumatol which produced a massive explosion. The benefits of the shaped charge were not to be discovered until about 1940. The grenade, known as the No. 44 anti-tank grenade, had the same percussion mechanism as the No. 35 which allowed detonation to occur on direct contact with the tank. Although this punched a hole in the side of British steel plate it only produced a large bulge in the mild steel of the German tanks. However, this was enough to kill or injure the occupants from the concussion.

Anti-tank engagements took place at close range so the 8 in rod had little time to stabilize the flight of the grenade, thus a calico tail was added to ensure that the grenade flew straight and hit the target squarely. It allowed the grenade to be fired at almost point-blank range and still hit the mark correctly. An improved grenade, the No. 46, was filled with a cast explosive instead of alumatol powder. This increased the explosive power of the grenade and a steel base disc replaced the dished tin one of the earlier grenade so that more explosive could be put into the body. An improved detonator was also developed but the war ended before the grenade could enter service.

CHAPTER 7

New Ways to Throw New Bombs – Grenade Launchers 1916–18

The first grenade that could double as a hand grenade and a rifle grenade was the Mills. It was also the first time-fused rifle grenade. This fact, combined with its lever mechanism, presented a number of problems that had to be resolved before the Mills rifle grenade could become a viable proposition. The solutions eventually led to a method of launching rifle grenades without recourse to rods, although the first Mills rifle grenades were fitted with short ones. However, these were eliminated with the cup discharger. This device might not have been developed without the Mills and its lever although it came to be used with grenades that had no lever.

The desire to do away with the rods was shared by the rifle grenadiers who had to lug them about and the research departments in the UK. Steel was a precious commodity and rifle grenade rods used a lot of it. In 1917 it was calculated that 50,000 15 in rods required 7 tons of steel. Considering that this was the approximate consumption per week, this amounted to some 364 tons of steel a year. As far as transporting the rods was concerned, the grenadier had his work cut out. It was an unenviable job to have to carry up to sixteen rodded grenades at a time; although not in battle, only as a workhorse. Sixteen weighed in the region of 20 lb. Furthermore, the rods had to be protected against accidental damage as well as mud which could render them unusable. Eight or sixteen rifle grenades made for an awkward and unwieldy load that was not easy to carry down trenches with all their bays and traverses and tight corners.

Various carriers were tried. In the spring of 1917, trials were conducted with an experimental pattern of carrier designed at one of the workshops. It consisted of a tin cylinder with a lid at each end to hold eight rodded grenades, four at each end, the rods passing through holes in a central wooden partition. As it was not contemplated that the grenades would normally form part of the permanent equipment of the rifle grenadier in battle, it was primarily a means of carrying them forward quickly when required. It was envisaged that it could be carried by a rifle grenadier with relative ease (it had a sling), without interfering with his use of the rifle and bayonet, although it is hard to see how anyone could bring his rifle to bear if he was lugging rifle grenades about. Basketwork containers, lined with waterproof material, were also tried. The trial showed that it was difficult to remove and replace the lid of the tin version and that the carrier was too heavy, difficult to carry down trenches and very noticeable in the open. The basketwork version and an ordinary haversack with a board fixed in the bottom, perforated with six holes for the rods with an extension to protect them, were both thought to be better alternatives. In the end, however, none were judged to be superior to the old style bucket pattern and it had all been a bit of a waste of time.

That sort of conclusion was not uncommon. At about the same time that the rodded grenade carriers were being trialled, a bandoleer with spring hooks to carry sixteen hand grenades was tried out. It was worn over the left shoulder and under the right arm, with the hooks opening in front and facing downwards; as the grenades were taken out and used, the belt was merely slipped round. It seemed like a good idea but it did not work in practice. The hooks were too weak to hold the grenades during rapid movements. Had the hooks been stronger, however, it would have been difficult to insert and withdraw the grenades. Moreover, the bandoleer got in the way of the box respirator which had become the standard issue gas mask by then. In any case, sixteen grenades were simply too many to carry. The bandoleer was dropped.

That the Mills – for which the bandoleer grenade dispenser had been designed – could be adapted to become a rifle grenade was an inbuilt feature of the grenade, albeit unintentional. The requirement of all rifle grenades at that time was the ability of the body to take a rod. No other design of hand grenade had the potential to house a rod. The Mills could do it because it had a base plug (closing the hole into which the centre-piece was inserted), originally made of aluminium, a soft alloy or brass. None of these materials was strong enough to withstand the stresses of launching a grenade: the steel rod was pushed through the base plug. However, it was but a simple matter to replace the plug with one made of a something stronger. Steel was used first but this was later replaced with one of cast iron in the interests of economy. This had a 0.25 in diameter screw-threaded hole bored in it to take a 5.5 in long rod. It was launched by a 35-grain cordite blank but this was later replaced by a standard 43-grain cartridge used for launching all rodded grenades.

The problem with the Mills was not so much the provision of a rod but how to keep the lever in place once the pin had been removed prior to firing from the rifle. If the lever could not be retained, the striker would hit the cap and ignite the fuse; the grenade would

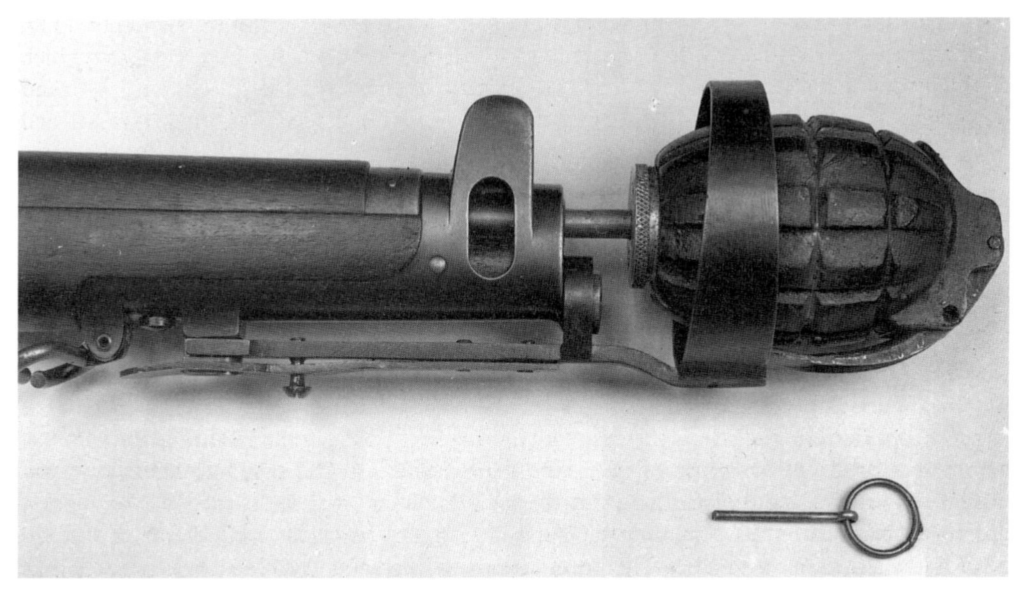

No. 4 Mk I grenade cup made in three parts and fitted to the rifle's bayonet attachment points. This had the advantage of doing away with the necessity of fitting the bayonet to fire rifle grenades. The rod has not been fully inserted in the barrel. (IWM)

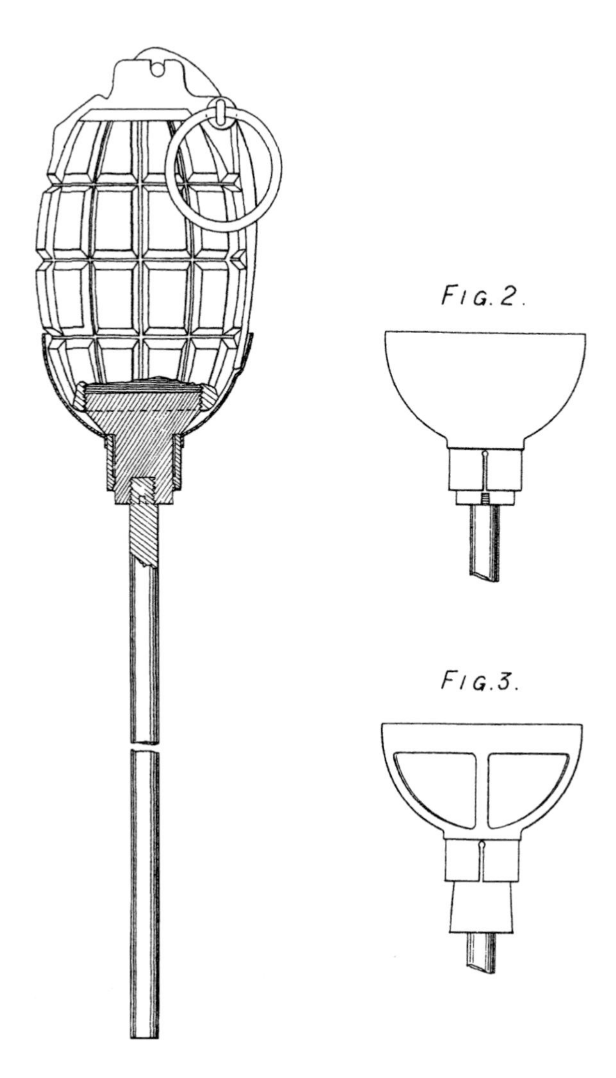

Hale's invention (UK patent 109,273) for firing a Mills rifle grenade using a form of cup to retain the lever, only this one is attached to the rod assembly rather than to the rifle. The cup is held in place by an annular clip that sets back on discharge, allowing the cup to fall back and release the lever. In a simpler version, the lever is retained by a metal strip attached to the clip. The grenade needed a specially machined base plug for the clip in both cases.

detonate long before the grenadier was ready to discharge it from the rifle. The answer was the grenade cup, a clever piece of designing that was simple and easy to manufacture and which was secured to the rifle with the bayonet. Made from sheet steel, the No. 1 Mk I grenade cup, consisted of a one-piece stem and ring, the latter having a diameter slightly greater than that of the Mills. The stem fitted under the muzzle so that the ring was positioned about 2.75 inches in front and concentrically with the barrel. The sides of the stem curved up round the nose cap of the rifle, the bottom of the curved part having a slot cut in it to allow the bayonet ring to engage the lug on the nose cap. The end of the stem

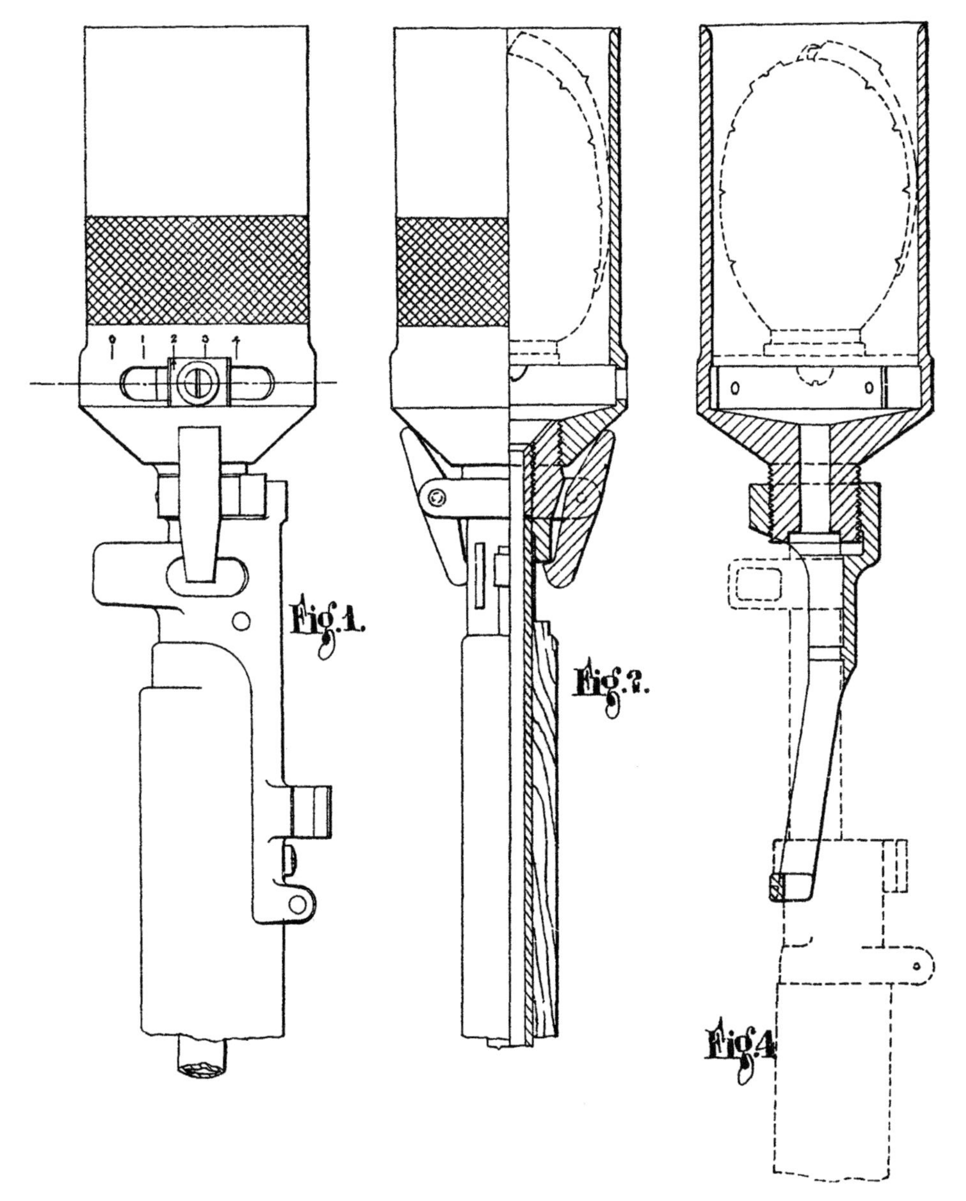

Robert Burn's cup discharger (UK patent 126,692). The rifle on the right is a P14 and the discharger required a different form of adapter for it to be fitted to the muzzle.

was forked so that it went round the bar that engaged the slot in the pommel of the bayonet. When the bayonet was fitted, the grenade cup was firmly fixed in place. With the grenade loaded in the rifle, the ring prevented the lever from releasing until the grenade was fired. A later variation was the No. 4 Mk I cup which was made in three pieces and could be fitted to the rifle without the bayonet as it was fixed to the rifle via the bayonet attachment points.

The Mills in its rodded form was designated the No. 23 Mk I. Brothers thought that this was the 'most useful development of the grenade' which was introduced with the cup in 1916. By the middle of following year, the Mills had been redesigned and reintroduced as the No. 23 Mk III which was essentially the same as the No. 36 Mk I. This, instead of being adapted to take a rod, was intended to be fired from an entirely new device which did away with the rod. The cup discharger not only made the rod redundant but increased the range by as much as two and half times that of the rodded grenade and provided the grenadier with a much easier method of varying the range. Moreover, the discharger allowed grenades to be thrown more accurately than rodded grenades.

Trials with the cup discharger were carried out in France during the spring of 1917 and were so successful that GHQ immediately requested a supply of ninety-six per battalion and 'a reserve of 10% on the Lines of Communication'. By October the dischargers were being delivered but the discharger only entered widespread use in the last few months of the war. The cup discharger was known by several names, mostly derived from its inventor, Robert Burn, a New Zealander who owned an engineering business in Petone and in 1917 was a lieutenant in the New Zealand Mechanical Transport section. He filed a patent application in February and another in August and these were combined in UK patent 126,692 granted to him in May 1919.

The discharger consisted of a 2.5 in steel cylinder about 4 in long with a solid, truncated cone at its base which could be screwed on to an adapter block, pierced by a hole the size of the rifle bore, and shaped to fit flush with the muzzle and engage the bayonet lug. The whole assembly was secured firmly in place by two pawls, the hooked ends of which engaged the oval holes in the muzzle cap while the opposite ends bore against the cone of the discharger. The Mills was furnished with a gas check disc which fitted the bore of the discharger so that the propelling gases were sealed behind the grenade and acted over the whole of the area of the disc until the grenade left the cup. The grenade was fitted with a 7-second fuse when fired from the Burn discharger.

The range of the discharger could be altered with an adjustable gas port in the base of the cylindrical part of the device that allowed propellant gases to escape below the grenade gas check. Following the trials, a mechanical defect was found in the design of the gas port, necessitating modifications. The gas port was opened or closed by a sliding shutter and was graduated according to range. With the rifle held at 45° and the port fully open, the grenade reached 80 yd; with it fully closed the range was 200 yd. In December 1917 G.R. Thatcher filed a patent application for an improved gas port system in which a sliding ring with a series of holes in it could be rotated about the base of the cylinder which also had a series of holes. This became UK patent 129,740 and appears to have been used on later versions of the discharger.

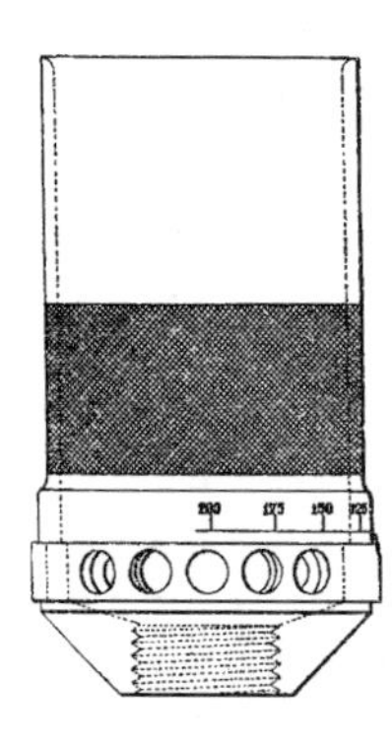

Thatcher's adaptation of Burn's discharger (UK patent 129,740).

Experiments were subsequently conducted with the No. 34 Egg grenade although this required a narrower-bore discharger which the Army Council was not keen to sanction, arguing that it would require too much steel and the rifle grenadier did not want to have to carry two dischargers. As far as the consumption of

How to launch a grenade from the Burn discharger. This Royal Engineer is wearing a box respirator. (IWM)

materials was concerned, the Army Council was mistaken, as a second discharger would actually reduce the amount of steel used for rifle grenades. The egg grenade could be fired to an even greater distance than the Mills, up to about 500 yd.

Although the Burn discharger, irrespective of which grenades were fired from it, had considerable advantages over the rodded grenade it was not perfect. There were problems with the propelling cartridge which caused a bright flash when the gas port was open. The recoil was heavy but if the power of the cartridge was reduced to make it more comfortable, the maximum range would be reduced to a mere 150 yd. The Mills was heavy and made heavier by the necessity of gas check discs. And the procedure for fastening the cup to the rifle, involving screwing the cup part to the block with the pawls, which had to be engaged to fix it firmly to the rifle, was not ideal; 'a feature which will in future designs be eliminated', hoped Brothers in 1919.

The idea was not a bad one, just its embodiment, since precision was once again necessary in the manufacture of the various components of the discharger if they were to fit together correctly. The fact that the pawls had to press against the cone of the discharger meant that the cone had to be made very precisely otherwise unequal pressure was exerted on them, preventing a firm grip of the rifle. Vibration from a series of discharges caused the cup to tilt if the pawls were not equalized so that the seal between the discharger and the muzzle was lost. The propellant gases were very hot and travelled at high velocity so that they very quickly eroded any gap to a much bigger one and damaged the screw thread of the adapter block so that the join between the block and cylinder seized up.

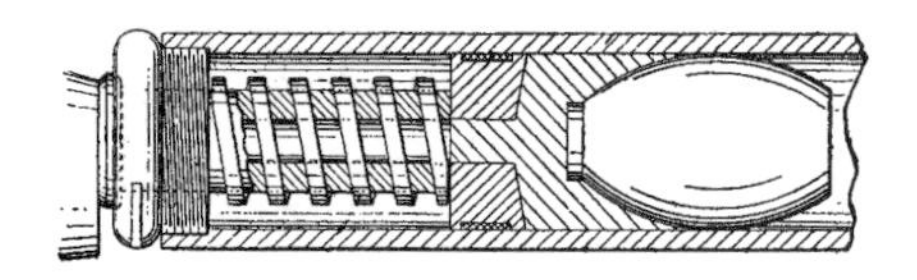

A form of cup discharger invented by A.L. Chevallier and H.J. Blanch (UK patent 101,108) in early 1916. The cup is a slidable sleeve that fits over the barrel. A wooden sabot centres the grenade. On firing, the sleeve moves forward against a spring which absorbs some of the recoil.

The propellant gases also tended to erode the holes in the gas port, reducing the range that was supposed to be obtained for a particular setting. Doubt was cast on the value of altering range with such a system in any case, because of the effects of wind, air temperature and rain. Wind, in particular, had a considerable effect especially if the grenade was fired into it. Moreover, doubt was expressed after the war whether 'the average man in the excitement of action would trouble to adjust a mechanical device of this nature'. There may have been some truth in this concern but if men could be trained to use the Mills as a hand grenade correctly, so that the number of accidents was significantly reduced, then they could also be trained to use the discharger correctly.

Range was intertwined with the size of the grenade and the maximum recoil the rifle could withstand. Experiments showed that the maximum velocity at which a No. 23 Mills, which weighed 27.5 oz with the gas check, could be safely fired was 140 ft per second which threw it out to approximately 150 yd. On the other hand, a 17.5 oz grenade could be fired at 220 ft per second to more than 300 yd. Range was also affected by the length of the cup; the longer it was, the greater the time spent by the gases in propelling the grenade, so it travelled further as a result. However, a longer cup made for greater recoil.

French troops armed with Viven-Bessière grenade dischargers. Note that the two soldiers in the foreground are resting the butts of their rifles against their hips rather than on the ground. This is not a posed shot. (The Times History of the War)

The cup discharger was a variation of a French device invented by engineers Jean Viven and Gustave Bessière in 1916 which saw widespread use in the French Army and was later adopted by the Americans when they entered the war. It was also used by the British from 1917. The inventors were granted two UK patents for the device and its ammunition, 100,700 and 104,836, and a third, 109,498, for a branched double-tube device. Their launcher was simply a large-bore muzzle attachment that fired a special grenade designed for it but whereas the Burn discharger used blank cartridges, the Viven-Bessière used the normal ball ammunition.

The grenade had an axial bore through which the bullet travelled and the expanding gases following it propelled the grenade out of the discharger. The bullet also acted as an obturator to seal the gases during its passage through the grenade and imparted rotation to it. A fuse-triggering device on the top of the grenade was activated by the bullet deflecting a lever. Either time-fused or percussion-fused grenades could be fired from it. Like the Burn device, the Viven-Bessière suffered from being a piece of precision engineering. If the grenade did not sit squarely in the tube which depended on the precision of the bore, and if tube was not squarely attached to the muzzle, the bullet would strike the side of the bore.

From the earliest days of the rifle grenade, the butt of the rifle had to be held firmly against the ground to fire it because the recoil was too severe to fire it from the

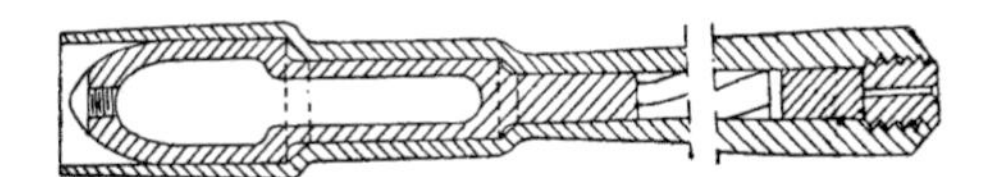

Viven and Bessière's first UK patent application, dating from 1915 (granted as 102,371). The drawing shows a barrel extension with 'two . . . gradually increasing diameters'.

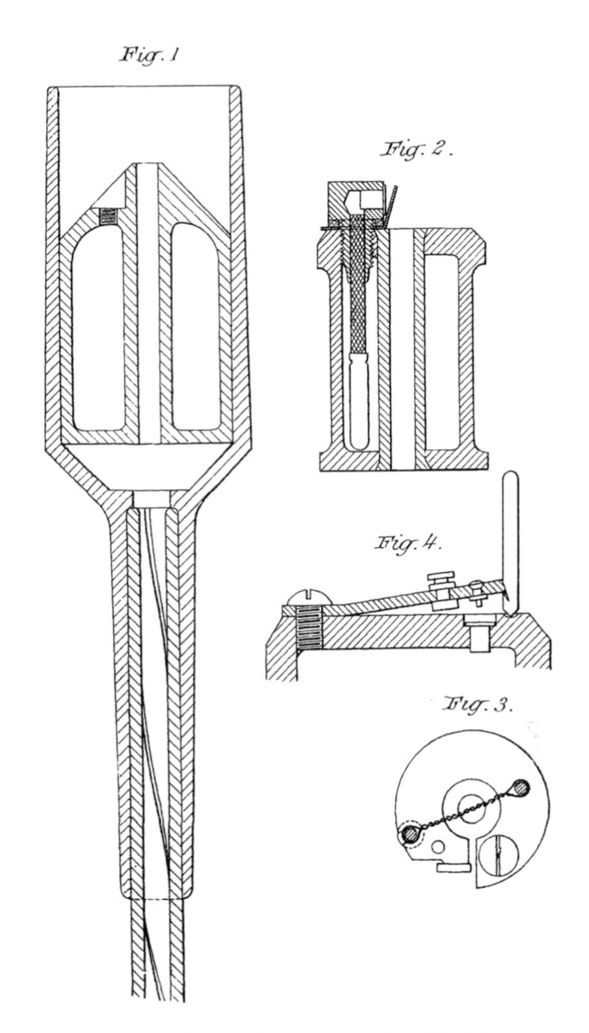

Viven and Bessière's second UK patent, 100,700. The reason it has a lower number than the earlier application is because the second one was granted first. Details of the grenade arming system are illustrated in the right-hand figures. Top: *time-fused version of the grenade.* Middle: *percussion-fused version.* Bottom: *detail of percussion fuse, the large disc in fig. 3 extending diagonally from the screw in fig. 4.*

shoulder. As a consequence of this, wooden stands or cradles were devised to support the rifle. The first ones were no more than improvisations from suitable lengths of timber. In February 1915 the 1st Cameronians used an double A-frame arranged on its side and provided it with a seat for the grenadier. However, being so close to the rifle grenade when it was fired was not encouraged in case of a premature at the muzzle, although similar devices seem to have been common for a while at least.

By mid-1915, the Second Army Workshops were making devices for firing rifle grenades. The device was quite sophisticated, allowing elevation and direction adjustments and may have been a simplified copy of a German apparatus for holding a rifle which incorporated a recoil-absorbing spring. According to Todhunter's description and sketch, it consisted of a platform with a turntable on which was a holder that could be pivoted in the vertical plane, all of which was cast in brass using old cartridge cases. The turntable and the holder were graduated to improve accuracy. The barrel from a long rifle (from a Lee Metford, for example) was cut to the length of the barrel in the SMLE service rifle and secured in the holder. Todhunter's report in June 1915 implied that the only limiting factor in the provision of this apparatus was the supply of brass which was also being used to make trench mortars. There is nothing to suggest

February 1915 and a 1st Cameronian prepares to fire a No. 3 rifle grenade. The rifle is fixed in an improvised timber stand. This is yet another posed shot. In reality, the rifle grenadier would fire the rifle by a lanyard while he was well out of harm's way. (IWM)

A German rifle grenade stand, 1915. Although heavily retouched, this photograph, from The Times History of the War, *shows the stand quite well. Unlike the crude wooden device used by the 1st Cameronians, it is made of metal and is adjustable for elevation. The rifle is clamped into a cradle with the butt clamped to a curved metal track, the latter's position on which could be altered. It may have been this device that inspired Kneeshaw. The grenade appears to be the 1914 Rifle Grenade without its bowled tin disk.*

how many were being made or how effective it was, but judging from the other devices designed and made at the workshop it was probably a useful addition to the armoury.

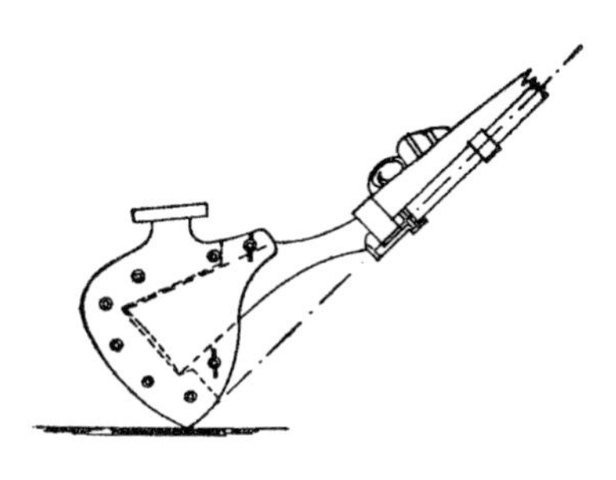

The Gauldies' device for firing rifle grenades (UK patent 102,755).

A few inventors tried their hands at devising suitable stands, among them K. and W. Gauldie who came up with what must have been one of the most unusable, not to say unsafe, gadgets imaginable. It was an approximately triangular plate with curved sides that was supposed to be bolted to the butt. Two of the curved sides met at a sharp apex and this was supposed to be the sole point of contact with the ground. To make matters more difficult the apex was to be aligned with the axis of the barrel. The idea was that this would prevent rotational displacement when the grenade was fired. The plate was even provided with a seat for the poor grenadier. It is not hard to imagine what would have happened had anyone been foolish enough to try this device, which became UK patent 102,755.

A couple of months after the Gauldies filed their application in January 1916, Wilfred Kneeshaw, a second lieutenant in the 4th Battalion, Royal Welch Fusiliers, filed an application for a more realistic stand (UK patent 101,441). It consisted of a rectangular base with four stabilizing arms which could be weighed down with sandbags to absorb the recoil. A pair of braced uprights at the front end of the base had a pivotable cradle to support the fore-end of the rifle just in front of the magazine. In fact, the fore-end was fastened to it otherwise the recoil would make the rifle jump out as soon as the grenade was fired. The butt was supported in a padded shoe that could be securely bolted to a curved trough. By pivoting the rifle in the cradle, the butt could be moved to a different position in the trough so that the rifle pointed at a different angle to allow grenades to be fired to different distances as required. This stand must have been used by Kneeshaw in France before he brought the idea to England to have it patented, so it is not unreasonable to assume that this was a workable device. However, there appears to be no documentary evidence to show that it was used.

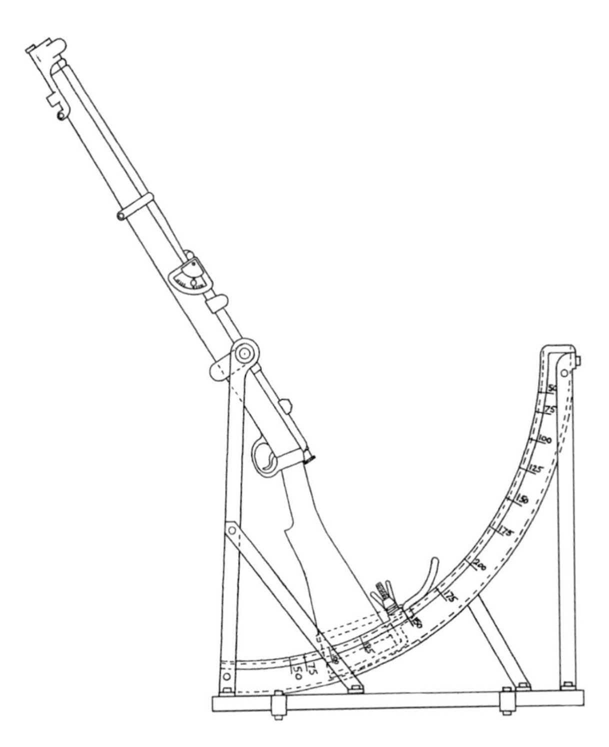

Kneeshaw's stand for firing rifle grenades (UK patent 101,441).

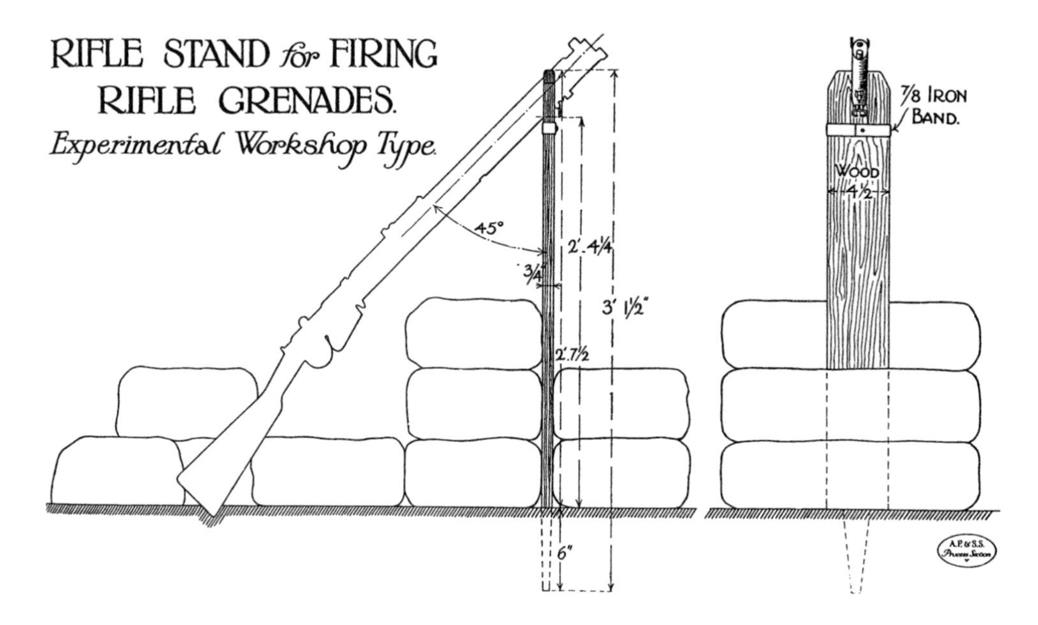

The experimental workshop design of rifle stand illustrated in 'Notes on Inventions and New Stores No. 2', July–August 1917. (MUN 4/3590)

In the summer of 1917, the Royal Engineer workshops designed a much more simple stand in which the rifle was set at 45°. It was no more than an upright ¾-inch thick slab of wood 2 feet 7.5 inches in length and 4.5 inches wide with a slot cut in the top to rest the muzzle of the rifle and a 6-inch spike to stick it in the ground. Again, sandbags were used to steady the stand and the rifle. The rifle's forward sling swivel was relied on to stop the rifle jumping out of the slot with the recoil and range was altered by using the rubber rings and range cards. The butt could be moved sideways to some extent to make corrections for line. This was an 'experimental workshop type' described in 'Notes on Inventions and New Stores No. 2' for July–August 1917. Since it was not mentioned in subsequent 'Notes' there is nothing to indicate whether it proved to be successful in operation.

The combination of grenade and rifle was effective but inconvenient as it meant that the rifle could not be used for its original purpose of firing ball ammunition. Moreover, although the need for stands rendered the rifle grenade less mobile, it was nevertheless more mobile as a weapon than the light trench mortar which fired a bigger bomb to a greater distance. To some extent, the rifle grenade and the light trench mortar encroached on each other's territory but the matter was never resolved because the tactical use of rifle grenades was never clarified. Rifle grenades tended to be used to attack snipers, mortar positions, pillboxes and strong points but the light mortar could do the same job more effectively. However, there were more rifle grenadiers in a battalion than light mortars and the rifle grenade was clearly an infantry weapon whereas the light mortar was somewhere between the infantry and the artillery. This lack of clarity about who was responsible for which weapon and about which one should be used in which circumstance led some people to think that an entirely new weapon was needed by the infantry, one that could fire grenades to rifle grenade distances and which was truly mobile.

These grenade guns as they were called had only one function: to fire grenades. The advantage to this was that they allowed the rifle to return to its original role. There were, however, a number of difficulties, not the least of them being that the grenade gun was an additional item of equipment for the soldier to carry, and some of them fired their own special ammunition that further added to the infantryman's burden. By 1917, when the grenade gun was being seriously considered by research departments like the Munitions Inventions Department, the rifle-fired bullet was no longer contemplated by the majority of the infantry as their principal means of killing the enemy. There were numerous directives that emphasized the need to shoot the enemy, when the rifle could be brought to bear, rather than relying on the grenade, irrespective of how it arrived at the enemy's feet. The truth was that the average infantryman had more faith in explosives than bullets for dealing with the enemy and by 1917 he had more experience with grenades than musketry. In this respect, the opinion of those responsible for approving new weapons was rather out of touch with what the soldier at the Front was actually doing, despite the directives, which in one sense were merely trying to restore the status quo of the rifle. However, these things are never as clear-cut as making a simple choice between yes and no.

It would appear that only two grenade guns received serious attention and these were quite dissimilar weapons. The first was a shoulder-fired grenade launcher invented by an engineer called Leonard Thring following conversations with officer friends at home on leave from France. They impressed on him that such a weapon was sorely needed. Thring noted their suggestions and devised a recoil-absorbing grenade-thrower that could be fired from the shoulder, for which he applied for two patents in January 1916 (granted as 124,469 and 124,478 in 1919 – the first one was for a special sighting device for the gun). In essence, it

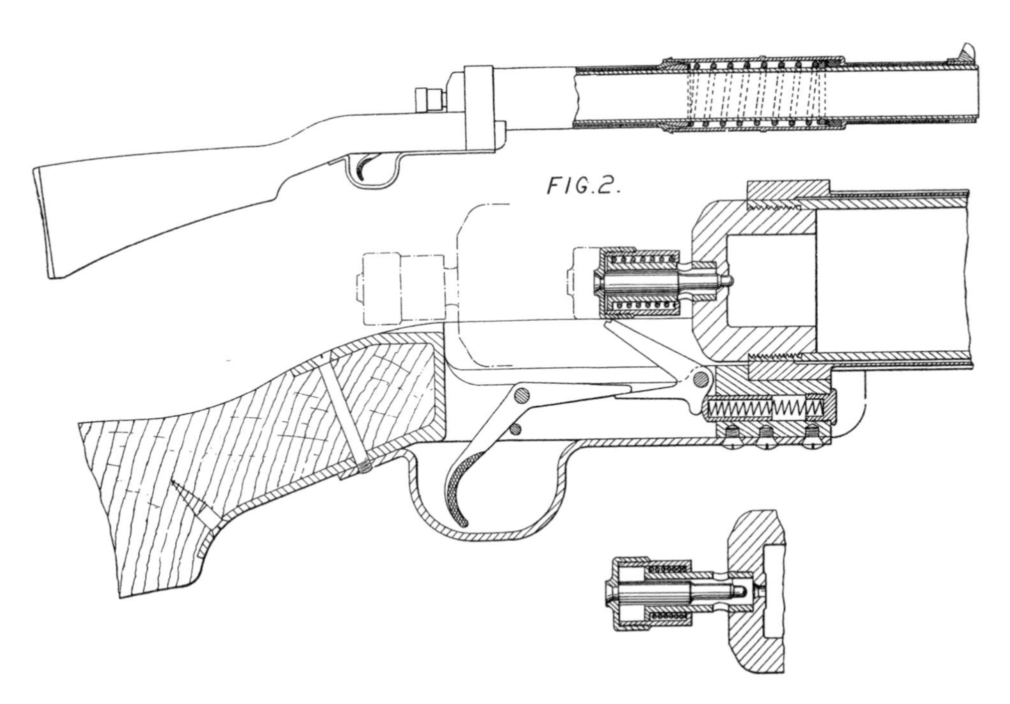

Thring's grenade gun, the subject of UK patent 124,478. These drawings illustrate the trigger mechanism and the recoil system. Note that the breech moves back over the fore-end towards the firer's face.

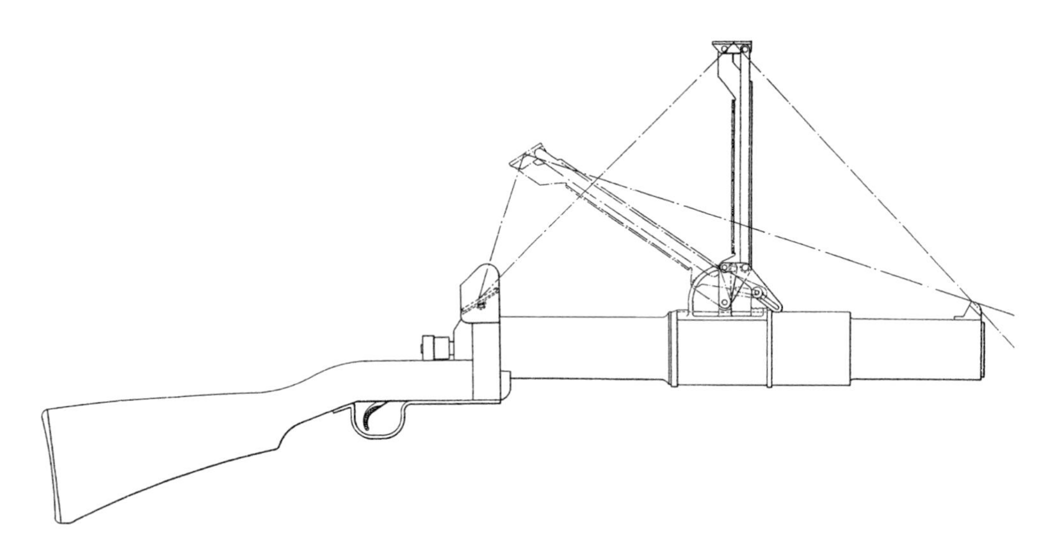

The sighting device on the Thring grenade gun, described in UK patent 124,469. A mirror is mounted at the top of the folding frame.

was simply a smooth-bore barrel (a length of steel tube) clamped to a wooden stock. It was not unlike the M79 grenade launchers used by the US Army in the 1960s except that Thring's device used a recoil-absorbing mechanism. This mechanism consisted of a recoil spring that encircled part of the barrel, and a ring of 'brake blocks' behind the spring, all of which were covered by a tubular casing joined to another tube, inside which was the barrel. This mechanism stayed put while the barrel travelled backwards when the gun was fired. It was rather too complicated to work well.

The Munitions Inventions Department gave the gun a series of trials but by April 1917 it had been turned down because it required special ammunition, was too cumbersome and the recoil was excessive. It is worth noting that when Thring invented his gun and its ammunition, which did not require a rod, rodded grenades were the only sort of rifle grenade available and these were nothing like 100 per cent reliable; the cup discharger had yet to make its appearance. By the time it was turned down, however, the cup discharger was undergoing successful trials. Moreover, the cup discharger was lighter and simpler and did not require special ammunition. Had the cup discharger not been invented it is likely that the Munitions Inventions Department would have persisted with the Thring gun. For his part, Thring entertained loftier thoughts about the usefulness of his invention and envisaged that it would replace the Stokes mortar, a somewhat unrealistic fantasy. He did not take the rejection lying down. Astonishingly, his patent agents (the firm of Kilburn and Strode which still exists) wrote to the parliamentary secretary, Ministry of Munitions, in July to argue their client's case. This was not the sort of thing that patent agents do as a general rule but it appears that Thring was a friend as well as a client. Even so, the letter changed nothing.

But there may have been another explanation for the department's unwillingness to persist with Thring's gun: the Munitions Inventions Department was developing its own design which may have been inspired by it. In the early part of 1918, the department conducted comparative trials with 'various guns for firing grenades' and its own design produced the best results. It was more versatile than the Thring as it did not require special ammunition and the grenade could be launched by both blank and bulleted rounds, using the Lee Enfield rifle mechanism (the Thring had its own design). The grenades which it fired did not have an axial bore to allow the bullet to go through them like with the Viven-Bessière; the bullet actually hit the base of the grenade to launch it. The gun was not intended to be fired from the shoulder and could be fitted with a base plate for resting it on the ground, or with a short shaft, the whole thing weighing in the region of 12 lb. It appears that the barrel which took the grenade was interchangeable with the Burn discharger or a 50 mm design that was evidently under test as well. The 50 mm discharger seems to have been a French design used for firing a grenade with an axial bore. This may have been a Viven-Bessière device.

Another of the grenade guns used in the trial was probably F.V. Lister's converted shotgun for firing Mills grenades for which he filed a patent application in March 1916 (granted as 124,765). Various bomb-throwers for firing special grenades were invented during 1915 and 1916 but none of them proved to be sufficiently interesting to warrant serious consideration. There were, of course, a number of contraptions for throwing hand grenades apart from the catapults and spring guns. These were aids to the thrower rather than substitutes for his arm and included P.D. Malloch's 'hand-device for throwing bombs' that worked on a simple mechanical principle and the 'hand-device for

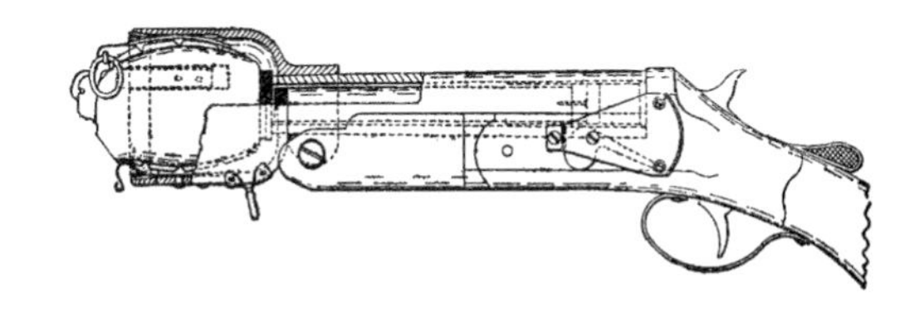

The Lister grenade gun, a converted shotgun, the subject of UK patent 124,765. The triangular shape in front of the hammer is a clinometer. The grenade is retained in the cup by clips.

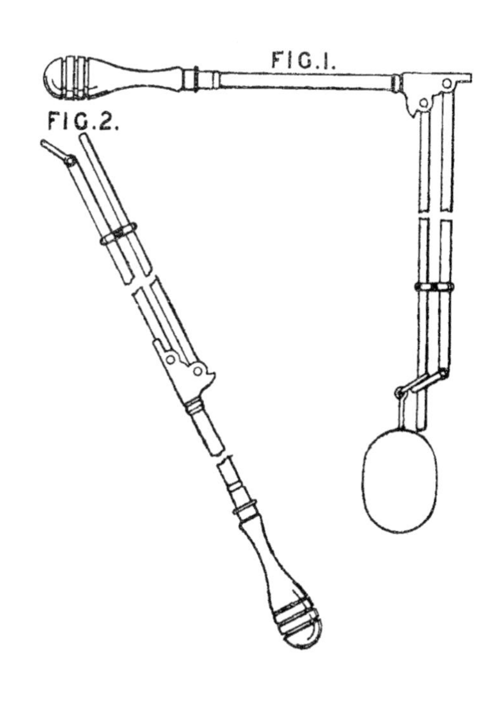

P.D. Malloch's mechanical grenade-thrower (UK Patent 103,379). Note the hook on the end of one arm for pulling the pin.

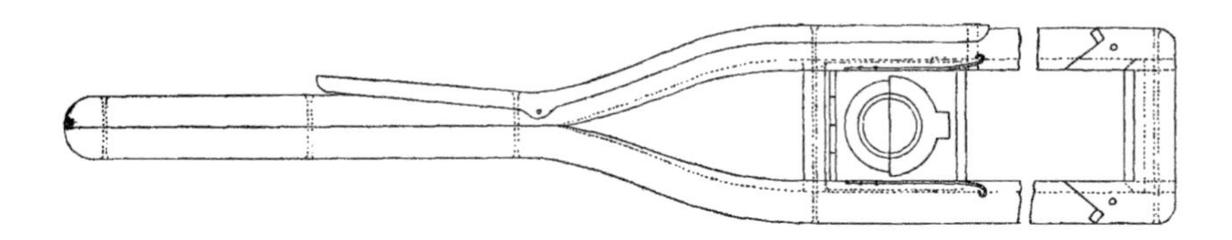

Bomb-throwing bat for throwing the Mills, subject of UK patent 104,376. Gripping the bat's lever releases the bomb-carrier which moves up guides when the bat is swung. Spring clips holding the two-part carrier together slip into special notches, allowing the carrier to open and release the bomb.

throwing the Mills bomb' invented by Storch and Davis, a bat with a sliding bomb-carrier. Neither seems to have excited much interest. The only other device to undergo lengthy trials, including troop trials in France, was the Temple device. This appears to have been a cross between a small trench mortar and a grenade gun and was fed by a magazine.

According to the description in 'Notes on Inventions and New Stores No. 1', published in the spring of 1917, it could be 'carried either on the chest on a breast plate fitted with straps, or on the bayonet boss of the rifle'. It consisted of

> a magazine containing six separate barrels each with a cartridge chamber. Four magazines can be carried on the breast plate and one on the rifle. Each chamber is loaded with a special cartridge which is caused to set back on a pin in the base of the chamber by insertion of the rod of the grenade. The grenade is jerked down towards the base, and the explosion of the cartridge thus caused, forces a disc up the barrel expelling the grenade rod with little noise and with no flash. The safety pin of the grenade is withdrawn automatically in flight by means of a small weight attached to the ring of the safety pin – the set back of the weight on shock of discharge withdrawing the pin. To eject the cartridges, the magazine has to be unscrewed bodily and a rod inserted down each barrel. It is then reloaded and replaced. The range is about 75 yards, and the accuracy depends on the angle at which the apparatus is held either on the chest, or on the rifle. The weight of each magazine loaded is about 3½ lbs.

It raises the question of why this curious device should have been seriously viewed as suitable for front-line use as it seems too absurd to be workable. Moreover, the potential for accidents seems enormous.

Temple brought his invention to France to demonstrate it in the spring of 1917 and 'both forms proved very satisfactory, and attained all the advantages claimed . . . by the inventor'. These evidently concerned accuracy, rate of fire and lack of noise and flash. Remarkably, GHQ seemed to believe that there were other similar devices in Britain just waiting for a comparative trial in France as it asked the Army Council for 'all available throwers of the present pattern, both for firing from the chest and for firing from the rifle [to] be sent out at once for practical trials'. This must have been received with some bafflement. GHQ was no doubt disappointed not to receive a variety of similar devices but merely a note informing them that such things did not exist. So keen was GHQ to try out the Temple device at the Front that it immediately asked for 200 of them and 10,000 cartridges.

Nothing seems to have come of it although a Munitions Inventions Department report from May 1918 mentioned a Temple bomb-thrower which looked promising and for which copper driving bands were not needed for the bombs. A 2 lb charge threw a 220 lb bomb 1,225 yd at 59°. This was clearly not the same device.

One of the last grenades that the Munitions Inventions Department was keen to develop was a 'rebounding grenade' that did not explode on impact but rebounded to explode in the air. It was a percussion grenade based on the Stewart pattern. However, lest anyone think that this was another weird idea from the Heath Robinson school, a rebounding mortar bomb was already being used by the German Army (described in Chapter 2). It was the effectiveness of this device that persuaded the Munitions Inventions Department that the British Army should have one as well. It never got one.

CHAPTER 8

A Tale of Two Stokes – Mortars 1915–18

If there was one outstanding invention of the war, it was the Stokes mortar. This remarkably simple weapon was not only vastly superior to any other mortar but it was cheap to make and significantly increased the firepower available to the infantry. Like Mills, Stokes had no experience of weapons before he set about designing the mortar but whereas Mills found little difficulty in getting his grenade accepted Stokes met considerable resistance to his design. This was partly because his inexperience led him down blind alleys and partly because of the changing responsibilities of the various research and development departments and the creation of new ones. It meant that no single department had sole jurisdiction – there were too many cooks. It was to prove a long hard road for Stokes before the mortar was finally accepted. The poor performance of the early designs of the ammunition did not make it any easier.

Wilfrid Stokes and his mortar, demonstrating its lightness and the ease with which it could be carried. Initially, Stokes crews carried their mortars in this fashion but they were too easily picked out by German observers, who quickly brought down a barrage on them. (The Times History of the War)

In late 1914, when Frederick Wilfrid Stokes learned of the Army's desperate need for trench mortars, he was fifty-four years old and chairman and managing director of an engineering company in Ipswich called Ransomes & Rapier, which made very unwarlike machinery such as cranes, pumps and gas cylinders. Although he knew nothing about guns, like so many leading inventors of the time, he was a good engineer who knew how to solve engineering problems. In 1918 he claimed that it was exactly because of his lack of knowledge of things military that he was able to come up with such a simple design. He abhorred the tendency towards increasing complexity and advocated the setting up of a new department, the 'Simplification of Designs Department' which if it did its job could reduce production times and costs. Needless to say, no one took him seriously. But he had a point. It was partly because his design was so simple that he had so much trouble getting

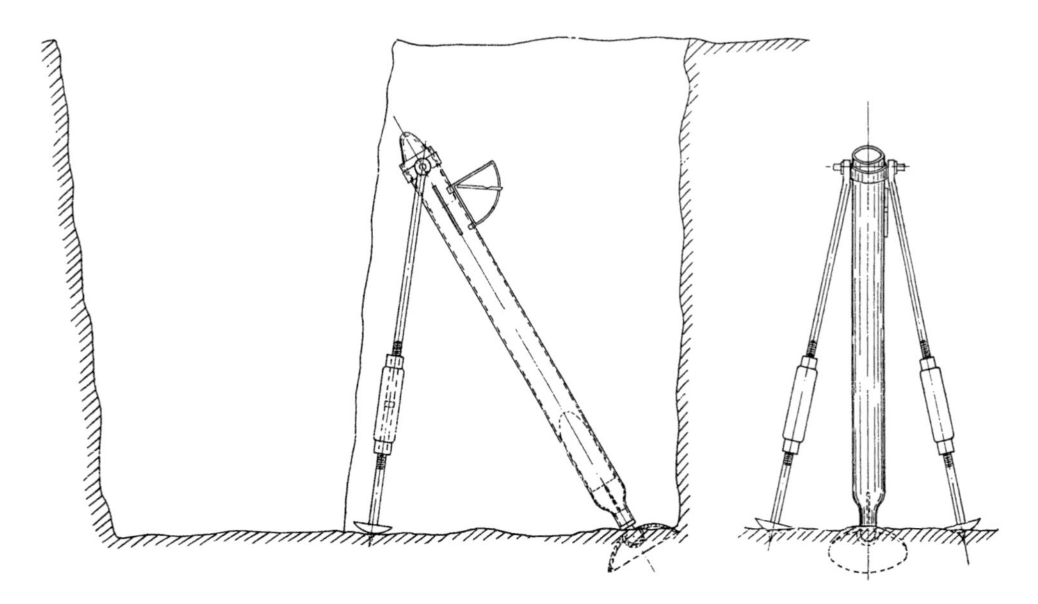

Wilfrid Stokes's original drawings for his mortar which he sent to the War Office in December 1914. (T 173/453)

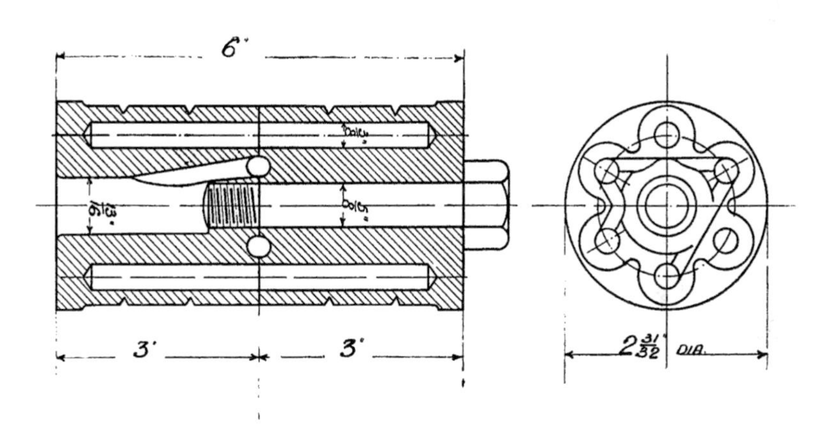

The bouncing bomb originally intended to be fired from the mortar. Note the six explosive compartments, the central propellant compartment and the connecting passages. (T 173/453)

it accepted, although in fairness to the departments that dealt with him, the early mortar and ammunition were decidedly imperfect. By the end of the war, his mortar was held up as the epitome of simplicity and effectiveness in weapon design.

Stokes was asked to design something to help ease the Army's predicament by a journalist friend who had visited the Front. In a remarkably short time he came up with a design of a simple length of tubing supported on two adjustable legs which fired a rather more complicated shell made of cast iron. This consisted of seven chambers, one of which housed the propellant,

The first mortar made by Wilfrid Stokes which he used for his initial tests. (T 173/453)

the other six containing explosive charges. The idea was that the shell should land in an enemy trench where one of the chambers would detonate and send the shell to another location until the next one exploded sending it to another and so on until the six chambers had all been fired. It could have been called a rebounding bomb. The tube or barrel had an integral firing spike in the base which detonated the propellant when the shell slid down the barrel and hit it. In this way, the mortar could fire as many shells as could be slid down the barrel, one after the other. The recoil was absorbed by a bowl of cast iron at the base of the barrel.

He sent the design to the War Office in December 1914 who thought it was unworkable and turned it down. Undeterred, he went back to the drawing board and 'acting on the courage of my own conviction . . . I had a primitive gun made. At the works of Messrs. Ransomes and Rapier, Ltd, Ipswich, out a piece of drawn tube, and a shell out of a piece of bar.' A trial firing shot the first shell to a greater distance than he had anticipated and he 'nearly took refuge in a cottage'. Encouraged by the results, he went back to the War Office and a trial was arranged at the Shoeburyness Test Centre for 30 January 1915. However, this did not go at all well. Accuracy and range were unacceptably poor. The Director of Artillery turned down the mortar after a second trial the following month.

Stokes remained optimistic, though, and concluded that although the concept was sound he had much to do to turn it into a workable weapon system. He decided that the 'bouncing cracker bomb' was not such a good idea after all after trying different approaches, none of which succeeded, and proceeded to design a more conventional shell. He was also told that the War Office was not interested in a bouncing bomb (although it would change its mind in 1918 when it discovered the Germans had one). Further, he realized that his knowledge of propellants and explosives was so limited that using black powder for both was the only way forward, although he soon moved on to experimenting with high explosives. He had to learn as he went.

Over the next few months, he devoted his weekends to developing the mortar and shell, conducting trials of his own to test his modifications. The mortar itself was easier to improve than the shell, which was something of a headache, but he was determined to produce a weapon and shell that would be of real value to the war effort. As far as the mortar was concerned he had four objectives:

1. Simplicity in manufacture.
2. Simplicity and speed in firing.
3. Lightness and portability.
4. Quickness and ease in setting up, and change of objective.

Initially, the barrel was made by boring a steel tube but the quicker process of cold drawing was found to produce accurate barrels. The bottom end was bottlenecked with machinery used in the manufacture of gas cylinders, readily at hand in Ransomes & Rapier's works. The legs on the first production mortars were a pair of inverted A-frames with elevating and traversing gear although his earliest designs had even simpler strut-like supports that were quite flimsy in comparison to the legs the mortar ended up with in the field. The early A-frames proved to be rather difficult to set up properly in the field and liable to damage when set up incorrectly, so after about 2,000 mortars had been produced a heavier tubular design replaced them. When the war ended, a refinement of nested springs was in development to absorb some of the recoil and prevent damage to the mortar if it had been badly set up.

This example of the first service pattern of the mortar is set on a display stand. The first type of leg is clearly visible. Note the shell with the fuse facing the camera and the shell-release device on the side of the barrel near the muzzle. (T 173/453)

The second service pattern with stronger legs. The shell-release device has been omitted. Note the periscope and canvas muzzle cap hanging from the elevating gear. One of the three depressions in the base plate can be seen; the middle one is occupied by the breech end of the mortar. These allowed some degree of traverse. (T 173/453)

The design of the striker proved to be more difficult than Stokes had first thought because as he put it in 1918 'I started off on the wrong track'. Originally, the striker was pointed so that it struck the propellant cartridge in the centre of the shell, the gases blowing past it. However, fouling from the remnants of the cartridge was severe and there was no chamber in which the propellant could be burned efficiently. He tried a square-ended striker with a completely enclosed chamber for the cartridge. The results were disastrous. The shell split and the barrel nearly burst. After that, he made pressure calculations first to check if what he was proposing was safe.

With the calculations he now made, he determined the correct thickness of the cold-drawn barrel to withstand the pressure generated by the propellant in the expansion chamber at the breech end. The chamber was important to the operation of the mortar. The propellant he eventually chose was ballistite and this could generate a pressure of more than 40 tons per square inch when it completely filled a chamber. The expansion chamber reduced the pressure to about 1.75 tons per square inch for a 3 in bore. He tested the calculations with a barrel that was reduced to a thickness of 1/16 in for 2 ft. Firing ten rounds from it proved that it suffered no deformation.

After much trial and error, Stokes at last came up with a workable design of shell. He had a lot of trouble with the shell tumbling in flight because it would not stabilize nose first, a problem that was caused by the unrifled barrel. Since he did not want to put rifling in it, he put fins on the shell. Although this worked, the design was for some reason unacceptable to the War Office so Stokes had to start again. The final design was a simple cylinder, originally made of cast iron but quickly changed to steel tubing which contained about three times as much explosive as an 18-pounder shell. The ends of the cylinder were screwed in place and the diameters of these had to be precision machined within very close tolerances to ensure that windage losses remained consistent.

To overcome the fouling problems with the original propellant cartridge, Stokes designed a cartridge chamber for the shell that projected downwards from the rear of the shell and which was vented to allow the gases to escape and propel the shell. The size, number and position of holes had to be determined empirically and it soon became apparent that the cartridge holder had to be made from high-quality material to avoid splitting when the cartridge was fired. The propellant was contained in a shotgun cartridge case. Various cases were tried and he eventually selected Eley as the best (the 3 in mortar used a 12-bore while the later 4 in used a 4-bore). Having selected ballistite, a combination of nitroglycerine and nitrocellulose made by Nobel, as the most suitable propellant and having determined the right amount of fulminate of mercury for the initiating cap, Stokes was dismayed to discover that on one day things would go well while on the next he could not reproduce the same results. He made adjustments to correct the faults only to find that the following day the same problem reappeared. This phenomenon bedevilled him for some time before he discovered that the unpredictable variations were due to changes in temperature.

In the meantime, he had shown the improved mortar to the War Office once more and trials were held in March and April at Woolwich. These were reasonably successful and all that remained was approval from the Deputy Director of Artillery, Major-General Bingham (this was before he joined the Design Department of the Ministry of Munitions). Although GHQ had submitted repeated requests for a new mortar and the Stokes fitted the bill, Bingham told Stokes that the Army already had enough mortars and did not need a new one. He refused to sanction its manufacture. It seemed that all the time and money that Stokes had invested in his mortar (he had spent about six months and £3,000 on its development) had been for nothing.

However, all was not lost. By now, the Ministry of Munitions had been created and it decided to take an interest in the mortar, arranging yet another trial. At this latest demonstration, Stokes met Captain Sutton, RE, who had returned wounded from the Dardanelles but with the specific instruction to find a suitable mortar for use in the peninsula where the mortar situation was dire. The Stokes mortar impressed him and he persuaded Lloyd George and Churchill to attend another demonstration on 30 June. They too were impressed with it and Lloyd George agreed to the manufacture of the Stokes mortar and its shells. There was one proviso, however. All the wrinkles had to be ironed out first so that it worked perfectly.

Even Stokes had to admit, it was still far from perfect. For one thing, the shell's fuse was not giving the best performance. A solution to the fuse problem was suggested by a Captain West of the Royal Engineers (who may have been the same West who invented the Spring Gun): why not use the Mills fuse and lever mechanism. Stokes agreed. The time fuse that was eventually used was an adaptation of the Mills mechanism but it went through at least three modifications before an acceptable fuse was developed.

In August the mortar underwent another series of trials, this time for the Ordnance Committee. They agreed that it was better than the 3.7 in mortar but were unhappy with the shells, which still needed improvement. Nevertheless, Lloyd George instructed that 200 mortars should now be manufactured. To the displeasure of the Trench Warfare Department, Stokes proceeded to organize about forty companies, including Ransomes & Rapier, to fulfil the order. Somewhat pointlessly, the department countermanded this and placed the orders with firms of its own choice. The official sanction to make the mortar came from the Ordnance Board in September. However, Munitions Design decreed that 1,000 shells had to be successfully fired from six Stokes mortars before it could be used on operations. It was not until yet more trials had been completed in March 1916, this time to look at its rapid-fire capabilities, that the mortar at last became operational and even then only smoke rounds were fired from it.

It was firing high explosive before too long, which it could do at a considerable rate – between twenty and thirty rounds a minute. The limiting factor was the skill of the loader and the supply of ammunition. Robert Graves recalled the battalion trench mortar officer

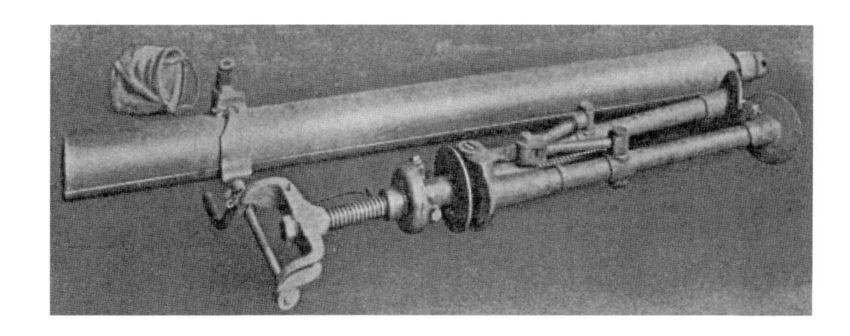

The legs have been removed for transport. (T 173/453)

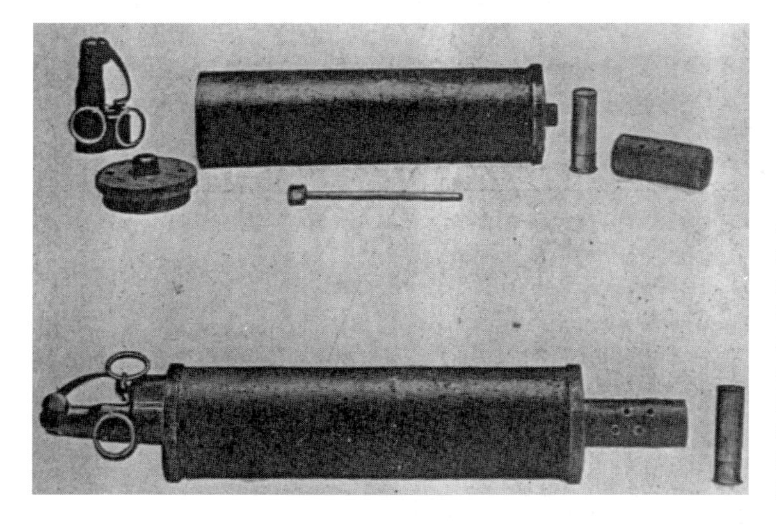

High-explosive 3 in round. The top view shows the components including the cartridge and its holder, detonator and fuse mechanism. The latter is a modified Mills mechanism. Note the holes in the cartridge holder. (T 173/453)

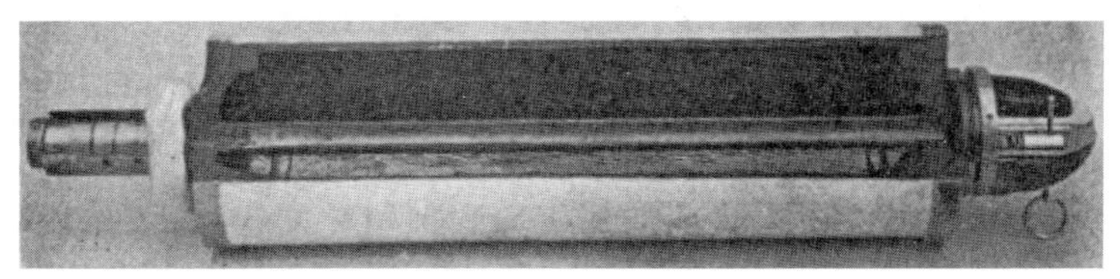

A 4 in gas shell sectionalized. Note the propellant increment ring around the cartridge holder. (T 173/453)

enthusing over his two new Stokes mortars which he described as 'beauties', explaining that he could 'put four or five shells into the air at once'. Yet the first Stokes did not always perform as expected. During a raid by the Royal Welch Fusiliers in April 1916, the two mortars detailed to silence a machine-gun developed faults and failed to fire more than a few rounds. But on most occasions the Stokes did sterling work in destroying enemy machine-guns and trench mortars. Frank Richards was full of praise for them because of their high rate of fire and condemned the 3.7 in mortars they replaced as 'clumsy' and more dangerous 'to ourselves than they were to the enemy, having a short range and the shell often bursting in the gun'.

The original Stokes had a system whereby it was fired in the same way as the existing service mortars, in other words, slowly and with a lanyard. It was actually fitted with an arrangement at the muzzle so that the shell did not drop on to the firing pin until the lanyard was pulled. This was slow and tedious, not to say unnecessary, but it had been imposed on the mortar for reasons of safety. However, the thinking behind this had the existing service mortars in mind and failed to take into account the entirely different firing method of the Stokes. The system was quickly dispensed with as it became apparent that it was superfluous.

After the 3 in Stokes entered service, very little was changed apart from the legs and it remained much the same at the end of the war as when it was introduced in 1916. Later, a 4 in model was introduced but the 3 in was the more common type. Improvements were made to the elevating and traversing gear to make the Stokes more accurate and stronger and a deflection scale was added so that correct deflections could be read for every 5° of elevation. This was necessary because altering the elevation affected the traverse. The shell also remained little changed apart from slight modifications that became necessary to help production and to correct minor defects that field use threw up. The propellant charges consisted of three 12-bore cartridges with different fillings which gave ranges of 50–430 yd. The maximum range was achieved with the red cartridge but it caused a lot of prematures and

A view of the Stokes clinometer showing the long-range settings. Range in yards and time of flight are marked. The manufacturer's name is also visible – N.E. Hamsay of Newcastle and London. (T 173/453)

A Portuguese Stokes crew near Neuve Chapelle, June 1917. Note the wooden bed for the base plate, introduced to prevent the mortar sinking in soft ground. (IWM)

casualties were common so it was withdrawn. However, Captain Newton of the Second Army Workshop found a remedy. He used a 12-bore cartridge of propellant as a primary charge and supplemented it with a ring of additional ballistite placed round the cartridge holder. The ring was made of fabric and had to be kept dry.

Not only did this solve the problem of prematures but it increased the range by more than 60 per cent so that the 3 in Stokes could throw a shell to 700 yd. The ballistite ring was later replaced by cordite rings which extended the range to 800 yd. Unfortunately, the cordite had the disadvantage of producing a considerable flash as well as blast at the muzzle. Moreover, there were difficulties in getting hold of cordite of the right thickness; it was essential that the propellant did not burn too quickly otherwise the pressure in the barrel would become too great. To get round these flaws, experiments were conducted with EC3 sporting powder which was flashless and gave little blast. Photographic celluloid was used to contain the powder but it was not entirely satisfactory as it did not burn consistently, which caused erratic shooting. This had not been resolved before the war ended.

By mid-1917 the Stokes had surpassed the poor reputation of the early mortars and was being hailed as a battle-winning weapon by GHQ which issued notes about its accomplishments to encourage similar endeavours. 'Employment of 3-inch Stokes Mortars in Recent Fighting' issued in June 1917 (which could mean that it referred to Arras in April or the more recent battle at Messines) gave several examples. A preparatory barrage of 4 minutes prior to a brigade attack had the objective of destroying five machine-guns at 550 yd range for which two ballistite rings with a green cartridge were used. 'The machine-guns did not fire and the attack was successful.' On another occasion, a party of Germans was seen to be setting up a light mortar. A Stokes fired on them and the second round made them retreat, leaving the mortar exposed. The Stokes fired eight rounds for registration and then proceeded to destroy the mortar with three direct hits. The Stokes was even used to shepherd potential prisoners forward from their trenches so that they had no choice but to surrender.

By the middle of 1918 another increase in range was needed and Newton proposed putting tail fins on the bombs, which must have struck Stokes as rather ironic considering that his proposal to use tails had been turned down in 1915. Although the tails increased the range to 1,800 yd, the accuracy left a lot to be desired. In the end, a tailed bomb of a French design was adopted. Following this, experiments with lighter bombs (7 lb as opposed to 11 lb) led to another French bomb being adopted. This was a streamlined Brandt design (UK patent 131,258) used with the company's pneumatic mortar which was fired with compressed air. This was in service with the French Army. The Brandt mortar shell made use of the incremental ring charges and it was possible for the Stokes to fire a Brandt shell to 2,500 yd. The French charges did not produce accurate shooting, though, so a British charge was developed. The Brandt shell did not enter service before the close of hostilities.

Six months after the introduction of the 3 in Stokes, the pistol head igniter with Bickford fuse being used on the shells was still giving a lot of trouble. Prematures and blinds were far too common so when it was declared obsolete it was replaced with an all-ways fuse (No. 146) but this turned out to be dangerous to handle and it did not perform well. Improvements to the fuse reduced the prematures to an acceptable level but blinds were still occurring too often and by the end of the war the problem had still not been entirely eliminated.

On 27 July 1915 Stokes filed two patent applications, one for the mortar, the other for the shell with the cartridge in the base, using the same firm of patent agents as Thring was to use for his grenade gun. The patents were subsequently granted as 10,882/15 and 10,883/15. On 11 January 1916 the Ministry of Munitions offered Stokes £10,000 as a one-off payment for a licence to manufacture the mortar and its ammunition. Moreover, he was assured that the sum would not be reduced by the special tax on war profits; if he had to be pay the tax the Ministry would refund the money. The Ministry also offered a royalty of £1 per mortar and 1*d* (approximately 0.4p) per shell manufactured. The terms also allowed Stokes to apply for foreign patents provided publication came after the end of the war (which, in effect, meant that he would have to wait until after the war to file any foreign application) and permitted the mortar to be manufactured by or for Allied governments, provided the UK gave prior approval. Two days after the offer, Stokes accepted.

The Stokes formed the basis of a new medium 6 in mortar introduced in mid-1917 to replace the 2 in medium which was far from reliable as the ammunition was prone to prematures. In addition, its range was inadequate. This new mortar was a development of the Stokes undertaken by Newton who was now at the Trench Warfare Department, although he embarked on its development while still at the Second Army Workshop. He set out a list of eight requirements that the new mortar had to satisfy.

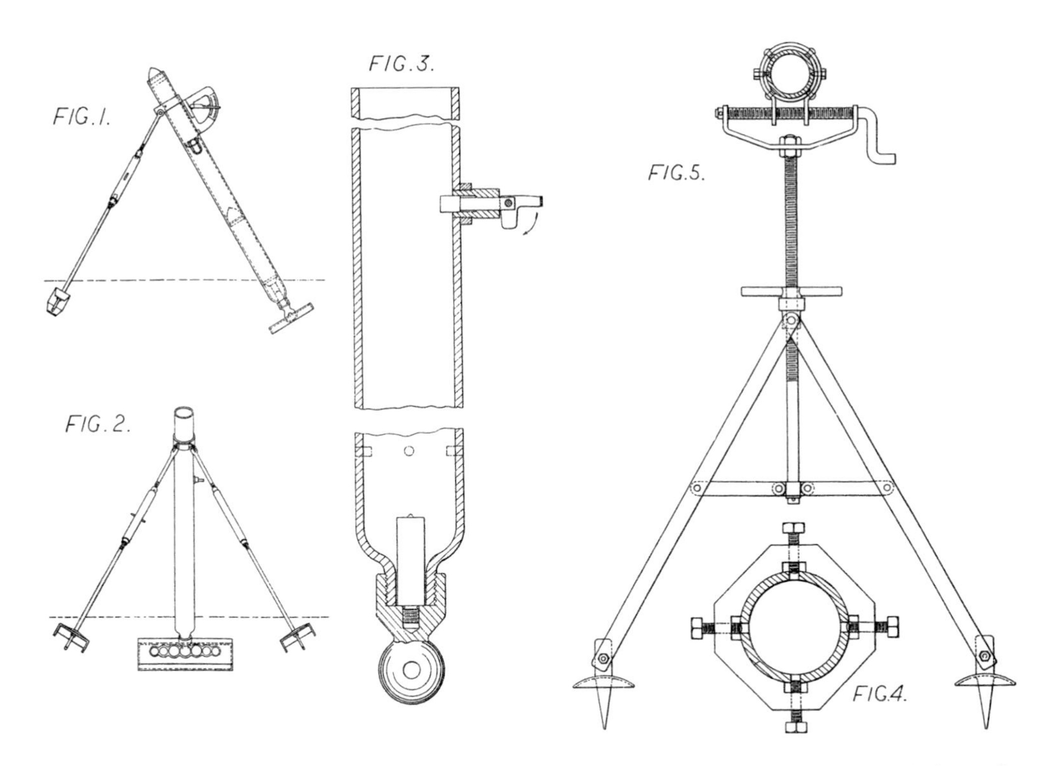

Left: *The drawings from Stokes's first mortar patent, 10,882. Note the cartridge holder on the base of the shell in fig. 1 and the shell-releasing device illustrated in figs 2 and 3. Note also the firing pin and that it can be removed with the base cap.* Right: *Legs for the mortar as illustrated in 10,882.*

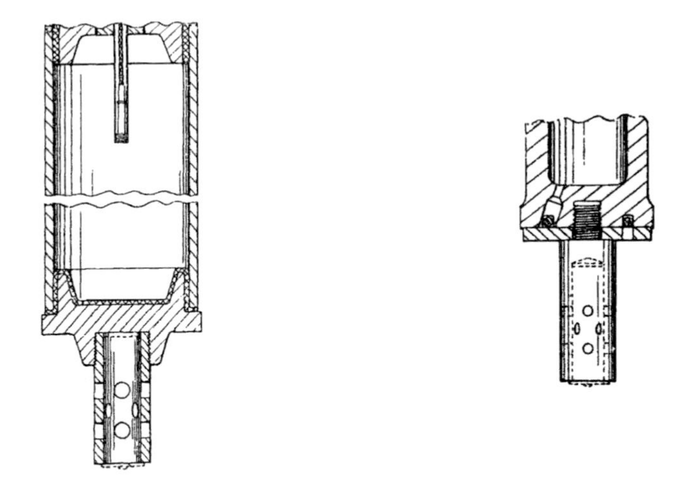

Left: *Stokes mortar bomb as illustrated in UK patent 10,883. The propellant cartridge holder is screwed into the base and is pierced with several holes to allow the gases to escape. Note the thickness of the base. The cartridge is the dotted line in the holder.* Right: *An alternative shell base described in 10,883. This is a time-fused shell. The hole on the right-hand side circles the base and enters the explosive cavity as shown on the left-hand side. This passage contains the time fuse which is ignited by the flash of the propellant on discharge.*

1. There must be no flash and little noise when fired.
2. High rate of fire.
3. The weight of the weapon must be at a minimum.
4. The range should be as great as possible, the weight of the barrel being the limiting factor.
5. The bomb had to convey the maximum amount of explosive.
6. The bomb had to be capable of demolition work yet destroy wire and personnel without making big craters.
7. The fragmentation of the bomb should be such that the danger zone was confined to an area occupied by the enemy and no splinters should be projected back into friendly troops.
8. The mortar and its ammunition should be easy to manufacture and easy to use in the field.

A 6-inch diameter for the barrel was a compromise that would meet these criteria, capable of delivering 12 lb of explosive. A 6-inch bomb would have better penetration characteristics than the 2-inch toffee-apple bombs, which were about 9 inches in diameter. Providing the bomb with a modified 107 Newton fuse ensured that instantaneous detonation would destroy wire entanglements without producing craters. Gun cotton yarn was chosen as the propellant although this was not a popular choice but there were very few prematures or accidents using this propellant. By the end of the war, 38,000 6 in mortar rounds were being manufactured every week.

As far as speed of operation of the mortar was concerned, Newton realized that the obvious answer was to use a system similar to that of the Stokes. Moreover, this reduced the number of working parts to a minimum which in the muddy conditions of the trenches was an important consideration; mud was a serious problem with early mortars, fouling the firing mechanisms. Newton did not adopt the striker and cartridge-holder method of firing the bombs of the Stokes but elected to use defective small arms cartridges fitted with integral strikers and a flat stud in the barrel to arrest the bomb's passage down the barrel, similar to that used on the old 3.7 in and 4 in rifled muzzle-loaded mortars. The use of the cartridges helped to prevent misfires and was cheap whereas the cartridge holder used on Stokes shells had to be machined from steel and drilled with holes. The cartridges contained gun cotton yarn dusted with black powder.

Newton chose to adopt a slightly different system from Stokes because of the occasional difficulty created by the striker being slightly eccentric which caused misfires. If the percussion cap was eccentric this produced the same problem. Because of this, the striker used by the 6 in was later adapted for use with the 3 in and 4 in Stokes. He also devised a safer method of dealing with misfires which was a 'very unpleasant business' especially for an inexperienced crew. Instead of having to remove a misfire by hand, he designed a 'miss fire plug through which a slow burning time fuze could be inserted'. By lighting the fuse, a misfired round (often caused by a defective cap) could be ejected safely.

Newton discovered that by adding slow-burning cordite or smokeless powders to the gun cotton yarn contained in the cambric bags, the range could be doubled from 1,000 yd to 2,000 yd without having to increase the thickness of the barrel; it was ultimately thickened slightly. It was through this discovery that Newton had the idea for the ring charges later adopted for the Stokes, increasing its range from 300 yd to over 800 yd, without having to make any alterations to the mortar. Having proved successful with the Stokes, the same principle was applied to the 9.45 in mortar. It helped to solve the problem of fizzles while improving the accuracy at 1,100 yd from 93 yd at 45° elevation to about 12 yd. This improvement was possible because of the increase in consistency of propellant gas pressure.

The additional charges for the 6 in were contained in cambric bags rather than rings as the design of the bomb would not allow rings to be placed round its tail. Four bags of gun cotton were used and up to four bags of cordite could be added. As with other mortars, the 6 in produced a muzzle flash which could be a nuisance when trying to conceal a position from the enemy. Guy Chapman noted the 'violet flame of a 6 inch Stokes repeated time and time again' as it fired in the twilight of early evening. The first 6 in Newton mortars (also known as the Stokes-Newton) were cast in brass from used cartridge cases, then machined. Newton also experimented with adding rifling using machinery made locally (this was while he was still at the Second Army Workshop) but he abandoned the idea when it became apparent that it was an unnecessary complication which would inevitably slow down production. Its rate of fire was eight rounds a minute.

The increase in range with the extra charges meant that the mounting was stressed more than originally intended and its wooden platform had to be strengthened with a sub-bed which provided a larger surface area and increased the mortar's stability. The elevating and traversing gear also had to be strengthened. These were a source of considerable problems in the field. They consisted of two guys of threaded steel bolts, anchored to the base by extension bars. The threaded bolts could be screwed into open receivers that were hooked to the barrel. By screwing the bolts in or out the mortar could be trained on to a given target but they had an unfortunate tendency to break and had to be replaced by stronger ones. At much the same time, the method of attaching them to the barrel was changed.

But none of this did anything to remedy a basic flaw in the gear: if the barrel was traversed, the elevation was altered and if the elevation was changed the traverse was affected. Moreover, the scale inscribed on the barrel was not mathematically accurate. This was of little consequence when the ranges were 1,000 yd or less but as soon as the extra charges increased the range it became a serious problem. Vickers and Armstrong Whitworth were asked to find a solution but one was not forthcoming before the end of the war. There was also disagreement over the worth of any change to the mortar that would make it more complicated.

Newton's 50 lb finned bombs remained in service from the introduction of the mortar despite problems when extra propellant bags were used. The increased charge tended to buckle the tail. Various remedies were tried including corrugating the fins to strengthen them and putting stiffening struts between them but the problem persisted.

No other mortar entered British service, apart from the Livens oil can mortar (*see* Chapter 9) although many were presented to the research departments for their approval. Some underwent trials. A French design, the Claude was trialled in 1917 but it appeared to suffer from prematures although later French trials at Bourges disproved this. The most important of all the criteria that any mortar had to satisfy was simplicity. Anything that was deemed to be complex did not really stand a chance. Many weapons fell into this category, rifled mortars included. A company called the Midland Gun Company designed a 3 in trench mortar with a rifled barrel which it called the BEF Trench Howitzer. The inspiration for this device had evidently been the many unexploded trench mortar shells lying on captured enemy territory due to faulty ammunition and careless gunners who, when stressed, often failed to withdraw the safety pins before firing. It was designed to have a range of 1,500 yd and had a specially designed, muzzle-loading shell with a copper driving band. There was a foolproof detonation device which decreased the percentage of duds and speeded up the rate of fire. It was alleged to be capable of firing thirty rounds a minute. The Munitions Inventions Department turned it down.

An even more complicated weapon was a magazine-fed device with a rifled barrel submitted by Captain Stanley Frederick Stokes, Royal Engineers, who was unrelated to Wilfrid Stokes of Ransomes & Rapier. This was supposed to fire shells at an incredible rate, machine-gun fashion. When Captain Stokes approached the Munitions Inventions Department in August 1915, he was unaware of the other Stokes. The captain's mortar had a

Captain Stanley Stokes's mortar in the closed firing position with one round in the breech. A loaded magazine is ready to feed its six shells into the mortar. A publicity shot from a brochure produced by Alley & MacLellan Ltd. (MUN 7/273)

Another shot from the Alley & MacLellan brochure showing the open position. The mortar weighed 209 lb not including ammunition. (MUN 7/273)

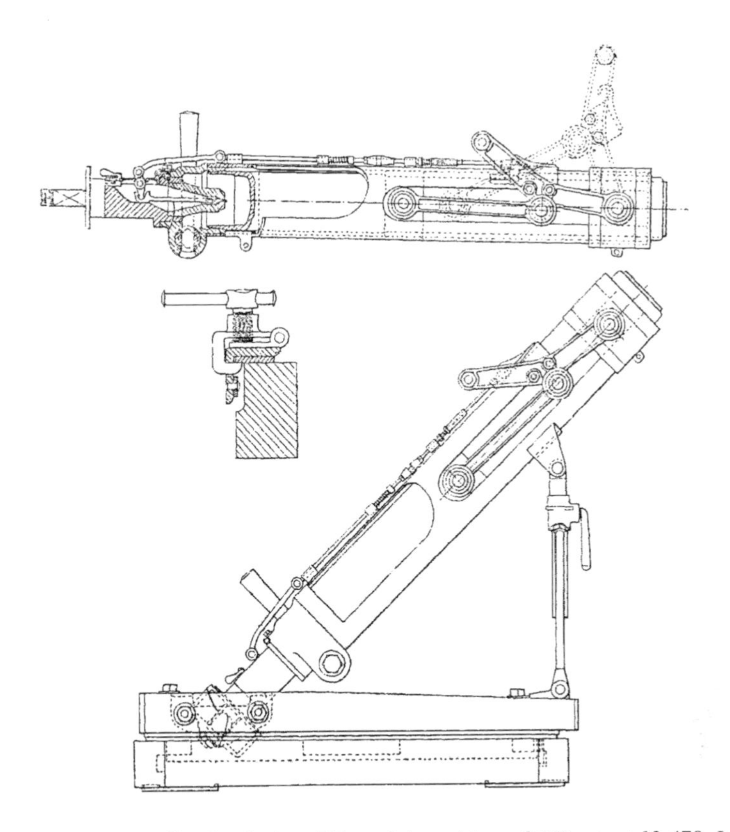

The mortar invented by Captain Stanley Stokes, RE, and the subject of UK patent 12,478. Its complexity compared with Wilfrid Stokes's mortar is easy to see.

3.25 in bore and a range of 1,000 yd, firing a 10 lb shell. The department was not keen on it so Captain Stokes took it to the engineering firm of Beard & Fitch who undertook to develop it. The cost of the modifications was estimated at £100–£200. The first trial was held in November 1915, followed by another at the Grenade School, Marsden Park, Godstone on 18 December, this time with the Mk II. This second trial went badly, with a lot of misfires and jams, a shell finally bursting in the barrel so that the chamber burst. The next round fortunately misfired, otherwise a bad accident might have occurred. It was rejected on 27 January 1916.

In February Captain Stokes injured his hand, breaking a couple of fingers, while experimenting with shells for the mortar. His medical board proceedings file suggests that the weapon was being taken up but this was wishful thinking on Stokes's part who wilfully misled the board. In the meantime, showing remarkable faith in his invention, Stokes had proceeded to file patent applications in August 1915, which subsequently became UK patents 12,477/15 and 12,478/15 although they were not granted until 1919 by which time it had become rather academic. In June the New Trench Gun Syndicate obtained the patent rights. The design was modified by engineers Alley & MacLellan, the previous firm having lost patience and cut their loses. In September 1916 Alley & MacLellan spent yet more time and money perfecting the gun to fire fifty 4 in, 10 lb shells per minute. By now, the costs had escalated to over £400. It made no difference, the mortar was still rejected.

Following Captain Stokes's medical board proceedings, much to his chagrin he found he was to be posted to India and began to feel unfairly put upon by the authorities who were not in the least bit sympathetic to his cause. He returned to Chatham Barracks in September. In the meantime, his wife wrote to Lloyd George to plead her husband's case and her letter was passed to the Munitions Inventions Department who told her that the mortar had been rejected. Captain Stokes was nothing if not persistent. He never accepted any rejection as final and kept up his campaign to get his weapon accepted.

A report in January 1918 listed the mortar's shortcomings. It was not mobile enough. The parts were difficult to keep free of rust; it was highly susceptible to mud and water. It was dangerous when it jammed – the operator was liable to get his head blown off. If the striker broke, it was far from easy to replace. The mortar needed an excessive number of spares. Fouling by unburned celluloid caused misfires. It was considered highly improbable that the weapon would ever enter service. This was a polite way of rejecting a dangerous and unreliable contraption that could have caused a disproportionate number of friendly casualties.

There were a number of mortars that worked on the principles of expanding liquids, i.e. hydraulic mortars. Gogu Constantinesco, a Rumanian engineer, and W. Haddon, both of the Haddon Engineering Works in Alperton, Middlesex, devised such a mortar and filed a patent application on 19 June 1916. This was eventually granted as UK patent 16,280. At about the same time, Constantinesco was in the process of designing a hydraulic interrupter gear for aircraft machine-guns to enable them to be fired through the propeller without shooting the propeller to pieces. This was based on one of his earlier inventions, a hydraulic drill used in

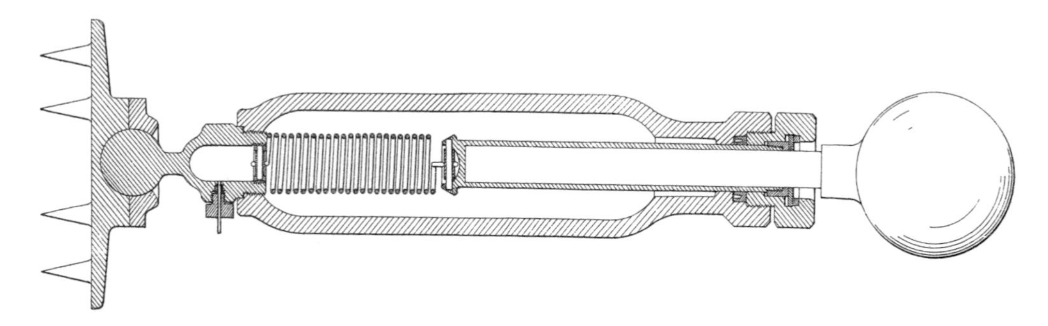

Gogu Constantinesco invented this hydraulic mortar (UK patent 16,280) in 1916. This drawing illustrates one embodiment for firing toffee-apple rounds. Note the fluid chamber at the breech.

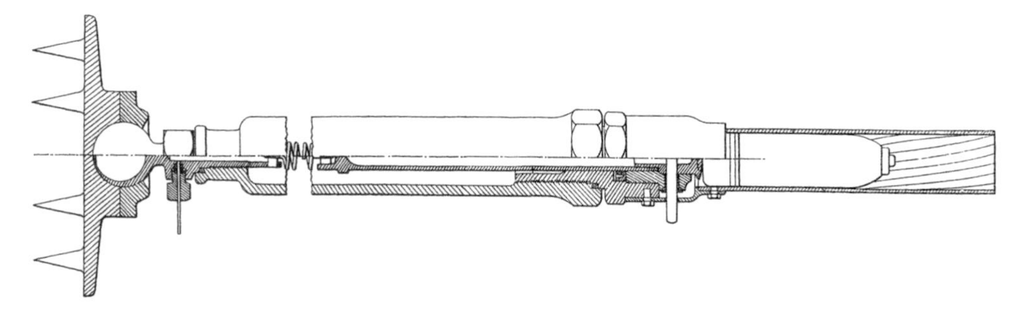

Another embodiment of Constantinesco's invention showing a rifled barrel for firing 75 mm shells.

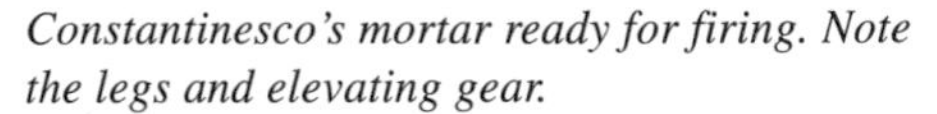

Constantinesco's mortar ready for firing. Note the legs and elevating gear.

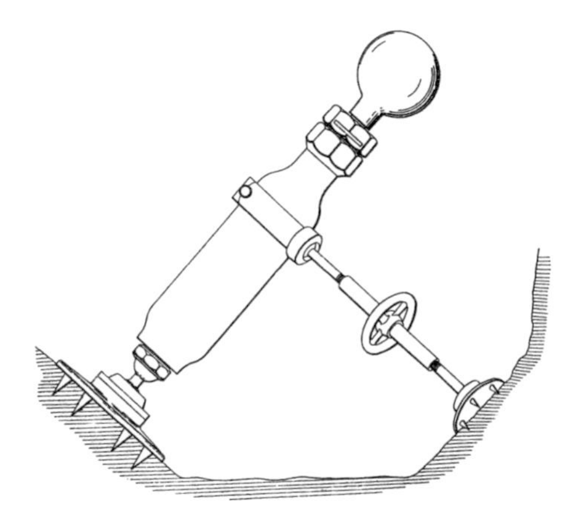

Side view of the hydraulic mortar.

mining. The interrupter gear entered service in 1917 and was in general use by the end of the war. The interrupter gear eventually won him an award from the Royal Commission on Awards to Inventors. With J.R. Middleton, he filed a second patent application for another mortar in March 1917 which was granted as UK patent 128,595 but the piston in this one was operated by explosion of a propellant.

He was not so fortunate with his mortars as he was with his interrupter gear. They were both rejected by the Munitions Inventions Department. The truth was that irrespective of any merits in its favour, a hydraulic mortar was not a practical weapon for the trenches. It was an ingenious device, and no doubt Constantinesco was an expert when it came to hydraulics, but his mortar was too complex and would have required specialist equipment and personnel to maintain it. The one described in UK patent 16,280 was intended to fire 75 mm artillery shells. It consisted of a cylinder, mounted on a ball joint, in which was a piston that was drawn back towards the base by a powerful spring. A rifled barrel was mounted on the mouth of the cylinder and a shear pin or disc at the mouth held the piston in a cocked position. The shell was inserted in the barrel and the head of the piston abutted the base of the shell. A chamber at the bottom of the cylinder and below the spring was pumped full of liquid (water or oil), the pressure rising until it reached the correct level, shearing the pin and allowing the piston to propel the shell up the barrel. A major disadvantage of the hydraulic mortar was the necessity of pumping the liquid which would have required a lot of hard work on the part of the operator. It would not have been popular with mortar crews.

Some mortars were operated by compressed air. The Germans copied a French compressed air mortar. A 105 mm model fired finned projectiles to about 2,500 yd. A regulator was used to adjust the pressure and therefore the range. The Germans also used a 150 mm model. Compressed air mortars may have been silent, as were hydraulic mortars, but they were technically more complex than conventional mortars and required skilled operators specially trained in their use. The problem of noise and flash occupied the minds of many inventors and various noise reduction devices that could be fitted to mortars were invented but none of them seem to have been really effective or practical. Some were given trials and a Temple device was fitted to the 2 in toffee-apple mortar.

The Brandt pneumatic mortar with compressed air cylinder photographed in August 1918. Someone has lodged a shell in the muzzle, presumably for effect, although it appears to be about to fall out. Note the leather muzzle cap suspended from the barrel. (IWM)

Experiments were carried out with a number of heavy trench mortars including a 9.45 in version of the 6 in Newton but the mounting was not strong enough so it was abandoned. A Thornycroft mortar of the same calibre was considered. This was a modified service 9.45 in with a separate explosion chamber (as opposed to an expansion chamber) from which the propellant gases passed into the breech but it was considered to be an unnecessary complication which only added weight. Moreover, for safety reasons the chamber had to be cooled every few rounds after rapid firing before it could be reloaded. The advantage of having a separate chamber of this sort was the reduction of stress on the tail fins so that they were less prone to buckling. It was turned down.

Vickers and Armstrong Whitworth both submitted large-calibre, rifled breech-loaders which were described as 'finely made pieces of ordnance'. The Vickers had a calibre of 9.2 in while the Armstrong Whitworth was a monster of 11 in. The Armstrong Whitworth mortar was trialled but found to be no more accurate than the 9.45 in already in service and since the projectile weighed 200 lb, which was far too heavy, no further action was taken. The Vickers was not even given a trial.

The main objection to these weapons was that they were too complicated to manufacture and would divert skilled workmen from the production of artillery as well as needing skilled

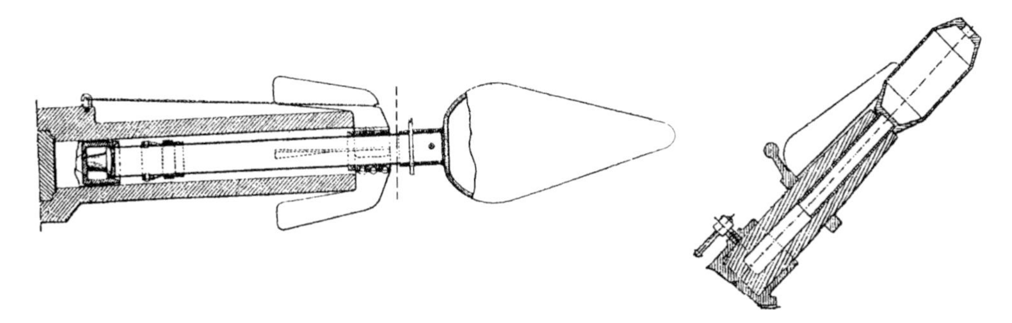

Left: *E. Schneider's mortar shell with stem and fins.* Right: *UK patent 127,285, granted to the French company Soc. Anon pour l'Exploitation des Procédés Westinghouse-Leblanc. The stem is hollow so that the propellant gases do not interfere with the fins. The adjustable collar round the barrel, just below the fins, allowed range adjustments by varying the size of the combustion chamber behind the stem. The mortar was the subject of UK patent 125,413.*

artificers to maintain them in the field. Armstrong Whitworth also submitted a 10 in rifled muzzle-loaded mortar but again its accuracy was no improvement over the 9.45 in and the shell was far too heavy. It had some novel features, none of which counted in its favour since they added complication rather than providing simplicity. It was the subject of at least one patent, and possibly two (13,445/15 and 125,475). It had a separate explosion chamber and a small breech block. The opening from the chamber to the barrel was filled by a piston fitted to the base of the shell to allow the pressure to build up to the necessary pressure before projecting it from the barrel. This was just another unwanted complication.

In the end, only simple mortars interested the research departments and the Army. Despite Wilfrid Stokes's criticism of government departments making things unnecessarily complicated, every complex device was turned down.

CHAPTER 9

Oil Cans and Projectors – Livens, Flame and Gas 1915–18

Perhaps the strangest mortar to emerge during the war was the oil can mortar invented by Captain Livens, RE, which was designed to throw incendiaries rather than high explosive. At the time he conceived the idea, he was in command of the Flammenwerfer Company (which he had commanded since its inception in 1915), one of the Special Companies of the Royal Engineers and was in France to use the flame projectors to silence enemy machine-guns in the Somme offensive. However, he faced a serious problem of range: the weapons could not be fired from the British line because it was too far away from the German trenches for the stream of flame to reach, as the projector only had a range of 110 yd. He hit upon the idea of a simple mortar to throw oil-based incendiaries in bombs rather than project fire out of a nozzle.

The mortar was indeed very simple, so simple in fact as to almost defy logic. Nevertheless, reasoned thought was at the heart of the invention. The oil for the flame projector was stored in 12-gallon drums, made of ⅟₁₆-inch thick sheet steel. These were approximately 12 inches in diameter and 20 inches tall. According to Livens 'when the top was removed [it] formed a very simple mortar tube'. Such a tube seemed an unlikely candidate from which to fire mortar rounds since logic suggested that it would not withstand much of a charge before bursting. Nothing ventured, nothing gained, Livens decided to give it a go, setting some drums in the ground at 45°. The projectiles for these unlikely mortars were equally unusual, being made from Army Service Corps 3-gallon round-section drums. These were about 12 in deep and were used for transporting lubricating oil. These were no more than tin cans with soldered bases. The soldered joints were the weakest points and needed to be supported in some way. Livens reasoned that if the force of propulsion could be made to act perpendicularly to the base of the 3-gallon drum, the side wall would be strong enough to keep the bomb in one piece.

For much the same reason, the flat base of the 12-gallon drum mortar tube would be the strongest part of the mortar as it would be supported directly by the ground and the walls would not have to withstand great pressure. To satisfy these two requirements, Livens had some discs of wood cut to a diameter about 1 in less than that of the mortar tube but greater than the diameter of the 3-gallon can. He now had all the components. All he had to do was to see if it would work.

A small charge of a few ounces of black powder was put inside the larger drum and the wooden disc placed on top. The smaller drum, containing 'very inflammable Persian distillate', was then put inside the larger drum. The fuse consisted of streamers of oily sacking tied to the handle of the 3-gallon can which was ignited by the flash of discharge. A trial run showed that the 3-gallon can could be thrown 200 yd and stay in one piece until it hit the ground, when it burst open, spilling its contents which were then ignited by the burning streamers. It was remarkably effective. A few refinements were necessary, however, such as putting blocks on the wooden disc to ensure that the charge was always the same volume and evenly spread. Livens also decided that it would be wise to put the powder in some sort of waterproof 'cartridge' and experimented with slightly different sizes of disc. It had taken Livens less than a week, from inception to usable weapon.

The mortar not only worked but it was simple to use and tube and bomb could be carried by one man, one under each arm. When used in earnest the effect was devastating. A salvo of 100 oil can mortar bombs was in Livens's words 'most impressive, and a considerable area of ground was smothered in burning oil'. He later demonstrated the mortar to the King when he visited France. The oil can mortar was first used against machine-gun positions at La Boiselle on the night of 25 July 1916 as the Australians were attacking Pozières. Livens received orders at 11 p.m. on the preceding day and a dawn reconnaissance of the enemy positions revealed two strong points, each of which 'consisted of ring trenches at the junction of other trenches'. These contained machine-guns with good fields of fire over the area of No Man's Land that the attacking infantry would have to cross.

Another strong point was discovered at the eleventh hour, after the reconnaissance had been completed and this too needed to be dealt with. This meant that the force of 120 oil can mortars had to be divided into three as there was no time to bring up another section of mortars from their base nearly 20 miles away to deal with the third strong point. The equipment was brought as far forward in daylight as it was possible to take a lorry without being detected. The section commanded by Livens had another 200 yd of open ground to cross via a track that was shelled every time anyone was seen on it, and the light would not permit this to be crossed until 6 p.m. It was made more complicated by the fact that the British bombardment was due to start at 8.30 p.m. To avoid short rounds and the inevitable German retaliatory bombardment, the carrying party had to have completed their job of taking the equipment as close to the German line as possible and returned before the bombardment started. Unfortunately, the party consisted of inexperienced men who had never been in the trenches before and they did not arrive at the dangerous section until exactly the moment the bombardment started. Despite seeing another, unconnected, party of four get blown to pieces, they somehow managed to get most things up to the proper place, although some equipment was left about 70 yd away and was very difficult to find in the dark.

Livens and his team had eighty mortars to set up and load, the most difficult part of which was splicing the eighty fuses into powder junction boxes that would allow the entire eighty to fire at once. They were installed almost side by side 'in the parados of an old piece of German communication trench' and were due to be fired at 12.30 p.m., H-hour of the attack. Everything was ready with 10 minutes to go, so everyone not needed for the firing was withdrawn to safety in readiness for the inevitable German counter-bombardment once the flashes from the mortars were seen. At 12.30 p.m., they were fired 'and the bursting cans made a fine splash of flame all over the German machine-gun posts'. The machine-guns never fired a shot. Within the next 3 minutes, a heavy barrage landed on the mortar position and it 'became very unpleasant'.

The next morning revealed that none of the mortars had escaped the barrage. More importantly, though, all the mortars had worked perfectly. Even when a mortar did burst, its bomb was actually propelled further than when the mortar remained intact. Later experiments showed that the bomb would invariably travel at least two-thirds of the maximum range when the mortar burst. To be on the safe side, Livens designed a fuse that would not arm until the bomb had travelled a minimum distance so that if one did fall short it would be blind.

Not content with what he had achieved, Livens now proceeded to improve on the mortar and its bomb and these became the second pattern. By now, the terms being applied to these

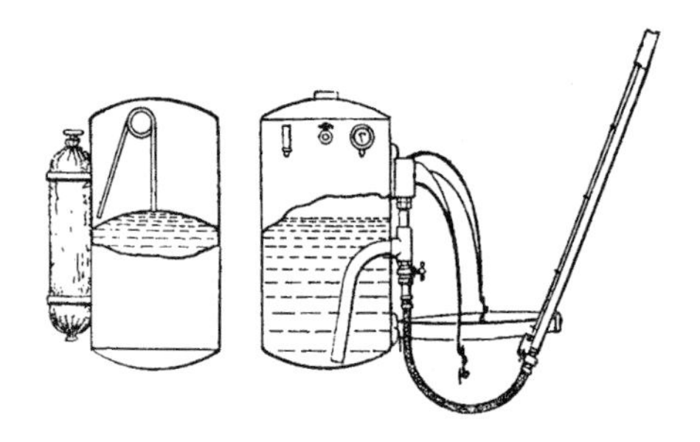

R. Fiedler's patent (30,161/10) for a portable flamethrower, dating from 1910.

improvised devices were 'oil drums' and 'portable cans for carrying oil up trenches' the latter shortly becoming 'portable cans'. For reasons of secrecy, these terms stuck, although the bomb soon became known as the Livens Drum. Even before the first operational use of the devices, Livens had sent sketches to Haig at the latter's request, copies going to the Trench Warfare Supply Department with a request for suitable drums. What arrived shortly afterwards was not quite what he had hoped for. The 'mortar' drums were 4 ft long but only 9.5 inches in diameter and had no tops, while the 'bomb' cans each had 'a separate compartment which, curiously enough just held a Mills grenade'. This was supposed to hold 'a priming charge of petrol'.

The second pattern of the mortar had a range of 350 yd with a bomb that weighed 60 lb when filled. The empty can weighed 18 lb so the ratio of filling weight to container weight was three to one. As Livens put it, this was 'extraordinarily economical'. The mortar and its bomb must have been the most cost-effective weapon of the war. The oil can mortar was also used to great effect during the attack on the Messines Ridge in June 1917. 'A lake of fire' was reported to have been created by 'a salvo of 100 Livens Incendiary Drums' and the term 'boiling oil' was used. Because of the success of the incendiary mortar the idea was

German Flammenwerfer, *late 1916.* (ILN)

French soldiers test a captured German flamethrower, September 1915. The cylinders are in the foreground while the hose operators are in the middle distance. (ILN)

extended to gas as a filling for the bombs rather than incendiaries. This subsequently became the Livens Projector, an incredibly powerful gas weapon and arguably the most effective of the war.

The Germans were the first to use gas and were the first to use flamethrowers, both in 1915. The history of the British response to both is inextricably intertwined with Livens, although the flame projectors (as flamethrowers were known) and gas dispensing apparatus were not at all alike. Nevertheless, through Livens the flame projector led via the oil can mortar to the Livens Projector. The history of gas warfare in the First World War may be short in terms of years but in terms of complexity it is a vast subject which can only be touched upon here. The focus here is on Livens who was a driving force in the development of both gas weapons and flame projectors.

The Germans first used flamethrowers against the British at Hooge at the end of July 1915 during the Second Battle of Ypres. Captain Hitchcock of the Leinsters described the 'liquid fire' attack as 'most demoralising' launched by 'a number of men carrying on their backs a tank similar to a potato-spraying device with a hose. From this jet issued forth a flame of liquid which was estimated could shoot some 30 to 50 yards.' Despite the surprise and the horror the flamethrower induced in the defenders, few men became casualties from burns. The flamethrower was operated by two men, one to carry the tanks, the other to aim the hose. The Leinsters were 'instructed to aim at those who carried the flame-spraying device, who made a good target'. The fuel tank of at least one unfortunate German carrying a flamethrower was hit during the attack and it 'blew up with a colossal burst'.

Before their operational use against the British, flamethrowers had been used against the French and on the Eastern Front. The French captured flamethrowing equipment which was subsequently demonstrated to both the French and British troops. In March 1915 the Royal Welch Fusiliers attended such a demonstration. It was not an unqualified success since 'premature operation scorched some of the Staff, to the unconcealed delight of the infantry'. James Jack witnessed another demonstration in September 1916 and was of the opinion that such weapons were unsuitable for trench warfare, a view shared by many. He had a point. None of the flamethrowers used during the war was truly portable and the fuel, a mixture of heavy and light oils propelled by nitrogen or deoxygenated air, was not entirely safe especially if some oxygen was left in the air. It was not until the 1940s and the invention of a thickening agent called napalm – a derivative of naphthenic acid and palmitic acid (hence the name) that turned the liquid fuel into a gel which was much easier to project with less chance of the fuel burning back to the projector – that flamethrowers became really effective. Moreover, the unthickened oils used in the First World War had a tendency to burn up before reaching the target so that very little fuel actually made contact with it. Napalm overcame these problems.

The German use of flamethrowers at Hooge demanded an immediate response, except that the British had no similar devices. An experimental programme was quickly started to devise long-range as well portable flamethrowers that one man could carry and operate. Private enterprise was already ahead of the game. Joseph Menchen, an American with experience of industrial fuel burners, had approached Colonel Jackson in February 1915, claiming that he could make a flamethrower despite having no experience of such things – he believed that there was probably very little difference between burners and flamethrowers. Jackson, keen to encourage new lines of development, asked him to design two types, a short-range model and a long-range one.

The short-range portable model was ready for trials in April and although it seems to have performed well with a respectable, if not outstanding, range of about 20 yd, the device was rejected. The long-range model consisted of four cylindrical fuel tanks joined in series to a single discharge tube with a nozzle along with an equal number of compressed air cylinders, each cylinder being fed by an air bottle. Although this trial model had everything joined in series, Menchen thought that it would work equally well if they were joined in parallel or even radially. The fuel and the propelling gas were released with valves that were arranged to ensure that the fuel was released before the gas. It had a range of about 100 yd but was rather too complicated to be of practical value in the trenches, of which Menchen, unlike Livens, had no experience. Menchen, like so many inventors, had sufficient faith in his devices to believe that it was worth his while filing four patent applications in late 1915. He was subsequently granted three patents, two of the applications having been combined at a later date (14,715/15 was concerned with the flamethrower as a whole, 14,716/15 was concerned with the valve system, and 16,062/15 was concerned with the nozzle and ignition system).

Meanwhile, a French company, Hersent, had also developed a flamethrower which was the subject of two UK patents. The application filed on 27 March 1915, concerned with the flamethrower unit, became 7,524/15 while the second filed on 4 November related to the ignition system and was granted as 15,581/15. The Hersent device was simpler than Menchen's. Captain Vincent, one of the team developing British flamethrowers for the Trench Warfare Department, borrowed some the features of the Hersent device, and assisted by Captain Hay came up with a 'knapsack' model that had a range of about 35 yd. Vincent demonstrated it at Wembley on 15 December 1915. The trial went well but the device only had a fuel capacity of 6.5 gallons which allowed just 17–18 seconds of flame. The apparatus was no lightweight at 80–85 lb but fortunately for the operator it was well distributed.

There were, however, grave doubts about the usefulness of a one-man flamethrower. GHQ did not believe that it was suitable for the conditions in France. It was suggested that if the knapsack flamethrower was adopted, the fuel would have to be sprayed on the ground, then ignited with a firework instead of projecting fuel and igniting it at the nozzle. This rather odd and unrealistic idea came about because of a genuine fear that the operator might be sniped by the enemy so that the flame could be turned on friendly troops, although how spraying the fuel on the ground first avoided getting sniped is rather obscure. Strangely, the idea that it could be used to clear pillboxes or blockhouses, as flamethrowers were used in the Second World War, never seems to have crossed anyone's mind (although in fairness these did not become widespread until 1917). The only use that could be suggested for the device was in street fighting, a somewhat absurd notion at that time since there was no prospect whatsoever of street fighting occurring in the near future.

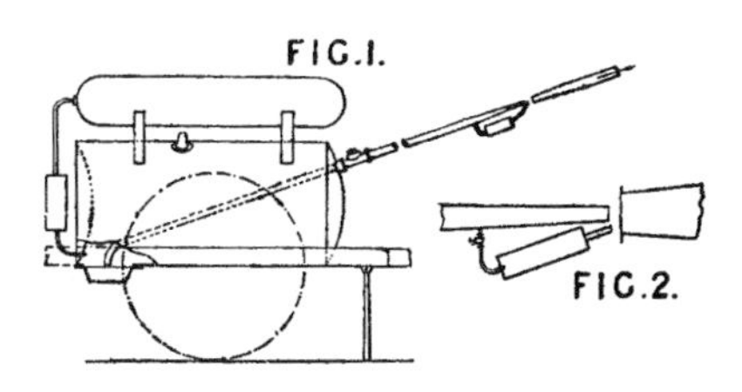

Drawing from one of Hersent's patents (7,524/15) for a flamethrower mounted on a truck. Fig. 2 shows the ignition system for injecting a more flammable liquid into the stream which is mixed in the tube on the right.

None of the one-man flamethrowers that were trialled during the war, mostly during 1915 and 1916, was ever really considered suitable for trench warfare. All were rejected for Army use although some found their way to France only to be dismissed out of hand by GHQ. Only the Navy showed a real interest and used Hay one-man models during the 1918 raid on Zeebrugge.

The flamethrower trials held at Wembley on 15 December also saw the demonstration of two other types that could be described as medium and heavy, the former having been designed by Vincent. The medium was a semi-portable device with a range of between 40 yd and 60 yd and a crew of two, while the heavy or battery model had a crew of eight. During the course of the trial of the semi-portable flame projector, one of the compressed air cylinders burst and the operator was severely burned, along with Vincent. The cause of the accident was put down to a rivet shearing and the manufacturer of the Duralumin cylinder, Vickers, was blamed. However, this does not appear to have influenced any decision about the viability of such equipment at the Front. At 230 lb, the equipment was too heavy to be carried and had to be transported on a special truck. The tanks had a capacity of 15 gallons which allowed a flame time of only 20 seconds. Despite the accident, it was considered to be simple and safe and was viewed more favourably than Menchen's device.

The battery model comprised four units, each with four 20-gallon fuel cylinders each of which could produce 11 seconds of flame. If two of the units worked together the flame time was 23 seconds and if all four were used in unison a discharge of 45–50 seconds duration could be achieved. The equipment was provided with a quick shut-off valve which could be used to throw a continuous succession of balls of flame 80–85 yd for 3–3.5 minutes with an average of four balls per cylinder or sixteen for the battery as a whole. Because of the length of the jet (and because this was unthickened fuel) the wind direction and strength made a considerable difference to the range as well as to the accuracy.

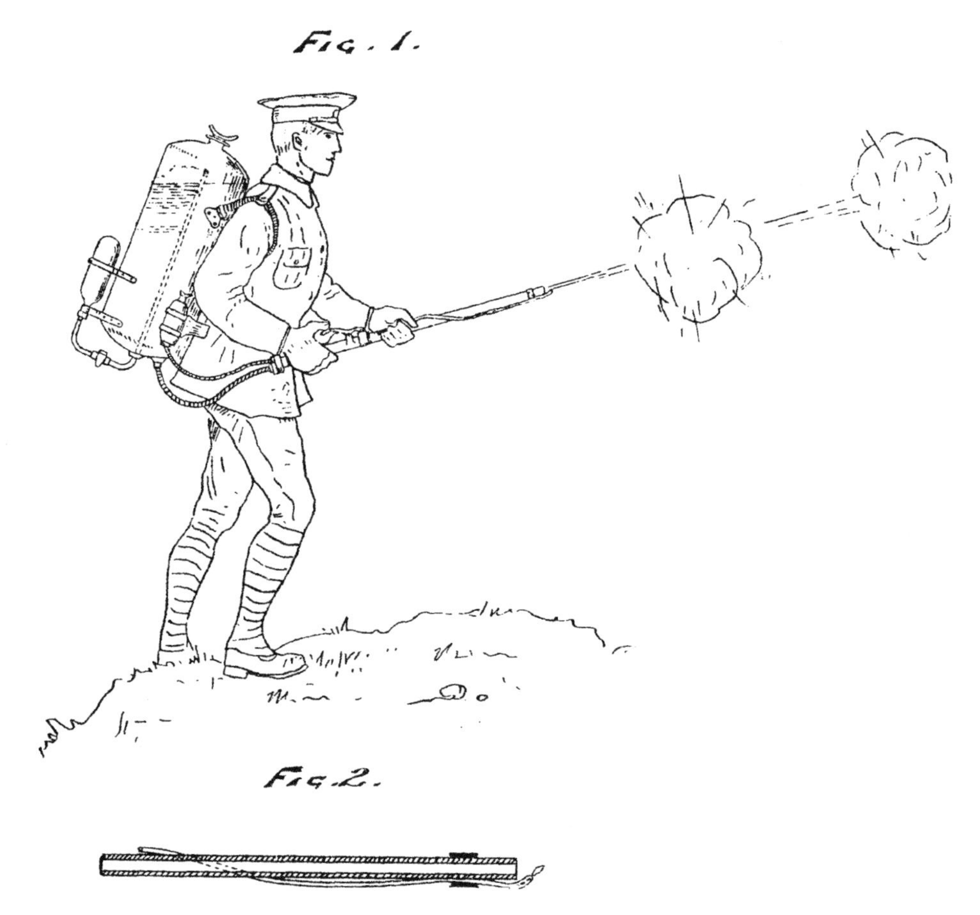

William Hall's portable flamethrower (UK patent 15,288/15). Note the lever for projecting 'puffs of flame' rather than a continuous stream. The specification stated that in a continuous stream 90 per cent of the fuel is wasted.

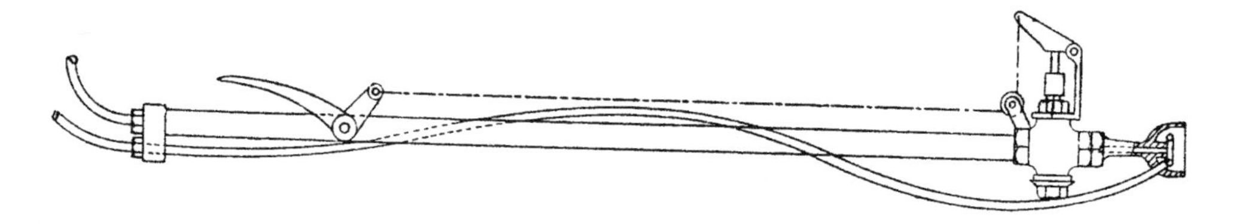

Drawing of the lever attached to the nozzle valve from Hall's patent.

Having successfully fired the projector to a more than respectable distance, it was decided to try igniting the stream of liquid after it had left the nozzle to see if the range could be extended. It was recognized that the range was affected by the quantity of fuel that was burned up before reaching the target. To this end, the jet of fuel was ignited after the projector streamed instead of at the nozzle but the results were very disappointing. A meagre 40 yd was all that could be achieved by this method so it was abandoned.

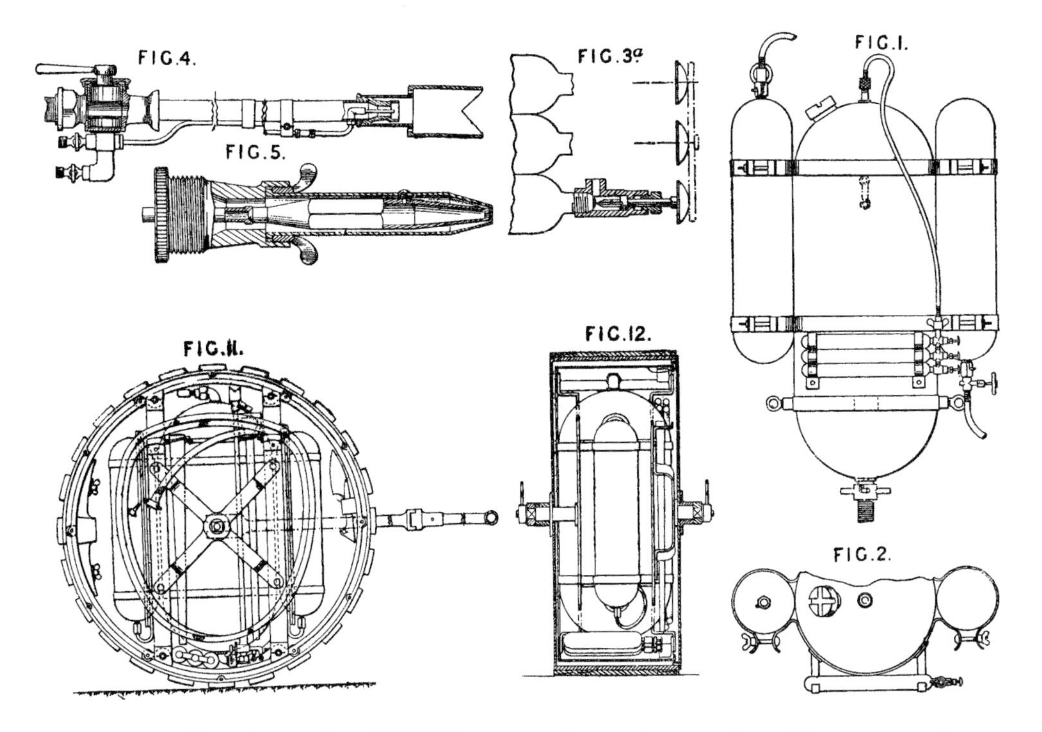

P.H. Lawrence's flamethrower from 1915. It has a complex nozzle system for mixing oxygen and chlorine gases (stored in the smaller side cylinders in fig. 1) to ignite the fuel which was 6 parts turpentine, 1 part carbon bisulphide and 2 parts phosphorus. It can be carried on the back or mounted in a roller as shown in fig. 11 'for rolling down a trench'. Although assigned a number (17,696), no patent was granted because the sealing fee was not paid.

What was needed was thickened fuel. Had anyone realized it, there was a thickener readily available – natural rubber. The ability of natural rubber to thicken fuel into a gel was not generally known at the time and, in any case, natural rubber was a strategic material already earmarked for a variety of essential war uses, not the least being vehicle tyres and obturator rings in artillery (these went inside the breech and sealed it when the propellant was fired, ensuring no gas leakage). The use of rubber would have transformed flamethrowers from dangerous Heath Robinson contraptions to truly effective weapons.

The battery model was a much more formidable weapon than either the semi-portable or knapsack models but it had one considerable disadvantage – its size. The battery weighed 2,500 lb and was 16.5 ft long and 4 ft 6 in high. It would be neither easy to take into the front line nor easy to conceal once it was there, yet it was a similar device that Livens took to France with the intention of using it during the Somme battles. Livens did not like the two-man flamethrower demonstrated at Wembley on 15 December, considering it to be badly designed and unsuitable for the trenches. He set about designing an alternative better suited to trench conditions. He had already conducted his own experiments with a one-man device of his own invention. Livens enlisted the help of his father at the firm of Rushton Proctor in Lincoln and between them they designed and built two types including a large battery model.

It took Livens six months. There seems to have been a permanent difference of opinion between the researchers, the Army Council and GHQ about the usefulness of the devices. And although Livens was dismissive of Vincent's two-man device, the Army Council was still considering it and had ordered several sets, only to change its mind later. By June both types designed by Livens and his father were more or less ready. The Large Gallery flamethrower was a monster which bore an uncanny resemblance to a mechanical sea serpent with a long neck that curved up to a small head from which the fire would belch, fuel tank humps and a tail of gas cylinders. The idea was to bury it in an underground galley close to the German front line prior to an attack – no mean accomplishment considering its size – and raise its head through the covering earth to spray fire at the enemy. As Livens wrote later

> the only way to bring the business-end of the weapon near enough for the enemy to be in range was to install the apparatus in a mine-shaft, going forward from our front line towards the enemy, but mine-shafts require many days, if not weeks, to dig, and five yards a day is about the maximum progress possible on a quiet front in suitable ground. Therefore, while the Flammenwerfer was well suited to the purpose [for] which it was designed, the commencing phase of an offensive from an old established front where mining had gone on for many months, it was of little value during the subsequent fighting in the enemy's old lines to enlarge the initial gain.

The device consisted of seven sections of 9 in diameter pipe joined in series with a discharge nozzle on the end of a narrow pipe at the 'head' and twelve gas cylinders via a reservoir tank at the 'tail'. The 'head' could be raised hydraulically and was armoured so that it cut through the covering earth of the galley. The 9 in pipe was both tank and discharge pipe as it contained the first shot of fuel which was propelled up the pipe by the gas acting on a piston. The fuel was ignited at the nozzle by acetylene which ignited spontaneously in air. The acetylene was generated in situ by dripping water on to calcium carbide. Two further shots were provided by a series of five tanks above and connected to the 9 in tube. In all, the device contained 250 gallons of fuel.

The smaller flamethrower was a two-man device that contained 12 gallons of fuel in a single tank discharged by gas from another tank. It was not meant to be carried in action, however, and only had a range of 35 yd. In June 1916 six gallery models and twenty-four semi-portable models, both of Livens's design, were sent out to France to be set up for use in the forthcoming Somme offensive. Only four of the large models were prepared for action and only two of them were used successfully, the other two being lost through the effects of shellfire before they could be brought into action. On 1 July, the first day of the Battle of the Somme, the two Livens flamethrowers seared the German trenches a quarter of an hour before H-hour. About forty Germans were killed and many more terrified, but it is doubtful whether this made a significant difference to anything. The two-man flamethrowers saw action twice during July and again in September when the large model also saw further action. Apart from a couple of flames in 1917 and the Zeebrugge raid in 1918 that was the only use of British flamethrowers. Their contribution had been negligible.

There seems to have been an almost perpetual shortage of fuel for the flamethrowers and requests were regularly submitted to the War Office. On 19 June 1916, even before Livens's devices had been tried on the Somme, the Army Council stated that 'Flame Projectors already demanded will be used whenever an opportunity offers until they become unserviceable; they will not, however, be replaced'. Flamethrowers were not regarded as effective enough to warrant more equipment being sent out to France and Haig did not want them in any case. Experimentation was to halt forthwith.

The far simpler oil can mortar, which had arisen from the need to find an alternative way to attack the German trenches with incendiaries, was a much more effective weapon than any of the flamethrowers. The success of these mortars led to the idea that the mortars could be used to throw gas bombs at the Germans in the same manner. When the Germans first released chlorine from 5,000 cylinders at Ypres in April 1915, against Algerian troops of the French Army, the British Army wanted a response to this new threat. By September the Army was ready to release a gas cloud of its own against the Germans at the Battle of Loos. Although these and later uses of gas clouds proved to have a limited effect against an unprepared enemy, it was realized that there were simply too many variables to guarantee success. These were mostly connected with the weather (for example, air temperature, wind speed and direction) but were also related to how far the gas had to travel and the density of cylinders in the release area. There were instances where a simple change in wind direction completely threw all planning and timetables into disarray.

British portable flamethrower on board HMS Vindictive *following the Zeebrugge raid in 1918.* (ILN)

Livens knew that if gas was to be effective it had to be delivered in higher densities than could be achieved with gas clouds. In addition, greater control over the gas was essential. Although both artillery shells and mortar bombs were adapted to carry gas, the effect was still limited and measures could be taken by the enemy to minimize the number of casualties. Shells and bombs could neither carry a big enough payload nor produce a high concentration in one place. It occurred to Livens that by adapting his oil can mortar bombs to carry gas instead of flammable liquid it might be possible to lay down a very dense, localized cloud of gas, especially if a large number of mortars were fired simultaneously. He conducted some experiments which showed that the idea was not only sound but potentially even more destructive than his cans of petrol.

The gas projector was first used operationally in the capture of Thiepval in September 1916, followed by a repeat performance during the capture of Beaumont Hamel in November. These were not full-scale projector operations, merely trials to prove the concept. The proof was very convincing and General Sir Hubert Gough in command of the Fifth Army and his Chief of Staff General Neill Malcolm gave Livens all the cooperation he needed to develop the weapon in the field while keeping it secret from the Germans. Both recognized the potential of the weapon and arranged for the projector to be used only against positions that would be immediately taken by the infantry. This ensured that no information about the new weapon could be passed back to the German rear. Indeed, so successful were these precautions that the Germans were completely in the dark about the projector until well into 1917 and even then they did not know how the weapon worked.

Some of the reports that the Germans did manage to write were captured before they could be sent back to the German divisional staff. The reports assumed the attacks to be gas clouds released in the usual way but of far higher density. During the Thiepval attack about 1,100 lb of gas was fired at a frontage of only 80 yd and this formed a 'gas lake' that flooded the cellars of the ruined Thiepval Château, occupied by the German commander of the Thiepval garrison. He, along with at least 130 other German soldiers, were killed by the gas. At Serre, 200 Germans were killed and the German commander reported that the attack was 'of a new kind, of great intensity, delivered without warning' and was desperate to know what he should do against a future attack. He received an unhelpful reply 'to take the necessary precautions' but died before he could do anything.

On the day after the gas attack on Beaumont Hamel, the infantry took what remained of the village. Livens discovered a deep German dugout untouched by 'our heaviest shelling with twelve inch howitzers', with fifteen Germans, five rats and a cat all dead. They had died in the act of trying to escape and the evidence suggested that it had happened within a matter of a few seconds. This was not because the gas was any more lethal but because of its concentration.

> This dug-out was in the track of a cloud containing nearly a ton of gas, and the number of seconds in which these men were killed could be gauged almost exactly, because the three furthest from the entrance down which the gas had come, had had time to put their gas-masks on before they died, the fourth man had his mask half on, and the fifth had it to his face, the sixth out of the box, the seventh had opened the box, and completing the series, the eight[h] had his hand on the lid, while those in front were killed so quickly they had not had time even to think about their masks.

Livens likened the scene to 'a cinematographic series of photographs of German gas-mask drill'.

The well-trained German soldier could don his gas mask in less than 6 seconds. In all likelihood, the concentration of gas was so high that the normal gas mask was ineffective. What made the scene all the more remarkable was the fact that the centre of the beaten zone (the area into which all the drums were fired) was some 300 yd away and the nearest bomb or 'drum' had landed 280 yd from the entrance. The main target, the deep artillery-proof dugouts used by the German garrison, revealed an even more startling picture. When these were examined, they were found to contain approximately 300 dead, all of whom had been killed by the gas. This was the reason for the comparatively light casualties suffered by the infantry when it crossed No Man's Land to take the German positions. A similar attack on the nearby Y Ravine was equally successful. This was an astonishing vindication of the projector and gas drum projectile.

Having now established the effectiveness of the weapon (which, unlike the first oil can mortars, were made by Hartley & Sugden), Livens proceeded to improve on it. The acetylene welds of the early drums which contained the gas tended to become porous due to corrosion caused by moisture and chlorine (chlorine gas is made up of diatomic molecules of chlorine, hence the chemical formula Cl_2, but some chlorine atoms remain unattached and these readily dissolve in water to form hydrochloric acid). This would not have been a problem but for the fact that the drums were filled with the gas in the field and had to be stored until required for use. The filled drums had no fuse and relied on splitting open on impact. Thus, the drums were not inherently strong and there was always the danger of leaks or splits from rough handling.

Eventually, fire welding of $\frac{3}{16}$ in sheet was shown to be the best way to make gas-tight drums and these, like the first gas drums, were made by Stewart & Lloyd at their Coatbridge factory near Glasgow, as well as at their Birmingham factory. By the end of the war, 430,000 had been made. It is evident that the French also used the Livens Projector with drums of the same pattern and the Italians proposed to do likewise.

The projectors only had a range of 350 yd which, as the battles of the Somme developed, was quickly recognized as too short. Livens needed a more robust tube from which to project the gas drums, and discovering that 'a certain quantity of waste Mannesmann tubing in odd lengths' was left over from work done for the Admiralty he decided to experiment with this. (The Mannesmann process made seamless tubing from a metal bar with two eccentrically mounted rollers. The rollers simultaneously rotated the bar and forced it over a mandrel.) Livens selected 8 in diameter tubing which had to be at least 3 ft long to maintain a minimum length to calibre ratio of four to one which earlier experiments had shown to be essential for the 'parallel portion' of the bore if the projector was to fire a drum to a good range. Anything less than this caused the range to drop off drastically. The maximum weight of the projector had to be kept to 100 lb as this had been determined as the maximum load that could be carried without special equipment. The length and weight determined the thickness of the walls of the projector which were $\frac{3}{8}$ in thick. A black powder charge gave a range of 1,300 yd and was electrically ignited, the wires passing down the tube from the muzzle to the charge.

By now, the First, Third, Fourth and Fifth Armies were keen to get hold of as many of the projectors as possible. This required coordination with GHQ and General Thuillier as Director of Gas Services arranged with the Ministry of Munitions and the War Office to have as many projectors as possible manufactured in time for the forthcoming offensive in the spring of 1917. Livens attended the conference in the UK and remained in England to help deal with the technical problems that needed to be resolved. It was during this time that he perfected the drums. The projector had been transformed from an improvised device into a 'proper' weapon system. Throughout the whole process, Livens had not worked alone and he owed a debt of gratitude to many officers, as well as to his father, which he was only too willing to acknowledge. In fact, he made it plain that the credit for the invention should be shared equally between himself and his father. Without the support of the Director of the Trench Warfare Supply Department, the weapons would never have reached France in the numbers needed to make the impact they were about to make.

The Livens Projector was, of course, a mortar and the Livens Drum was a mortar bomb. The reason the projector was not called a mortar was logistical rather than secrecy although the term did help to obscure what the projector was. By avoiding calling the weapon a mortar meant that it was not classified as a gun. Guns came under the auspices of the Ordnance Board which would have been responsible for supplying the weapon. This would have inevitably slowed the supply process because of all the other guns which the Ordnance Board had to deal with. But if the weapon was called something else that did not suggest 'gun', it could be supplied to France by other means, i.e. the Trench Warfare Supply Department. The significance of all this was the speed with which Livens wanted the weapons supplied so that they could be used in the numbers necessary for them to be truly effective.

Vimy Ridge in April 1917 was the debut of the new projector. Half an hour after dawn broke, 2,000 were set up along a crescent of front above Arras and opposite Vimy Ridge. From an aircraft, Livens watched the drums burst on the German lines and the gas cloud drift over their positions. It travelled for more than 4 miles. The Germans believed that the 'Gas Minnen' had been propelled pneumatically or by catapults of prodigious proportions because they had heard nothing before the drums arrived. As Livens wrote later 'A catapult which would throw a 65 lb bomb well over a kilometre would have surprised even Archimedes'. The absence of noise was rather puzzling, however, since these projectors were far from quiet and 2,000 of them made a tremendous noise that could be heard 40 miles away over the noise of the artillery bombardment. Livens concluded that the noise was not associated with the gas drums partly because those on the receiving end tended to be dead so that there was little opportunity to communicate information with the rear. Moreover, the considerable flash of 2,000 projectors being fired simultaneously could have been mistaken for a mine being exploded. But this was pure speculation. The German casualties during the assault on Vimy Ridge were immense.

Even before Vimy Ridge, Livens had been experimenting with alternative propellants to black powder to increase the range of the projector. Newton, now a colonel and Deputy Controller of the Trench Warfare Department, provided invaluable assistance as did Colonel A.W. Crossley, Commandant of the Gas Warfare Experimental Ground at Porton Down. With the further assistance of Captain H. Goodwin, flake cordite was chosen as the propellant. However, this type of propellant needed an initial pressure of at least 1 ton per square inch for it to be burned properly. The space between the wall of the projector and the drum had to be reduced to achieve this level. It had always been a requirement that neither the tube nor the drum should be machined in any way as this would slow down production. The tolerances were consequently low. Therefore, Livens had to find a way of closing the gap that did not involve machining. He came up with a steel gas check fixed to the charge box.

The first trial with the cordite and gas check was held after Livens's return to England after Vimy Ridge. It was successful, the range being increased to 1,800 yd. He believed that this increase 'more than doubled the value of the weapon'. Later experiments with bombs of stronger construction showed that the range could be extended to 2,500 yd but these were not ready for use before the end of the war. With the weaker drums, the range could not be extended beyond 1,800 yd as the higher cordite charges needed to achieve the longer ranges tended to make the drums bulge which caused the projectors to burst.

In the autumn of 1917, Livens became a member of the Trench Warfare Committee. The committee took on the job of further development of the projector and several variations on the tube were developed to overcome the shortage of Mannesmann tubing. The most important of these were the wire-wound projectors and the forged projectors. The wire-wound projector was, in fact, a composite of lap-welded, ¼ in steel tubing fitted with a mild steel 'thimble' to strengthen the breech end and wound with 'a double layer of flat gun steel wire' which had a tensile strength of 90–100 tons per square inch. The Mannesmann projectors had a tensile strength of 40–50 tons per square inch whereas the ¼ in steel tubing only had a strength of 28–32 tons per square inch, but when it was wire-wound the finished projector was as strong as the Mannesmann projector and only a little heavier.

However, there were difficulties with wire-wound projectors because the gun wire was brittle and had to be protected against damage. There was also the problem of how to securely tie off the end of the wire. Moreover, the finished tube behaved differently from Mannesmann projectors. A 3⁄16 in radial bulge rippled up the lap-welded tube as the gas check travelled up it although it regained its shape afterwards. Nevertheless, this was a potential

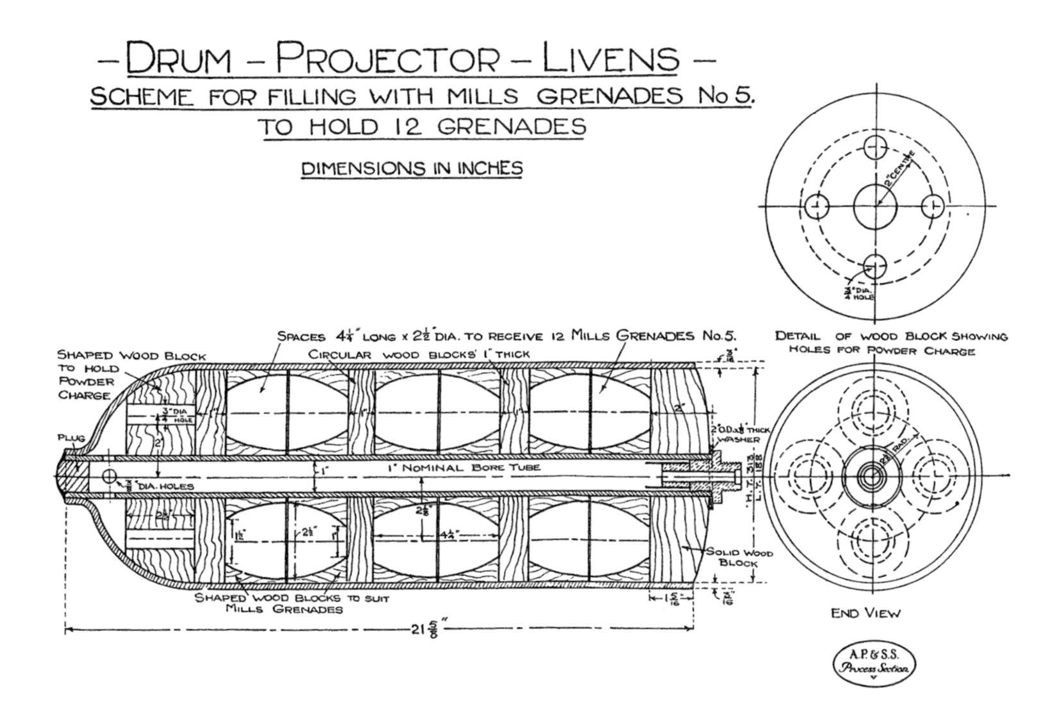

The Livens Projector. This shows an experimental method of launching twelve Mills grenades from the projector, illustrated in 'Notes on Inventions and New Stores No. 2', July–August 1917. (MUN 4/3590)

hazard as the wire and the tube were of different tensile strengths and permanent ripples could be left in the tube rendering it useless. Yet, such objections were regarded as unimportant since there was little in the way of an alternative; they just had to live with it. Large numbers of the wire-wound projectors saw action in France.

The forged projector was also produced in large numbers, several thousand being used in action. A billet of steel was forged on a hydraulic shell-press exerting pressure of 1,500 tons per square inch, followed by two drawing press operations. The inside was left slightly tapered towards the base by the process. The tube was subsequently cleaned and made uniform with an appropriate tool. The end was trimmed and the excess metal was turned off the exterior to reduce thickness and weight. That was all there was to it. It was an expensive process but on the plus side the projector was superior to any other with a longer range, the slight taper seeming to be a distinct advantage.

The projector was so effective that no one was surprised when the Germans began to make copies to return the favour. There were two types and although well made they were not a patch on the British originals. More seriously for the Germans, they failed to grasp the importance of using the projectors *en masse* to achieve the best results. One of the types had a rifled bore which was reputed to have a very long range but when tested by Livens he could only achieve 2,800 yd with it. It was also expensive to make and could not have been produced in large quantities because of its complexity. By the end of the war, the Allies had manufactured more than 150,000 projectors and more would have been used had they been available.

Livens declined to speculate on what might have been achieved had more projectors been available along with the necessary gas-filled bombs but he cited an operation where 600 projectors had been used to indicate the 'devastating nature' of the weapon. The operation took place near Passchendaele in October 1917. One night, two Special Companies of Royal Engineers fired 600 projectors in two groups. The German 80th and 81st Reserve Infantry Regiments, at whom the projectors were aimed, were nearly annihilated and another regiment suffered heavy casualties. In all, 2,500 Germans were killed in the operation. One reason for the high death toll was that the Germans had been caught in the middle of a relief but that did nothing to detract from the power of the weapon.

Besides the British and the French, the Americans also used the Livens Projector. The Italians had planned to use it but the war ended before they got the chance. The weapon certainly terrified the Germans, not just because of its devastating effects, but because they never knew when an attack would occur. Many of the gas attacks carried out by the British after Vimy Ridge in 1917 were conducted with Livens Projectors. The German Army suffered such high casualties from these attacks that its soldiers were forbidden to talk about the effects.

CHAPTER 10

Winners and Losers

The Army of 1918 was not the Army of 1914. Not only had the nature of the Army undergone a radical change through the creation of a 'citizen army' with an influx of officers and men with different political attitudes, different educations, different backgrounds, but many of the weapons with which this Army fought were very different from what the regulars and reservists of 1914 had been armed with. Moreover, tactical developments had been through a sea change.

The victories of 1918 were due more to these tactical developments than to any new weapon, although the two were inextricably intertwined. The notion that there was a war-winning weapon was a propaganda myth perpetuated during and after the war by men who had axes to grind, whether it was tank warfare or the incompetence of generals. No one, especially politicians, advocated a particular weapon with altruism in his heart. The truth is that had the tactical developments not occurred there would have been no victory for the Allies in 1918, if ever. It was how the infantry, artillery and air force were used cooperatively that made the difference. The new tactics used the destructive power of artillery much more scientifically and took into account the strengths and weaknesses of the 'new' weapons along with the benefits of air cooperation. By the end of the war, the British Army was a twentieth-century force; in 1914 it had been rooted in the nineteenth-century.

How weapons were used on a tactical level was the significant factor. Massed Livens Projectors, for example, used against a small area of enemy-held territory followed by the immediate taking of the ground by infantry was a formula that worked very effectively. When the Germans copied the projectors and tried to emulate the British successes they failed because they got the tactics wrong. Weapons such as the Mills grenade and the Stokes mortar had a tremendous impact on tactical developments, partly because they opened up new possibilities but also because they came to be relied on in ways undreamt of in 1914. Even by the middle of the war, troops were being castigated for over-reliance on hand and rifle grenades to the detriment of musketry but it made little difference to what soldiers did, partly because of the way training emphasized the grenade.

In some ways, this was an inevitable reactionary response by senior officers who had grown up with the importance of musketry inculcated in their thinking. Even old soldiers like Frank Richards deplored the loss of musketry skills. It took time for the benefits of effective and safe hand and rifle grenades to make themselves felt on tactical thinking. On the other hand, the front-line troops quickly became aware of the benefits of rifle grenades once they had been supplied with weapons they could rely on. By 1918 troops would rather use the Mills than the SMLE and shooting skills were nearly non-existent. But musketry never took a strong point or a concrete pillbox which could be efficiently silenced with a combination of hand and rifle grenades. Again it was the development of new tactics with new weapons that made it possible.

Similarly, the Stokes mortar was effective in destroying strong points and machine-guns when used in the right way. The earlier mortars could not have been used to do this. The realization that the new grenades and mortars could be relied on and that they could achieve things which their predecessors could not came about much more quickly than might have been the case with the old regulars because the civilian soldiers did not carry the same military baggage as the professionals. There was more to it than this, of course, because men like Newton, Livens and Jackson were professional soldiers and without them many of the developments in weapons would not have taken place nor reached the Front. Their inspired thinking, their energy to get things done and their willingness to experiment made a tremendous difference to what became available to the British soldier.

Development of new weapons was a continuous process. Even when a weapon had been adopted for service use, experimentation continued. Sometimes this was necessary because there were serious defects to be resolved. The early Mills and the early Stokes were far from perfect and there were numerous accidents. To some extent expedience had led to their adoption in the first place – the Army was in dire need. Most of the new devices given to the Army in 1915 were imperfect to a degree that would have caused an outcry in peacetime. In a sense, the best weapons rose to the surface although this is a slightly misleading statement. The popularity of the Mills put a damper on the development of other grenades. Had the timing of events been different, the Mills might never have attained the unassailable position it did. It was not necessarily the best that could have been developed. The same could not be said of the Stokes, however. Despite problems with the ammunition when it first entered service, it became an outstanding weapon. Moreover, nothing better emerged throughout the war. Like the Mills, it led to the development of other weapons: the Stokes-Newton 6 in mortar (the Mills led the way to the cup discharger).

The Stokes mortar was much more mobile than its predecessors but not so mobile that it could keep up with the infantry in an advance. This did not really become a problem until 1918. Nevertheless, from early 1917 onwards the question of mobility was addressed although not entirely successfully. It was, however, much easier to move and set up than previous mortars and, indeed, much more versatile. Part of the problem was the measures taken to make the weapon more stable on soft ground which were not compatible with mobility. Various mountings were looked at to solve the problem and ways of carrying the weapon were devised. In the end, it was a question of a different approach to using the weapon rather than of changing anything about the mortar that provided the answer. By mid-1918 it was even being considered as a possible anti-tank gun and anti-aircraft weapon although the former required a quite different mounting to enable the barrel to be brought to bear on the target.

The First World War was probably the first war in which weapons were developed in response to changing needs. This was mainly because the situation had never arisen before. Development of this type became commonplace during the Second World War and improvisation has long since become an accepted method of solving problems. In the 1991 Gulf War, improvisation in response to specific threats was not treated as anything out of the ordinary. Recognition of the fact that needs change with changing circumstances and that the flexibility to adapt is crucial stems in a large degree from the First World War. Rather than being hidebound by tradition and old-fashioned ways to the detriment of the conduct of the war, the development of new weapons, the willingness to use them and the desire to make them as efficient and safe as possible demonstrated that senior officers were more concerned with the welfare of their men than popular opinion has been manipulated to suggest. Without their consent and approval none of the new weapons would have found their way to the front and men like Newton would not have been encouraged. Newton ended the war a lieutenant-colonel and was awarded a CBE in 1920 for his contribution to the war effort. He was awarded $100,000 by the American government for his efforts, coming top of a US list of British war inventors.

Louis Jackson retired for the second time as an honorary major-general in November 1918. After his retirement, he contributed 'Fortifications and Siegecraft' to the eleventh edition of the *Encyclopaedia Britannica* and wrote articles on poison gas and military mining in the *Britannica*'s supplement. He was made a Commander of the Legion of Honour in 1917 and a KBE in 1918 for his contribution to the war. He died in 1946 aged ninety.

More than 75,000,000 Mills grenades were manufactured during the war. As the No. 36 grenade, the Mills remained in British service throughout the Second World War and was only retired in the 1970s. It is still in use today in some parts of the world. A television report in May 1998 about fighting somewhere in Africa showed a soldier proudly wearing a Mills on his belt. Neither the French nor the Germans had a comparable grenade. Considering all the patents related to the Mills, it would appear that the Germans no more availed themselves of enemy literature on munitions and related topics, than did the British (with the exception of the Krupp article on mortars that led to the toffee-apple). Leeming's worries over the potential value of patent abridgements and complete specifications to the enemy was apparently unjustified as no one seems to have thought of looking at them.

After the war, a Royal Commission on Awards to Inventors was set up to look into rewarding inventors who had made significant contributions to the war. Those who thought they had a case submitted claims to the commission which then examined the evidence and heard depositions from expert witnesses to decide if the claim was valid and the size of any sum to be awarded. The Royal Commission awarded Mills £27,750. He also made quite a lot of money from the manufacture of the grenade (his companies made millions of them) and from his patents. Mills was knighted in 1922. He died in 1932 at the age of seventy-six.

Wilfrid Stokes was made a KBE in 1917. In the end, over 11,000 mortars entered service and more than 20,000,000 shells were fired from Stokes mortars (in 1919, Stokes thought that between 7,000,000 and 8,000,000 had been fired in British service). Stokes submitted his claim to the Royal Commission on 6 June 1919 and on 3 May 1921 he submitted an amended claim. Why there was a two-year gap is not certain but it may simply be that it took that long for the commission to get round to his claim; it was certainly very busy dealing with many others. What is clear from both claims is that the government had not paid him any of the royalties promised in 1916. He also wanted to be paid the £3,000 he had spent out of his own pocket in developing the mortar and the shell. Moreover, he wanted to be recompensed for supplying GHQ with a mortar and 100 shells for a demonstration in France before the mortar had been accepted. He also wanted all the other 2,000 rounds fired in demonstrations and trials to be taken into account. In support of his claim he pointed out that the inventor of the all-ways fuse that was used solely with the Stokes and which had been very troublesome had already received an award of £14,000.

During the course of the commission's investigation of his claim it emerged that the Stokes was more accurate and more destructive than the 18-pounder. It was evidently considered to be good if about 5 per cent of 18-pounder shells hit the target whereas the Stokes could be relied on to hit the target with 70 per cent of its shells. The cost of an 18-pounder shell was £6 but a Stokes shell cost only £2. Clearly, the Stokes was more cost-effective. It also transpired that the US government had paid him £100,000 for the patent rights and the Italian government had paid him £50,000. The Ministry of Munitions did not support his claim and thought that he had been paid enough already. It would appear that, in the end, he was made an award of only £10,000, a paltry sum considering the value of the Stokes to the British war effort. The Stokes was the basis of the modern mortar and in its more highly developed forms saw service throughout the Second World War and into the present day.

The Burn cup discharger remained in service into the Second World War. The Livens Projector went the way of all gas weapons after the war and was never used again. Catapults, so useful in the dark days of 1915, returned to the pages of history. The flamethrower did not come of age until the discovery of thickening agents and the invention of napalm in particular. In the Second World War, American flamethrowers saw widespread use in the Pacific against Japanese bunkers.

The First World War was a remarkably inventive time. The technological and tactical differences between 1914 and 1918 was a gulf wider than a mere four years. It should never be forgotten that these same weapons helped to kill millions.

APPENDIX

Patents Tables

Hand Grenades

Application Date	Patent Number	Inventors	Description
10/2/15	2,111	W. Mills	Mills grenade
10/2/15	2,139	W.M. Still & Sons, E.H. Still	Firing pin in handle operated by throwing
10/2/15	7,636	W. Mills	Lever locking mechanism; fitted with rod as rifle grenade
16/2/15	2,468 cognate 3,559/15	W. Mills	Development of Mills bomb
25/2/15	3,091	F.M. Hale	Firing pin in handle; development of Hale grenade described in 4,925/11
6/3/15	3,619	F.E. Baker	Fuse
10/3/15	11,747	C. Besozzi	Grenade
20/3/15	4,392	A.C. Roodhouse	Double spherical walls
20/3/15	4,407	J.F. Buckingham	Fuse
13/4/15	5,553	J.F. Buckingham	Fuse
13/4/15	5,564	J.F. Buckingham	Percussion fuse for spherical grenade
20/4/15	5,900	C.T.B. Sangster	Fuse
20/4/15	5,901	C.T.B. Sangster	Fuse
15/5/15	7,301	W. Mills	Clockwork delay fuse
9/7/15	10,047	L. Bekker, L. Lilienstern	Fuse. No patent granted; sealing fee not paid
20/7/15	10,515 cognate 11,103/15 & 12,867/15	W. Mills	Grenade
28/7/15	10,925	W. Mills, W. Morgan	Fuse
3/8/15	11,223 cognate 12,629/15	W. Mills	Addition to 2,468/15
3/8/15	100,325	W. Mills	Fuse
4/8/15	11,239	J. Gray	Grenade
9/8/15	11,494	P. Hanzer, C. Hanzer	Percussion fuse
10/8/15	11,551	L.L. Billant	Percussion fuse
12/8/15	11,679	J.A. Leeming, F.H. Brewerton F.A. Fraser	Grenade
8/9/15	12,889	J.A. Armstrong	Wheel-shaped grenade which can be rolled along ground or thrown
15/9/15	13,197	G.A. Smith	Fuse igniter of sulphuric acid with sugar and potassium chlorate
18/10/15	14,665	W. Mills, W. Morgan	Fuse
19/10/15	14,793	W. Breeze, Reason Manufacturing Co.	Time fuse
21/10/15	14,904	A.M. Flack	Double-walled grenade
12/11/15	15,984 cognate 16,218/15	H.D. Black, F.H. Brewerton, F.A. Fraser	Grenade
15/11/15	16,083	S.R. Parkes	Grenade
19/11/15	16,327	T.W. Adshead	Grenade
27/11/15	16,749	J. Walster, S. Walster	Fuse
1/12/15	102,479	K.W. Nielsen	Grenade with handle and shrapnel balls
6/12/15	171,144	J.J. Pouly, J.J.M. Daujard	Glass grenade with metal fittings
6/12/15	17,146	W.J. Mellersh-Jackson (Bombrini Parodi-Delfino)	Fuse

Application Date	Patent Number	Inventors	Description
11/12/15	17,397	C.W. Findlay	Manufacture of Mills centre-piece
14/12/15	17,494 cognate 17/16 & 77/16	J.R. Hamilton (J.D. Hamilton)	Double-walled spherical grenade with impact fuse
21/12/15	17,852	S.R. Parkes	Fuse
22/12/15	17,898	S.R. Parkes	Centre-piece
3/1/16	102,812	B.D. Barfleet, A.J.W. Millership	Grenade
10/1/16	102,830	E.B. Temple (formerly E. Bregeon)	Percussion fuse
13/1/16	102,390	R.W.B. Billinghurst	Grenade with all-direction percussion fuse
13/1/16	103,821	J.B. Semple	Tail unwinds in flight and arms grenade
15/1/16	102,279	H.A. Reincke, W.C. Macartney	Grenade with all-ways percussion fuse
18/1/16	103,009	S.R. Parkes	Safety device
21/1/16	102,173	J. Walker	Centre-piece
21/1/16	103,182	Sabulite Ltd, W.H. McCandlish	Percussion fuse for grenade armed in flight by wind-vane
28/1/16	103,353	S.R. Parkes	Time fuse
29/1/16	102,639	A.E. Teery	Fuse for grenade described in 7,636/15 (Mills)
3/2/16	105,932	H.K. Harris	Grenade
17/2/16	124,505	W. Mills	Fuse for Mills
22/2/16	100,718	J.E. Hearn	Grenade in shape of flask
23/2/16	104,204	O. Horton, A. Macpherson	All-ways percussion fuse for spherical grenade
7/3/16	104,539	J.A. Prestwich	Grenade
9/3/16	104,541	H.E. Asbury	Striker mechanism
9/3/16	104,542	H.E. Asbury	Related to 104,541
9/3/16	104,543	S.R. Parkes	Grenade
9/3/16	104,669	H.E. Asbury	Fuse
10/3/16	124,527	S.R. Parkes	Fuse
13/3/16	103,211	H.M. Knight	Practice grenade
4/4/16	13,405	E.W. Coleman	All-ways percussion fuse
12/4/16	105,400	G. Senior	Knife edges to alter flight when 'thrown in a particular manner'
19/4/16	105,417	G.T. Speir	Grenade
3/5/16	124,837	L.A. Daniels, C.A.P. Gardiner	DG grenade
6/5/16	101,196	H.C. Williamson	Grenade
15/5/16	125,100	F.W. Charmier, W. Curtis	Fuse
17/5/16	103,589	K.W. Nielsen	Addition to 102,479; percussion fuse for grenade with conical, flexible tail
5/6/16	102,332	H. Siegwart	Safety device
7/6/16	109,373	F.M. Hale	Mills rifle grenade
14/6/16	106,872	H. Austin	Percussion fuse
15/6/16	141,741	A. Dewandre, J. de Laminne	Fuse
15/6/16	141,742	A. Dewandre, J. de Laminne	Resilient lever to hold safety pin in place; relates to 141,741
15/6/16	141,743	A. Dewandre, J. de Laminne	Percussion cap holder; relates to 141,741 and 141,742
15/6/16	141,744	A. Dewandre, J. de Laminne	Igniting weak percussion cap; relates to 141,743
22/6/16	107,601	E.M. Shinkle	All-ways impact fuse
3/7/16	107,086	S.R. Parkes	Perforated line inside grenade to improve fragmentation
8/7/16	106,555	Oritur Manufacturing Co. J.W.G. Starkey	Manufacture of centre-piece
10/7/16	125,420	F.J.C. Carruthers	Percussion fuse
22/7/16	125,436	F.W. Charmier	Fuse for grenade and trench mortar bomb
4/8/16	124,493	W.J. Davey, E.W. Blake	Fuse
25/8/16	127,293	F.L. Leblanc	Fuse ignition

Application Date	Patent Number	Inventors	Description
1/9/16	125,599	S.R. Parkes	Percussion fuse
12/9/16	102,364	G.C. Salsbury	Centre-piece
14/9/16	103,094	J. Dubois	Grenade
11/10/16	127,279	L.L. Billant	Actuating mechanism
19/10/16	109,858	H.S. Valentine	Frictional fuse
20/10/16	102,917	J.E. Hearn, T.D. Galer	Plugs for grenades
6/11/16	110,915	R.S. O'Neil	Fuse
16/11/16	111,161	E.B. Temple	Percussion fuse
21/12/16	110,068	F.J.J. Gibbons	Fuse for Mills
5/2/17	111,949	F.J.J. Gibbons	Safety pin for Mills lever
14/3/17	126,740	Vickers Ltd, F.G.L. Johnson	Smoke composition for grenades
11/5/17	127,650	E. Sernagiotto, G. Orsi	Liquid filling producing asphyxiating vapour
22/5/17	115,897	P.E. Cheeseman	Fuse
27/7/17	121,272	F.N. Brondby	Percussion fuse
1/10/17	117,734	Dover Ltd, H.W. Dover	Lever for hand grenade
4/10/17	119,678	G.A. Shaw	Grenade
20/11/17	114,122	A.B. Gibbons	Manufacture of centre-piece of Mills
17/6/18	136,857	E.C.R. Marks	Disc-shaped grenade with disc-shaped bullets
11/10/18	123,028	F.J.J. Gibbons	Dummy hand grenade

Rifle-Grenades & Launchers

Application Date	Patent Number	Inventors	Description
2/7/15	16,869	Société de Construction Batignolles (précédement Ernest Gouin et Cie)	Rifle grenade
13/7/15	10,165 cognate 11,113/15	M.E. Brett (C.W. Cole)	Muzzle attachment
13/7/15	10,195 cognate 11,113/15	M.E. Brett (C.W. Cole)	Muzzle extension; uses blank cartridge
30/7/15	100,432	C.S. Walker	Cartridges for rifle grenades fed with rods; cartridge fitted to rod; gas checks
31/7/15	101,095	S. Rogozea	Muzzle extension; grenade has tubular tail which fits over extension; claw and notch arrangement to reduce recoil
22/9/15	13,510 cognate 13,511/15	S.C. Davidson	Constant angle and charge, range determined by venting system
20/11/15	102,371	J. Vivien, G. Bessière	Muzzle extension for grenade which may have short rod; includes grenade
27/11/15	103,109	A. Gauchet	Rifle grenade
8/12/15	17,245	N.L. Fynmore	Auxiliary time fuse to extend range
14/1/16	100,700	J. Vivien, G. Bessière	Muzzle attachment; bullet through centre of grenade
21/1/16	124,478	L.G.P. Thring	Muzzle-loaded launcher with shoulder stock and recoil reducing system
24/1/16	103,012	K. Gauldie, W. Gauldie	Rifle grenade with percussion fuse
18/2/16	124,507	J. Neale	Automatic igniter for time fuse in rifle grenade
21/2/16	101,108	A.L. Chevallier, H.J. Blanch	Muzzle attachment with sliding sleeve, spring, piston and wooden sabot
13/3/16	124,765	F.V. Lister	Cut-down shotgun barrel with socket for grenade
18/4/16	105,945	C.T.B. Sangster	Rifle grenade
1/5/16	101,193	L.W. Williams	Rifle grenade in two parts with rod attachment
2/5/16	105,427	S.R. Parkes	Rifle grenade with time fuse
3/6/16	125,129	C.T.B. Sangster	Rifle grenade
15/6/16	107,195	A. Dewandre, J. de Laminne	Blunderbuss for firing grenade with peripheral ribs

Application Date	Patent Number	Inventors	Description
25/7/16	109,066	W. Mills	Impact fuse for rodded rifle grenade
26/9/16	104,836	J. Vivien, G. Bessière	Addition to 100,700
26/9/16	109,498	J. Vivien, G. Bessière	Branched muzzle attachment
7/10/16	109,509	Guns & Munitions Ltd, V.C. Doubleday	Mechanism for releasing grenade's lever
20/10/16	107,893	C.T.B. Sangster	Rifle grenade with wind-vane arming device
20/10/16	124,775	C.T.B. Sangster	Rifle grenade with wind-vane arming device
24/10/16	112,954	T.D. Macfarlane, A.J. Penney	Rifle grenade
20/12/16	109,363	M. Barnett	Rod for rifle grenade
5/1/17	126,353	A.L. Chevallier	Spring-mounted muzzle attachment; grenade has hollow tailpiece
24/1/17	130,404	E.A.F. Naud	Fuse
2/2/17	113,126	M. Barnett	Ribbed reinforcing sleeve for barrel
7/2/17	130,406	E.A.F. Naud	Grenade with light cylindrical body and ogival ends to increase range
14/2/17	126,692	R. Burn	Cup discharger
7/3/17	126,733	M. Giorgi	Drawn steel tube attached to muzzle for firing grenade with bullet
29/3/17	128,315	R. Frugier	Funnel-shaped muzzle extension; grenade has hollow cylindrical tail which fits over funnel and is left behind when grenade launched. No patent granted; sealing fee not paid
23/4/17	109,944	K. Hagen	Grenade tube attached to barrel via muzzle extension with hole for bullet gases to propel grenade. Range and recoil modified by different-sized holes
23/6/17	117,064	E. Piersantelli	Crescent-shaped butt of launcher rests on ground or against shoulder; tail of bomb fits in barrel and holds rifle cartridge
18/9/17	119,218	N.W. Aasen	Launching tube mounted parallel to rifle barrel with connecting hole between, with valve in base of tube to regulate gas flow. Void
25/9/17	118,179	D. Kouskoff	Rodded projectile with knife blades on front end for cutting wire
10/10/17	119,852	E. Piersantelli	Addition to 117,064
5/11/17	129,368	S.C. Davidson	Addition to 13,510/15
15/12/17	129,740	G.R. Thatcher	Cup discharger with vent holes
21/2/18	123,182	L.H. Carroll	Grenade with central air passage and cloth tail
22/5/18	127,231	F.N. Brondby	Device for varying range of rifle grenades with tail sleeve and wings; sleeve fits over barrel or extension, the extent of fit determining range
29/5/18	148,766	E. Piersantelli	Three-piece tube with shock-absorbing springs
12/6/18	125,817	J.M. Kaylar	Fires winged projectiles
10/8/18	131,288	E. Brandt	Projectile with fins

Rests for Firing Rifle Grenades

Application Date	Patent Number	Inventors	Description
24/1/16	102,755	K. Gauldie, W. Gauldie	A curved butt attachment
23/3/16	101,441	W.S. Kneeshaw	Rifle stand

Grenade-Throwing Devices

Application Date	Patent Number	Inventors	Description
25/11/14	23,044	M.J. Dawson	Spring-operated arm
2/3/15	100,132	F.F. Fornay	Rifled, breech-loaded spring-operated gun; includes projectile
13/3/15	100,177	Soc. Anon de Commentry-Fourchambault et Decazeville	Mechanical. Void
22/5/15	7,710	C.P. Leach, A.W. Gamage Ltd	Catapult
25/6/15	100,791	F. Schimmel	Mechanical, rotary action; includes pebble projectiles. Void
5/7/15	9,794	V.C. Doubleday	Device for igniting time fuse
22/7/15	10,662	R.T. Glascodine	Catapult using rubber strips
25/8/15	12,298	J. Robertson	Mechanical thrower
6/10/15	14,168	S.C. Davidson	Spring-operated
13/10/15	14,505	C.K. Pellett	Device for launching propeller-driven projectile
9/12/15	17,291 cognate 6,725/16	A. Wood, G. Wood	Pneumatic with chain linkage
10/12/15	124,523	L.M. Pourcel	Pneumatic
31/12/15	18,180	A. Carreras	Torsional spring
2/2/16	103,841	F.F. Mote	Bomb propelled by explosive gases
29/2/16	104,376	W. Storch, C.W. Davis	Bat-shaped thrower
4/3/16	104,672	M. Velin, F. Schimmel	Tube discharging time-fused bombs ignited electrically on discharge
10/3/16	103,379	P.D. Malloch	Hand-thrower
16/3/16	104,893	C.T. Crowden	Pneumatic
20/3/16	120,738	A.P. Lawrence	Mechanical
25/4/16	105,787	J. Gardner	Mechanical
12/5/16	106,141	J.S. Owens, J.M. de M. Vermehr	Magazine-fed
27/5/16	106,656	J.A. Hill	Spring-operated
9/6/16	107,045	J.A. Hill	Development of 106,656
31/8/16	125,597	C. Gori, G. Minucciani	Centrifugal-action; includes fuse for lenticular bomb
14/11/16	137,873	R. Burn	Pneumatic
23/3/17	128,595	G. Constantinesco, J.R. Middleton	Hydraulic piston operated by explosive discharge
26/3/17	116,305	G.P. van Wye	Mechanical
1/6/17	133,070	C. Gori, G. Minucciani	Addition to 125,597
2/6/17	116,330	R.E. Blacker	Spring-operated
8/8/17	126,536	E.S. Jones, S.A. Leblanc	Spring-operated

Trench Mortars

Application Date	Patent Number	Inventors	Description
13/1/15	100,016	F.H.P. Wallis	Mortar and mounting. Void
24/2/15	3,025	A. de M. Bellairs	Fired by explosive mixture of acetylene and air or oxygen
9/4/15	100,408	R.A. Bréviaire	Pneumatic, muzzle-loaded, with muzzle-flash suppressor. Void
24/6/15	125,413	Soc. Anon pour l'Exploitation des Procédés Westinghouse-Leblanc	Mortar; ammunition described in 14,477/15
24/6/15	125,612	Soc. Anon pour l'Exploitation des Procédés Westinghouse-Leblanc	Addition to 125,413; ranged by altering size of combustion chamber
2/7/15	16,869	Soc. de Construction des Batignolles (Précédement Ernest Gouin et Cie)	Mortar

Application Date	Patent Number	Inventors	Description
27/7/15	10,882	F.W.S. Stokes	Mortar
30/8/15	12,477	S.F. Stokes	Related to 12,478/15; regulation of gases for range
30/8/15	12,478 cognate 16,179/15	S.F. Stokes	Breech-loaded
21/9/15	13,445	Sir W.G. Armstrong Whitworth & Co., C. Wale, S.M. Murray	Muzzle-loaded stemmed projectiles launched by piston on discharge; relates to mortar and ammunition
22/9/15	13,510	S.C. Davidson	Tripod for constant angle of elevation; bypass vent for propellant gases
11/1/16	100,377	I. Quennehen, R. Moine, J. Fieschi, M. de Mery	Acetylene as propellant; each charge is separately produced
17/1/16	123,656	S.F. Stokes	Range by regulating release of propellant gases
29/1/16	124,489	E. Schneider	Recoil mechanism
2/2/16	103,841	F.F. Mote	Tripod mount
28/2/16	104,525	R.J.W. Dawson	Heated-wire ignition system
16/3/16	104,893	C.T. Crowden	Mounting
1/5/16	124,831	L. Johnstone	Valve for regulating propellant gases in Stokes
19/5/16	16,280	G. Constantinesco, W. Haddon	Hydraulic mortar
17/6/16	125,148	D. Samaia	Trench mortar with noise-reduction system
10/8/16	127,285	Soc. Anon pour l'Exploitation des Procédés Westinghouse-Leblanc	For firing super-calibre projectiles
21/8/16	125,475	Armstrong Whitworth & Co., Sir W.G. Wale, C. Wale	Combustion chamber for trench mortar
14/11/16	137,873	R. Burn	Tripod for trench mortar
12/12/16	126,324	W. Heap	Mounting
5/1/17	126353	A.L. Chevallier	Mounting
10/3/17	143,275	J.A.M. Goumarre	Tripod for mortar or MG
23/3/17	128,595	G. Constantinesco, J.R. Middleton	Mounting
14/5/17	143,268	G.C. Davidson, C.P. Caulkins	Mounting for light mortar
11/6/17	127,879	J.I. Thornycroft & Co., J.E. Thornycroft, T. Thornycroft	Mounting
27/10/17	129,351	A.J. Stone	Mounting
5/11/17	129,368	S.C. Davidson	Addition to 13,510/15
9/11/17	129,376	J.I. Thornycroft & Co., J.E. Thornycroft, T. Thornycroft	Mounting for light mortar
21/5/18	136,194	R.C. Dodgson	Mounting
20/7/18	127,150	A.S. Adams	Mounting
31/10/18	134,548	Soc. Anon pour l'Exploitation des Procédés Westinghouse-Leblanc	Automatic loading device for Stokes

Ammunition

Application Date	Patent Number	Inventors	Description
27/7/15	10,883	F.W.S. Stokes	Projectile for mortar described in 10,882
20/8/15	12,036	E. Schneider	Trench mortar projectile
10/9/15	12,985	C. Bingham	Trench bomb with fins
13/10/15	14,477	Soc. Anon pour l'Exploitation des Procédés Westinghouse-Leblanc	Ammunition for trench mortar described in 125,413
16/11/15	102,594	S.F. Stokes	Trench mortar projectile with propellant cartridge in base; for mortar described in 12,477/15 and 12,478/15
16/11/15	103,270	S.F. Stokes	Use of flat bands of leather, cardboard, vulcanite as gas check on trench mortar ammunition

Application Date	Patent Number	Inventors	Description
29/11/15	16,795 cognate 6,889/15	H. Greener	Ammunition for trench mortar
4/316	104,672	M. Velin, F. Schimmel	Projectiles
6/4/16	104,847	S.R. Parkes	Time fuse for trench mortar ammunition
13/4/16	124,809	F.W.S. Stokes	Trench mortar ammunition fuse
3/5/16	124,836	S.R. Parkes	Cartridge for Stokes ammunition
15/5/16	125,099	O.R. Williams	Ammunition for trench gun
6/7/16	125,411	H. Greener	Time fuse for trench mortar ammunition
10/8/16	127,285	Soc. Anon pour l'Exploitation des Procédés Westinghouse-Leblanc	Super-calibre trench mortar projectile with hollow tail-piece (fits inside barrel) and wings (outside barrel); relates to trench mortar described in 125,612
21/8/16	125,475	Armstrong Whitworth & Co.	Trench mortar ammunition
24/10/17	113,927	H. Wade (Compagnie Général d'Electricité)	Message-carrying projectile
18/1/18	124,473	L.G.P. Thring	Cartridges for trench mortar ammunition

Flamethrowers

Application Date	Patent Number	Inventors	Description
25/1/15	17,794	Schneider et Cie	Remote control vehicle. No patent granted; sealing fee not paid
27/3/15	7,524	J. Hersent, G. Hersent, J.A. Thirion	Gas-pressure operated (also applicable to fire extinguishers!)
18/10/15	14,715	J. Menchen	Valves ensure that gas cannot be turned on until liquid turned on
18/10/15	14,716	J. Menchen	Relates to valves for 14,715/15
29/10/15	15,288	W.A. Hall	Man portable
4/11/15	15,581	J. Hersent, G. Hersent, J.A. Thirion	Apparatus for projecting flaming liquid under gas pressure
13/11/15	16,062	J. Menchen	Specs 14,715/15 and 14,716/15 are referred to
17/12/15	17,696	P.H. Lawrence	Portable combined flamethrower. No patent granted; sealing fee not paid
29/12/15	18,119	A. Kitson	Man portable; relates to ignition. No patent granted; sealing fee not paid
11/5/16	125,097	P.H. Lawrence	Backpack flamethrower. No patent granted; sealing fee not paid
8/3/17	113,973	W.J. Lester	Tank fitted with flamethrower and electrified water projector
10/7/17	128,275	P.H. Lawrence	Man portable; propellant gas bottle inside tank of fuel; igniter cartridge. No patent granted; sealing fee not paid

Sources

UK Patents and Patent Abridgements, August 1914 – November 1918

Classes

9 (ii) ammunition
92 (i) ordnance and machine-gun carriages and mountings
92 (ii) ordnance and machine-guns
119 small arms

Public Record Office, Kew

MUN 4/190 – Sir Ernest Moir's secret patent
MUN 4/426 – MID reports; DG grenade
MUN 4/766 – publication of patents
MUN 4/2537 – catapult pouches
MUN 4/2557 – grenades
MUN 4/2604 – grenades
MUN 4/2627 – grenade dischargers
MUN 4/2656 – Trench Warfare Department papers
MUN 4/2679 – flamethrowers
MUN 4/2812 – Gamage catapult and West Spring Gun
MUN 4/3586 – intelligence on enemy weapons
MUN 4/3589 – intelligence on enemy weapons; 'Notes on Inventions and New Stores', mortars
MUN 4/3590 – intelligence on enemy weapons; 'Notes on Inventions and New Stores'
MUN 4/6878 – Trench Warfare Committee papers
MUN 5/196/1610/17 – instruction to pay royalties to Société de Construction de Batignolles
MUN 5/197/1640/7 – Newton Pippin rifle grenade
MUN 5/382/1600/8 – 'History of Trench Warfare Supply, Aug. 1914 – May 1915'
MUN 5/383/1600/14 – 'Development of Weapons used in Trench Warfare', including sections by Newton and Livens
MUN 7/273 – Captain Stokes's mortar

T 173/453 – Royal Commission on Awards to Inventors and related papers (W. Stokes)
T 173/802 – Royal Commission on Awards to Inventors and related papers (grenades)

WO 33/934 – 'Handbook on Bombs and Grenades'
WO 106/432 – mortars
WO 140/14 – Reports on Trials (Hythe)

Official Publications

CDS 74, *The Training and Employment of Grenadiers*, GHQ, October 1915

PUBLISHED BOOKS

Babington, Anthony. *Shell-Shock*, Leo Cooper, 1997
Bidwell, Shelford and Dominick Graham. *Fire-Power*, Allen & Unwin, 1982
Blunden, Edmund. *Undertones of War*, Cobden-Sanderson, 1928
Chapman, Guy. *A Passionate Prodigality*, Buchan & Enright, 1985
Dunn, J.C. *The War the Infantry Knew*, Jane's, 1987
Edmonds, Charles (Charles Carrington). *A Subaltern's War*, Peter Davis, 1929
Fleischer, Wolfgang. *German Trench Mortars and Infantry Weapons 1914–45*, Schiffer, 1996
Graham, Stephen. *A Private in the Guards*, Macmillan, 1919
Graves, Robert. *Goodbye to All That*, Cassell, 1957
Griffith, Paddy. *Battle Tactics of the Western Front*, Yale University Press, 1996
Griffith, Wyn. *Up to Mametz*, Faber, 1931
Hartcup, Guy. *The War of Invention*, Brassey's, 1988
Hitchcock, F.C. *'Stand To' A Diary of the Trenches 1915–1918*, Gliddon Books, 1988
Jünger, Ernst. *The Storm of Steel*, Chatto & Windus, 1929
Macdonald, Lyn. *1915, The Death of Innocence*, Headline, 1993
Richards, Frank. *Old Soldiers Never Die*, Faber, 1933
Sassoon, Siegfried. *Memoirs of an Infantry Officer*, Faber, 1965
Skennerton, Ian. *An Introduction to British Grenades*, Skennerton, 1988
——. *List of Changes*, vol. IV 1910–18, Skennerton, 1993
Temple, B.A. *World War 1 Armaments and the .303 British Cartridge*, Temple, 1995
Terraine, John. *General Jack's Diary*, Eyre & Spottiswoode, 1964
The Times History of the War, 21 vols, *The Times*, 1914–20
Vaughan, Edwin Campion. *Some Desperate Glory*, Macmillan, 1979

MAGAZINE ARTICLES

Bull, Stephen. 'Grenade Thrower – Granatenwerfer M1915/M1916' in *Military Illustrated*, No. 92
——. 'Deadly Toffee Apple' in *Military Illustrated*, No. 96
Holder, Paul. 'Roman Artillery' in *Military Illustrated*, No. 2
——. 'Roman Artillery' in *Military Illustrated*, No. 4
Scott, Peter T. 'An Awful Job – the search for a British flamethrower' in *Military Illustrated*, No. 98
The Illustrated London News, 1914–18

Index